Mythos

Healing into the light,

From the personal and collective trauma we
are all experiencing, to vibrant being.

Rhythm as portal to dreams,
the creative unconscious.

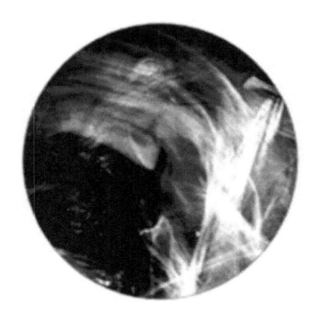

MYTHOS
DANCE OF PSYCHE
Rhythm of Consciousness

by

Dr. Christina Fragasso Kolakouskus Campbell

REGENT PRESS
Berkeley, California

ISBN 13: 978-1-58790-700-5
ISBN 10: 1-58790-700-3
Library of Congress Control Number: 2025900995

Readers should use caution as this book contains very serious
experience of trauma including abuse, persecution and holocaust.
This should be considered if the reader has
traumas that may be stimulated.

Manufactured in the U.S.A.
REGENT PRESS
www.regentpress.net

Table of Contents

Illustrations,
Watercolor of Dreams,
Photos of Dance

LAZER CLEANING OFF THE DUST OF THE ANCIENT BUST
Symbol of Ancient and Modern Healing

A Healer's Story, Mythos
    Wisdom and healing in an age of trauma and grief,
    The age of the bully and toxic environments:

Thus, Describes the emotional/spiritual conditions of our times:
    The traumatic effects of profit over people
    The traumatic effects of the Bully as gatekeeper of the profit motive.

A healing journey from trauma to Vibrant Human Being
    in an age of threat
    for self, culture, nature and the divine.

    Healer's psyche as mirror into the collective culture through
    Imagination in Rhythm: poetry, music and dance was portal to dreams,
    and depth of feeling; sourced insight into the personal, collective, and
    ancestral trauma.

It is exploration of the life force within through Sacred Dance:
    it is ancient and modern healing.
    The miracle and beauty of the life force that unites awakens.
    Unity as solution in an age of Tyranny.
    Rhythm: a unifying force in healing self, culture, nature and the divine.
    This is the Dance of Psyche:
    The Rhythm of Consciousness

Rhythm heals the split torn apart by trauma,

Inspires imagination in music and dance,

Taps the dream, the image which inspires hope for healing

Mirror into self and culture

Connects with the sacred, with the cosmos.

To become conscious, one becomes the dancer.

MY MOTHER'S QUOTE... NOW ON THE OTHER SIDE:

I have/call the imagination of the Universe.

My imagination works for me.

I am wisdom, the wisdom of life itself, is with me.

It is guiding my every thought and action in full achievement.

MY BROTHER'S QUOTE:

Imagination is an act of creation brought into reality by the ethos of an open mind and soul forged by courage.

AND

Revealed through you by the ultimate creator.

THIS IS MY PRAYER, MANTRA IN SOURCING MY WRITING.

My hope is to inspire through imagination and beauty in the depth of feeling in the human heart.

This is Healing Art.

MY BROTHER'S PHOTOGRAPHY
Dr. Walter Allen Campbell

VISION OF ARCHANGEL URIEL
Watercolor by Christina

Archangel Uriel

    Light of God

        Guardian of the Earth

        and Humankind

    Thank you for bringing down

        the touch of Sacred Fire.

    Inspire me to creative work

        so that my dream may come to earth.

    Your flame is vision prophesy,

        the poetry of truth.

    Set my creative spark ablaze

        so that my word and pen and hand

        bring light into the world.

    My intention is to bring light into the world

        From the darkness we face.

(Prayer card from Archangel Auriel's Church in New Mexico.)0.

DR. CHRISTINA CAMPBELL
Psychologist Specializing in the Treatment of Trauma,
Nurse, Healing Artist, Dancer
[Photo taken by neighbor: Beth Erickson]

Introduction to Book II

I am writing to all people who are concerned by the collective direction toward increasing mechanization and sterilization in the culture/world:

To those who would like to explore another way of looking at the problem;

To those who are worried about materialism and its effect on eroding the quality of our life, health and freedom;

To those who have been traumatized ty the collective machine: the homeless, our children who are left because parents are busy working, the victims of violence, children without food, those without healthcare, nurses and physicians who have little time for their patients, the mentally ill without care, mental health workers who no longer have adequate work in spite of the growing demand for their services, to those in prison, to the victims of hate, to the workers who have lost their jobs due to restructuring;

To the immigrants who are being threatened and deprived of their rights.

To those who have compassion for the victims of materialism.

To those who cannot keep up with the pace, for they may be the lucky ones who have not lost their soul.

To those who seek understanding of the collective, so that more individuals can make decisions that change the collective machine to become more humane.

This book is based on humanism. Concepts are relevant to human needs, feelings, moods and dreams. This way of knowing may be predictive. It is more of a first-person account than a third person one. There is a relationship between inquiry from personal experience and the acquisition of knowledge. It is both art and science.

Chapter 1

MYTHOS
DANCE OF PSYCHE:
Rhythm of Consciousness

THIS IS A HEALER'S STORY to shed light on the troubled times we live in. It is a journey from the dark night of the soul into the light. It is related to the personal and collective trauma we are experiencing using the arts, dance, and dreams as reflection and symbol of the psyche/ soul. Thus, describing the emotional/spiritual conditions of our times. It is a healer's journey through trauma for self and society. Through personal trauma, the collective trauma is reflected. Story created through imagination in music and dance. Imagination in rhythm is portal to the dream, shows the way to survival and peace.

Intuitive inquiry, a way of knowing through the body and movement shaping posture, rhythm, images and dreams, the creative unconscious; questions formed, insight gained, thus, integrating psyche and logos, art and science.

Mirroring the rhythm of the voice and movement, gesture, posture, facial expression is primal attachment in relationship.

It is depth of feeling. uniting self through visceral sensations from body, mind, emotions, and spirit.

Uniting with others, inspiring love.

Sourcing instinct, being and vibration,

Inspires love of nature, the earth, so we save her.

Attune to vulnerability allows us to experience threats to safety, so we can rescue self, culture, and nature.

The divine light and love is experienced, a spiritual reality: the stars, the cosmos, plants, animals, human beings, all beings are one.

This heals the split with self, culture, nature, and the divine.

Rhythm unites.

Important in an age of Tyranny which fractures the psyche and splits us from each other... through fractured truth.

Rhythm is a unifying force for healing self, culture, nature and the divine.

Dance Mythos is a healing story created through imagination in rhythm. Shapes the dance, the lucid dream, predicting the nighttime dream, Shows the way to survival and peace, from a commercialized mechanized world to one that has human values,

From trance, a robotic rhythm to one that is awake and alert, conscious of the threat to our human values through compassion, kindness and love, the light of being is found,

From the personal and collective trauma in society today, to vibrant being. Hope ignites:

The gold light of being is discovered in dance and in dreams.

Dance is a reflection of the psyche
Through Rhythm the soul is remembered
Time suspends itself reaching infinity
The present moment is past and future at once
Temporal space becomes infinite shaping itself in endless circles
    of death and rebirth
There is a flow of life — surrendering
We are the wind, fire, water and earth
Love, sorrow, anguish and joy
The body relaxes, becomes softer
Capable of experiencing life and vitality — of becoming vibrant human beings
Because we are the life force that is the cosmos — capable of experiencing
ourselves, expressing the story of our culture, being at one with nature
    and the divine
This is the Dance of Psyche: the Rhythm of Consciousness

This book : *MYTHOS: Dance of Psyche: Rhythm of Consciousness,* (2024) is a sequel to the first book: *Dance of Psyche: Rhythm of Consciousness* (2003). In the late 70's early 80's, I was very worried about the priority of profit taking over our culture. People were moving like machines as a way to survive, many motivated by greed and the desire to dominate over others for power, power through greed, and to separate from human needs and feelings: body, mind, spirit split. I wrote the following poem in 1982:

Modern Man moving fast in time,
Where are you going? Where is your heart? Beating to external rhythms,
believing bigger is better, more is better,
Precise,
Explicit,
Splits you into parts
Each moving precisely,
Separating you from yourself and others,
Win the mechanical heart,
Survive nuclear war,
Build more bombs to create peace. (Campbell, 1982)

The first book, *Dance of Psyche: Rhythm of Consciousness,* (2003) was a warning about a profit over people, hurry-up rhythm, and the effect it would have on our health and freedom: alienation, violence, war, and potential for fascism. Dance is used as symbol of the psyche, a personal and collective story is told through posture, rhythm, images and dreams. Thus, the emotional/spiritual conditions of our times were described in this way. This book was also about the denial of vulnerability in society related to human needs and feelings that drive alienation, make people sick and/or violent. It is the effect of a society that is based on materialism/profit on the human psyche. The writing is sensitive and heartfelt. Through healing journey through dance and art: illustrations, watercolor paintings of dreams and beautiful photography of dance shows movement across time and the life force, showed the way through trauma into the light. This is about the need to shift from robotic rhythm/trance state, fast in time and in rigidly defined ways, to natural rhythm which flows and is sustained in the moment. This gives people a way to be in their bodies and to feel, to become compassionate human beings. It is a philosophical shift from a mechanized, commercialized world to one that is human: from war to peace, and from trauma to wellbeing, and from a commercialized world to one that embraces human needs and values. (2003)

I raised the question, "Could this hurry-up robotic rhythm contribute to violence?" I gave the example of the violent incident involving the postal workers. Were the production quotas inhumane, driving those most vulnerable over the edge? In Treblinka, the concentration camp, Hitler gave the SS soldiers an order to get a large quote of Jews. Roma, children, disabled, the mentally ill, lesbians and homosexuals into the gas chamber every 10 minutes. The SS were busy looking at their watches obsessively counting oblivious to the horror taking place. The assumption here is that bottom line production quotas stripped of humanity numb the spirit and makes violence and human holocaust a reality. Thus, conditioned in the fabric of a society with a bottom-line mentality is a disregard for life. The Nazi movement was the ultimate machine.

Such is the nature of production oriented, bottom-line mentality, going faster in time doing more is addictive and numbing, leaving people lifeless, tired. One's inner feelings of vulnerability are threatened and the value for invulnerability and power becomes all encompassing. As people's nervous system numbs to the hectic pace, they become reactive, increasing their propensity for violence. Being strong and invulnerable becomes the norm: Robocops and Power Rangers increase in popularity (see illustration, p. 7). Tough guy rap becomes a popular rhythm, sometimes speaking out against oppression, but sometimes inciting violence.

On the tenth anniversary of the book I wrote, the book has come of age as people are more aware of the destructive effects of the profit motive and the corporate culture. People are working 24/7 in many cases and still have a hard time making ends meet. Bullying in society has increased in schools, universities, hospitals, and many of our institutions. Being up is often a job requirement and the truth has gone underground. Giving negative constructive feedback may get you fired. Double-speak is in. Talking-head quotes justify war and the exploitation of nature. Shootings are epidemic.

GANGSTA RAP. NAZI ROCK.

What's the difference?

When you see a Turk in a tram
And he looks at you annoyingly
Just stand up and give him a
good punch
And stab him seventeen times.

So don't follow me up and
down your market
Or your little chop suey ass
will be the target
Of a nationwide boycott
So pay respect to the black list
Or we'll burn your store right
down to a crisp
And then we'll see ya
▸ *'Cause you can't turn the ghetto*
into Black Korea.

By A.S. Ross
OF THE EXAMINER STAFF

THE FIRST SET OF LYRICS IS FROM A SONG titled "Final Victory," by Endsieg, one of Germany's neo-Nazi rock bands that play what a British expert on Eur pean hate groups describes as "Mein Kampf with a four-fo beat." Such records, distributed through shadowy right-wing o ganizations, rarely sell more than a few thousai copies each. Nevertheless, worried cor mentators point to them as further ev dence of a resurgence of the darke strains of European history.

The German government, i voking constitutional bans o "incitement to racial hatre and "demagoguery," and oth laws that agitate violen against foreigners, last mont banned a long list of white pow songs and outlawed some neo-Na bands.

The second set of lyrics is fro "Black Korea," by Ice Cube, Americe premier exponent of "gangsta" (gan ster) rap. Gangsta rap extols guns, co killing, race hate and misogyny, and i records sell in the millions. Ice Cube's la est, "The Predator," is the first rap albu

Picture and article from the San Francisco Chronicle,
Sunday, January 16, 1993

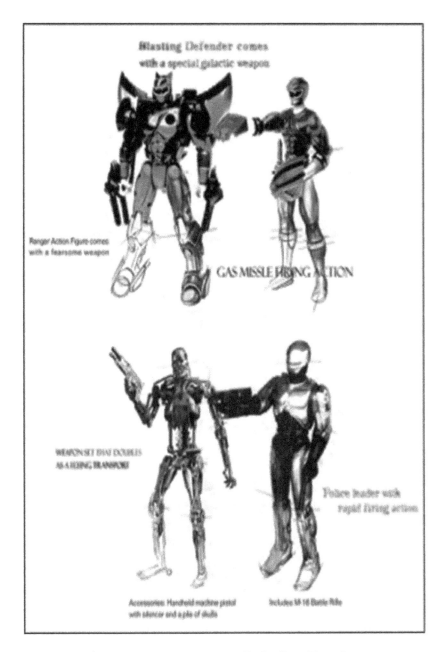

**Robo Toys: Power Rangers, RoboCop, Terminator
by Mathew Kimmins, Illustrator**

CARICATURE OF AL GORE
THE "TALKING HEAD", POLITICAL MACHINE
Cover from San Francisco Bay Guardian, August 9-15, 2000
Courtesy of artist, Andrew Vandakarr

Book Two: Mythos: Dance of Psyche: Rhythm of Consciousness

The dreams and dances from the first book gain more significance in this second book and are described in terms of relevance in today's society. A disembodiment through hurry-up rhythm has become more of a reality. It has affected our health and freedom with democracy in peril, health care and health compromised, violence in society ever present with reports of school shootings, and shootings in the street. There is danger in the rise of fascism and bullying, with the priority of greed in many of our institutions. The effect of a society that is based on materialism/profit on the human psyche is described; the inner sense of self becomes defective, powerless; violence becomes the solution which creates more suffering, fractures the self, splits society, disconnects from nature and the divine. This is collective trauma. In this second edition, from the Healer's journey, readers will discover that after the darkness of personal and collective trauma, the sacred light appears. Once again, Rhythm is described as a gateway to the collective unconscious and dreams. Dreams and dances related to Romani (Gypsy) Holocaust, possible past life, Tibetan medicine and Shamanism are also described. This is hope for healing in dark times, the way through trauma into the light. In this way, further insights into the dances and dreams continue to be explained through ancient and modern understanding of healing. The dances and dreams tap principles of Shamanism, Taoism, Hinduism, the ancient philosophies; then, Jungian psychology, integrating the Tao becoming the Tao of Jung; and then latest advances in psychology treating trauma, which includes the body, somatic methods.

The Inner Journey: The Dances of Psyche

There is a dance that is internal; it shapes itself in different postures to bring to life the waking dream. Underneath the fabric of everyday reality is a dreamscape containing images, colors, textures. Postures, rhythms, images and dreams are a gateway to the creative unconscious. Archetypes surface, mythology is created; story is told, both personal and collective. The dance is the symbol and reflection of the psyche, the rhythm of consciousness.

The following describes the creative process I used to develop choreography from my imagination. I was drawn to a rhythm, an image of a posture, a vision of the costume, including colors and textures. What arose was a personal but collective story describing a shift, an internal process from the fight against the machine to being human, from being traumatized to wellbeing.

Active imagination in dance is portal to images and dreams shaping a heartfelt story showing the way through the dark into the light, a healer's story through the dark night of the soul to the light. Rhythm as portal to the dream and the life force.

The Dances of Psyche are described:

The Dances of Psyche

Christina creates and performs authentic dance pieces based on psychological and social issues and perspectives, such as her moving and profound work, "Dances of Psyche." (Noelle Duncan, 2003)

In the dance, "Guernica, the Nazi and the Roma," named after Picasso's painting, she treats violence, trauma and alienation in society. Guernica conveys the horror of war, and the foretelling of the Neo-Nazi movement. Images that surfaced were the clock, the Nazi, and the robot.

After developing this dance, she had dreams of holocaust in the first week of August, 1989 and coincidently it was the anniversary of Romani Holocaust.

In her dance "Of Gentle Sorrow" she expresses grief at the loss of life and child.

In her "Fire Dance" she celebrate life, and the natural forces of fire and wind.

Lastly, "Venus: Goddess of Love & Peace" — an ecstatic dance celebrating the sacred light and this energy is offered to the audience.

The healing journey continues for self and society. These dances and dreams were premonitions of what is now a reality. In this second edition, I describe how they now reflect the emotional spiritual conditions of our times and continue through art, dreams and dance as reflection/symbols of the Psyche. soul, the Rhythm of Consciousness. Healer's sensitive and heartfelt story continues and shows the way through the personal and collective trauma and grief we are all experiencing, toward human values and a discovery of the life force that unites us all; the light of being is found in the dance. This healer's heartfelt story is created through imagination in rhythm as portal to images, dreams and depth of feeling shapes the choreography in dance. The dance concert developed and performed shows this healing journey; new reality is created. The dance and the dream show the way to survival and peace. This is a way out of loss and fear in becoming vibrant human being.

This is a healer's story; wisdom in an age of trauma and grief through rhythm as portal to imagination, dreams, and depth of feeling, and the beauty of the life force that unites awakens. Unity as solution in an age of tyranny.

Rhythm/vibration awakens the music and dance in the soul. Sensitive spirit can sense the inner vibration/rhythm and sense it in others, connect with the vibration of the divine. Singers, dancers, artists, source this collective feeling. It is life's mirror of attachment/relationship.

I use my psyche as mirror into the collective. Quoting from the first book:

"I believe that every theory that is created or work of art that is done is a reflection of the artist's or author's psyche and a reflection of the culture of that person, so that it is not only the art or theory but the description of the inner life that shapes the work of art is equally as important."

Psyche

The definition from ancient Greeks (Wikipedia, 2019) is relevant here.

Psyche means human soul, Goddess of the soul, Wife of Eros(cupid). Departed soul, spirit, ghost...God of love. Greek Goddess of the Soul.

Comes from the Greek word Psykhe, means the soul, mind, spirit or invisible animating entity which occupies the physical body.

Breath, spirit, soul.

I would say that dance is a reflection of the psyche/soul.

So, in this second book of *Dance of Psyche*, I continue to reveal the depth of my inner life revealing Healer's story for the personal and collective trauma and grief we are all experiencing in the age of the Bully. I am now partially retired and able to feel the effects of healing trauma of others, known as secondary trauma, and feeling strongly, the effects of toxic work environments and bully bosses. So, I share this experience for the healing and wisdom that hopefully will benefit others and society. This was a journey through the dark night of the soul. I sourced: integrating the experience of patients with toxic environments, my research looking at the relationship between stress/trauma and health and illness, and, lastly, I hope to inspire by sharing the light that appeared through, I believe many years doing dances from around the world as sacred prayer. Lastly, continued healing the traumas of loss and separation in childhood. Toxic work environments and events in present day society triggered these enormous losses. In this way, the dances and dreams are related to my inner life. I use my psyche to reflect on the emotional dynamics of our time. Rhythm is used as a reflection/symbol of the Psyche/Soul, the Rhythm of Consciousness.

This is an intuitive way of knowing through the body and body movement through posture, rhythm, images and dreams, sourcing depth of feeling, healing the split with self, culture, nature and the divine. Unity through rhythm to deal with tyranny. Dreams and images as hope for survival is a spiritual journey where the life force awakens. Imagination in rhythm, poetry, music and dance was portal to the dream, the image, the posture which sourced insight and healing; and shaped the dance. It was a doorway to the creative unconscious. Posture, rhythm, image is also a doorway into past memory and future hopes, an integration of all fractured debris into a collective whole, knitting together body with mind, mind with body, touching the spirit and the soul. Rhythm pulling these pieces together in a pendulum rhythm.: dark and light, ancient and modern, invisible and visible, bound and free, dependent and independent, from sickness to health, from violence to peace, from hate to love., sad to happy, fear to courage, rejection to acceptance, fear to love, past to present. Synchronicity is experienced across time and connects with the past and the future, past lives and future hopes, uniting present moment. This is the human palate of emotions shaping a variety of expressions, leading to acceptance of self and perceptions of beauty.

This healer's sensitive and heartfelt story was shaped in this way, and it continues. I use my psyche to reflect on the emotional dynamics of our times. Psyche means soul, the inner depth of feeling of the human being. Thus, rhythm accesses the underlying threat, fear, grief, sadness and joy through the way one moves. Rhythm makes the moods of humanity visible. It is reflected in the rhythm of the voice and movement, mirroring another in this way is primal attachment. As noted in the first book, the first song and dance are between the sound of the mother's voice and the fetus's movement in synchrony with Mom in utero. It is the song and dance of the psyche. Thus, dance is a reflection of the psyche, the rhythm of Consciousness.

Thus, music and dance are primal ways we relate to one another. Synchrony in gesture, facial expression, posture, rhythm is powerful, occurs in connection and love. The inner primal being, depth of feeling in relationship can be sourced through rhythm, music, and dance. It is a unifying force in healing the split with self, culture, nature and the divine. Synchrony is the expression of love and life, nature's mirror. Rhythm is nature's symphony. This visceral sensation in the body brings forth a feeling of beauty for other human beings, animals, the beauty of trees and rivers, water as life, the beauty of flowers, the rising and setting of the sun. The light and vibration of the divine is felt and becomes visible. This is the experience of the miracle of Life; it is the life force that unites, connects with the sacred, with the cosmos. The gold light of being is discovered in the dance and in the dream, consciousness is unity through truth, beauty, and love.

Rhythm is a mirror of life/healing force known since ancient times. Repeating from the first book:

Rhythm is a harmonious division of space and time that vibrates, sounds, organizes communicates and imparts knowledge. According to alternative theories and ancient mystics, there is a vibration or energy in space that holds knowledge of the Universe. Human beings are also energy fields that are organized through rhythm. Rhythm keeps us alive, the beating of the heart, the movement of the air through the lungs. The stars and sun circle in rhythmic patterns. It's as if the Universe dances and we are part of this great mystical dance. According to recent science and ancient mystics, we can acquire this knowledge through the rhythm of the breath, sound and movement. One can make daily life a moving meditation which is in concert with oneself, culture, nature and the divine. Knowledge can be acquired through the rhythm of the body and to become conscious, one becomes the dancer. (Campbell, 2003, p. 25)

Rhythm/vibration as mirror of life has been known since ancient times and is embedded in ancient practice of breathing and meditation of the Buddha, the whirling of the Dervish, the song and dance of the Shaman, and Shiva, the dance of the Universe. In studying dances from around the world: Greek, Persian, Indian, Flamenco, Tunisian, Middle Eastern, I did experience them as ancient healing rituals. I did compare them to present-day methods of healing trauma.

So, in this way, this writing is about body movement in attachment, trauma, health and illness. Without resonance through mirroring, the self is fractured and split from the whole, separating us from ourselves, others, nature and the divine. Rhythm is mirror of life, of relationship to self and others, reflective of culture, nature, and the divine... uniting all things. Mirroring through rhythm unites self, body, emotions and visceral sensation — with mind, awareness of thoughts and images, brings clarity of feelings and emotions and spirit, connects with the invisible, with ancestors past; it is both being and vibration.

The culture captured by hurry-up rhythm, bottom-line profit mentality has affected our health and freedom; contributed to alienation, violence, war and now fascism. The bully/tyrant is now the gatekeeper of the profit motive in many of our institutions and was in our capital. The bully is now our collective trauma. The emotional dynamics of toxic environments are described helping to validate underlying feelings and moods. And, saying again, Rhythm makes the invisible moods of humanity visible. Rhythm as reflection and symbol of the psyche is used to describe the emotional/spiritual conditions of our times. Thus, the underlying emotional issues that contribute to alienation and violence in today's American society are revealed in the fast paced/robotic rhythm/trance state; it reflects bottom-line profit mentality. World as machine is driven by values of production, efficiency and strength and denial of the body as the body is not profitable. Survival is equated with dominance and control over others. Thus, the vulnerable have become targets of the bully: the poor, minorities including blacks, Native Americans, indigenous populations, women, gays, disabled, and Jews. Those who speak the truth are also demeaned. So, hopefully, this edition will bring healing and empowerment through insight into these emotional dynamics, both the personal and collective dynamics of our times. This is a story about healing the alienation in society. The shift needed is from a commercialized, mechanized world, a robotic rhythm, a disembodiment to one that is embodied, connected to human needs and values; one that is awake and alert, conscious of the threat to these human values and the earth. Through depth of feeling for the other, an empathic connection, compassion, kindness and love and the light of being is found. This will heal the split with self and inspire beauty of diverse cultures and nature. Dance as a reflection of the psyche is powerful because of its ability to unite us. It is a healing journey in an age of personal and collective trauma toward human values and needs and a discovery of the life force that unites us all, the light of being is discovered; hope ignites in my dances and dreams. This is a journey through an intuitive way of knowing tapping the creative unconscious, sourcing knowledge across time, both ancient and modern, art and science. It is about healing trauma and a way to become a vibrant human being. The art that shows the life force dwelling beneath. Mark Franz:

The purpose of this kind of artistic expression is to reveal unearthly life dwelling beneath, to break the mirror of life so we may look being in the face. (Quoted in Jung, *Man and his Symbols*, 1964, p. 263)

Chapter 2

Recapturing Initiating Ideas from the First Book Relevant to this Second Edition

I BELIEVE THAT EVERY THEORY that is created or work of art that is done is a reflection of the artist's psyche and a reflection of the culture of that person, so that Freud's theory of psychoanalysis for hysteria was developed from his own hysterical conflicts, his theories were particularly relevant for a Victorian era, an era of sexual repression. And Jung's theories were developed from his own inner life. So, it is not only the theory that is important but the description of the inner life that shapes the work of art is equally important.

In reflecting on this statement, the first book was indeed reflective of our culture and my inner life of dreams, images expressed in story and dance theatre is reflective of our society today. The motive was to seek with all my heart to understand the nature of health and illness. I believe that the death of my father, the depression of my mother and the other tragedies in my life made me seek questions about the cause of illness and what keeps us healthy. I always had a hunch that stress and trauma may lead someone to become ill. What I was to find was something just a little different, which is the theme that ran through the first book and continues in the second. Rather than be swollen up by sorrow the rest of my life, I sought knowledge about health and illness and about healing.

I was my own greatest experiment. I was born in Orange Memorial Hospital in New Jersey in 1945 to Italian and Lithuanian/Russian second generation immigrants. My mother and father met in Manhattan during the war. My father was in the Army at Fort Hamilton, Brooklyn and my mother was a designer and draper at Bergdorf Goodman in Manhattan. They met at a WMCA dance during World War II. My father was a gentle, kind military man, and my mother was a very intelligent artist. My father was attracted to her because she was very vibrant. They struggled for survival during the depression. My father joined the army to escape the coal mines in Pennsylvania. His father left Russia/Lithuania to escape persecution. He was Roma (Gypsy) and was a horse trainer for the Aristocracy in Russia. My mother's father left Italy when his vineyards failed due to a severe drought. He came to the United States through Ellis Island and worked unloading fish at the Fulton Fish Market in Manhattan. He made enough money to send for his wife and four kids. He proceeded to open an Italian seafood restaurant in Jersey City. He became extremely successful and bought a farm in Matawan, New Jersey and then had another four kids. My grandfather was always a legend in my mind because of his generosity and success in business. Later, however, I found out that people would take their babies and children to my grandmother, my Nona, for healing. When they had a fever, she would anoint them with olive oil and hold them and their fever would often drop. She studied with several advanced healers in Italy. Later in life, I would realize that healing with the life force was my ancestral inheritance from her. I Received much guidance from her about how to access this energy.

THE OLD ITALIAN FISH MARKET
Painting done by Mother's Sister, Jeanette Fragsso Masi

My father left the Army and my mother left her job as dress designer to open an Italian Seafood market in New Jersey. My father would get up at 3:00 a.m. to travel to the Fulton Fish Market in Manhattan to buy the fish. He, actually, was the one who was excited to start this seafood business. It was a struggle for survival during these early years. In spite of the struggle, the extended families often got together for celebrations. It was very festive. I loved hearing the Italian, Lithuanian, and some Russian languages spoken. We spent many summers at the New Jersey Shore with my cousins playing at the beach. I loved my cousins very much. I remember I loved to move, you couldn't get me out of the water, and I loved to ride my bicycle, loved to dance and liked learning to play my violin. I also liked the culture in Manhattan. I loved the brooks and streams in Jersey. I inherited dance from both my mother and father. My mother auditioned on Broadway for a show, and they wanted her. She turned it down. My father loved the waltz and the Polka. So, lots of dance inheritance. I'm also pretty sure my

**ROSE MARIE FRAGASSO AND WALTER JOHN KOLOKOUSKUS
(CAMPBELL) THE ARTIST AND THE MILITARY MAN**

love for dances from around the world, particularly Turkish Gypsy dance, Karsilimas, and the fire of flamenco came from my Romani roots.

Tragedy struck early in life with my father developing a tumor in his chest. He was in and out of the VA Hospital for five years and died there when he was 39 years old. I just turned nine; my brother was ten. My uncle died two days later of a stroke, and we had a double funeral. My mother became extremely depressed, very frightened, and it stayed with her for most of her life. Much of this was due to toxic communication from her sisters. She began arguing with her family, rebelled, and moved to Florida where she continued to fight with them from 1500 miles away. Later another uncle, the father of my cousins, committed suicide. He was a father figure for me.

I identified with both my father and my mother — my father as the idealized military man and mother as the artist. I believe I am more of the artist, but I was drawn into the military as a nurse during the Vietnam War as a way to incorporate my father and work through his loss. My artist self and feminine nature came out in the military, and I was in big trouble. I met a very abusive Navy commander who raked me over the hot coals. I learned about scapegoating early in my career, and it took me over 27 years to figure out that it was not all me. This experience triggered my depression, which I have struggled with all my life. I also realized it was my weakness that made this experience as powerful as it was, because if I had a stronger sense of self, as I do now, it would not have been a big deal. In another respect, it was powerful enough to devote myself to healing trauma and the synchronistic bullying experiences of others. Now publishing the second book that has to do with bullying.

I learned how to survive by taking care of others. Becoming a nurse was one extension of early childhood. My struggle to be myself when I was in rigid systems was also a reenactment of early childhood. To be myself with a paranoid mother would have meant total rejection. I had the fear that if I came out, I would be destroyed. This made my love of art a difficult striving because in art one becomes visible. I became invisible to avoid the paranoid rages of my mother. However, she was very supportive in other ways. I just needed to avoid the topic of the relatives. She was also able to return to work and make a living, working as a dress designer in companies in Miami. At the same time, creating beauty out of nothing was a way to get relief from rigidity. Becoming the creative person that I am was a struggle because of this underlying fear; it was fraught with procrastination, boredom and extreme anxiety, followed by exhaustion. However, I must say I pushed down this fear when I spoke truth to power which I was often able to do. It was reaction formation.

I pursued advanced education, all the while studying dance on the side. It was a difficult striving because the healing arts did not pay the bills, so I continued to weave the best I could. My dissertation was on the treatment outcome of Hospice Care. In addition to looking at whether Hospice met the treatment objectives, I also researched the relationship of family dynamics and levels of depression with the onset of cancer. There was substantial but not conclusive evidence that depression and characterological patterns of dealing with stress precipitated the onset of cancer.

Out of the struggle, I created a continuing education program for nurses called Nursing Arts. It was a program that integrated the art and science of nursing courses describing the differences between the mechanistic underpinnings of the medical model and holistic theory. Family Systems Theory and the Dynamics of Illness, Creative Arts, Clinical Applications to Nursing, and lastly Therapeutic Touch, a healing method of laying on of the hands. I was helping to reshape mechanism in hospital systems and bringing out the humanity through the healing arts. Mechanism meant treating the body as a machine. If something goes wrong, the solution is to replace the part.

I began integrating dance into healing my own depression. I studied dance therapy and took a course in authentic movement. This dance therapy method was based on Jung's work in using active imagination to tap the unconscious. Many of the images, postures and rhythms that depicted archetypal themes were used to create choreography in dance.

The mythological dances were predictive of the dreams I would have when I was traumatized by a severe auto accident and my entire past trauma was painfully brought to the surface. The mythology was personal but also represented the collective unconscious of our time. One dream was being a Nazi Holocaust victim, perhaps a young Romani (Gypsy) girl who was separated from "her people" and placed in the gas chamber and perhaps may have been burned in the ovens. This metaphor or past life reality has made me extremely sensitive to the present sterilization of the culture, which focuses on bottom-line mentality and production versus the needs and values of human beings.

Throughout my career, I studied stress and trauma and discovered that one's traumas have a tendency to be repeated over and over again in one's life as a way to master the experience. There is repetition in thought, behavior, feeling and dreams.

The mythological dance pieces represented a shift from trauma to well-being. It was my internal struggle, breaking free from the rigid internal critical voice and being more humane to myself. This book is dedicated to those who wish to do the same.

I started to write the first book in 1982 and came up with the title, Dance of Psyche: Rhythm of Consciousness. Little did I know that in the future, knowledge about the significance of this title would so greatly expand. Many experiences as a nurse, as a trauma psychologist, and as a dancer combined to give me insight while writing this book. And my experience as a Navy Nurse during the Veit Nam era was extremely important in understanding the horror of war and witnessing the wounds of war.

It all began on the Greek dance floor at the Minerva Cafe in San Francisco in 1974. It was the height of the folk dancing era in the Bay Area when everyone was holding hands and dancing to cultural rhythms from many lands. The cafe was very authentically Greek. Old Greek women with their babushkas talked in dark corners and Greek sailors would periodically invade the cafe, dancing their Zimbetikos (a warrior dance), gulping down whiskey straight, and throwing their money around wildly. The

Christmas decorations were never taken down from year to year, and I can still remember the tissue bells that hung from the ceiling.

I found a spirited group of people in my first Greek dance class. The instructor was quite the Scorpio character, heavy in his style and a way with the women. He taught the feeling of the dance first through basic rhythms, the steps followed the feelings. We danced for two hours in the class in the back room of the cafe and danced the rest of the evening to a live Greek band. We all danced till two or three in the morning, laughing, telling jokes, letting go, and dancing, dancing, dancing. The dancers melted into one another — whirling, twirling, and kicking highly.

The dance helped to heal the torn fragments of my psyche by healing the split between myself and others. I became immensely curious about dance as healing art. I studied dance for the next 25 years, now 46 years total, and performed Egyptian, Tunisian, Persian, Turkish, and Arabic dances in Middle Eastern dance troops in the Bay Area. I could feel that these dances started in ancient temples as healing rituals. When dancing with other Middle Eastern dancers, I felt as if we were in those ancient temples. The sacred and the sensual were not separate. I could experience the divine in the dance. Mirroring the posture and rhythm of the other dancers had the capacity to unify us.

I studied the emerging dance therapists and started combining my interest in psyche with dance. I began developing a dance mythology from my feelings, my dreams and my images. I taught psychiatric nursing for many years and began to notice the relationship between the patients' patterns of movement and their psychodynamics. I started combining my interest in the psyche with movement. The students could get a better feeling of the patients' experience by mirroring their movement: the way the patients talked, walked, and expressed themselves.

It was about this time that I read Fritjof Capra's book, *The Tao of Physics* (1975, 2010), about a paradigm shift in science. Physicists were no longer viewing nature in terms of static materialism but from the field or force behind how things moved. The new physics were being compared to Eastern Mysticism. Science was changing the way of knowing about nature, away from an objective reality to a subjective one. This was very significant information as I felt the body had the capacity to give us intuitive information about ourselves and to explore our nature. Dance was a way to embody life and a way to unite us with all living things. This is the essence of Mysticism: union.

I was profoundly stuck by this idea, particularly the idea that the world we presently live in was conceptualized as a machine. Not only could I observe this mechanistic style in the culture, I could feel it. I felt like I was moving like a machine as a way to survive in the culture. It described what my experiences had been working in hospitals as a nurse. I felt like a robot in a disorganized system, checking IVs and administering medications. The healing art of care was practically nonexistent. It appeared very threatening to talk about the relationship of people's lives, traumas and stresses and how it affected their health or illness. It was taboo to talk about death.

Caring was often seen as incompetent or being too soft. It was difficult to integrate caring and technical competence, the art and science of care. I saw many flaws with the exclusion of the healing art to the soul worship of science. The ethics behind science for curiosity sake had not been challenged. Millions of dollars were spent in health care systems that mechanically dissected the problem, technologically making advances in diagnosis but failing miserably in terms of caring and healing. Checking accuracy in quantitative outcomes was valued; the myth was that the more precise the measurement, the better the cure. This was the hospital assembly line. The hospital machine. This problem is now being exacerbated by "managed care." It is more important than ever to look at this type of thinking because mechanism, a robotic rhythm embodied as a character trait, produces sickness and jeopardizes not only our health but our freedom.

Through dance and dance therapy, I healed my sense of alienation and fragmentation. Dance had the capacity to reestablish a feeling of life and wholeness and relationship to others. I could see the difference between moving robotically fast in time, detached, separated and fragmentd and feeling a sense of life and well being, "dancing." I discovered that movement is reflection of the psyche, a way to break the isolation, a way to get clarity about the need to make a shift in values from being a machine to "being" human.

I took a course in movement notation based on Laban's Theory which was simply a way to record quality of movement: how people move in time, how they use space, how they use their weight, and whether their movement was bound or free. In this course, I could experience different realities by combining different dimensions of time, space, weight, and flow. We were given an exercise to do haiku poetry using Laban's qualities to express the poetry. One woman's poetry in motion I will never forget. As she expressed herself, an inner life came to the surface, something I had never seen before. It was very beautiful. Experimenting with movement made possible the exploration of different realities, and in particular, the exploration of the inner life force within us all.

For my dissertation, I wanted to study something about the relationship of the style of movement to health from many different cultural perspectives. At the time, however, I felt I did not have enough expert help, for my advisors in educational psychology were traditional in their background. I did a quasi-experimental study evaluating the care of dying patients. I studied the psychodynamics of cancer patients, and although that seemed at the time far from my love of psyche and dance, it gave me more knowledge and hypotheses about the relationship between psychological stresses, between health and illness, and between life and death. It was in this study that I began to observe a relationship between belief, expectation and treatment outcome. The degree of hopelessness experienced by these patients was not due to the cancer, but due to a loss of hope about ever making a connection with the most important people in their lives. Many of the patients had difficulty with intimacy because of an inability to express vulnerability. Patients would tell me they thought they were "strong as iron." I began to see Illness as a denial of vulnerability and the psychodynamics of ill patients as symptomatic of problems in our culture.

There was another course I took that had a profound effect on my thinking and crystallized my ideas. The name of the course was Dance through Time, taught by Carol Teton. One could see the relationship between style of movement and world view through the centuries. I looked at the fifteenth through the seventeenth centuries. There it was — world view, concept of space and time from classical physics, and Cartesian philosophy reverberating across work, art, science, including dance. (Rust, 1969, pp.31-119) This insight contributed to the major assumption of this book — our reality shapes our movement in time and space, and affects the quality of our lives and our health.

I then made the connection between mechanism in our modern era and the most popular diseases of our time: heart disease, cancer, and addictive behaviors including drugs, cigarettes, alcohol, work, and destructive relationships. The psychodynamics of these diseases are related to mechanism: denial of feelings, emphasis on external reality, a belief in the idea that more is better, the valuing of production and perfection. Mechanism is expressed by moving too fast in time, taking no time to smell the roses, or to hold someone's hand and really feel their warmth. Illness can be seen as a disorder in rhythm and as an expression of alienation.

My own healing through therapy and dance also helped me see that I am part of this mechanistic society. I was caught up in achievement and subsequently realized it did not cure the underlying emptiness, and it interfered with my enjoyment of life. Mechanistic symbols (the Nazi, the robot, and the clock sense of time) came up in my images, dreams, posture, and rhythms that represented both my personal and collective unconscious. The push to go faster and faster was a way to numb the underlying feelings of helplessness and terror and grief and push down the pain of past trauma.

Finally, I became fascinated with the idea that rhythm was powerful in changing states of consciousness. I realized that from my dance experience and as a therapist. I used sculptures of the patients' families of origin. There was a rhythm of walking and talking that came out of the posture and put the patients back in time to past experiences with their family.

Later in my career, I studied EMDR (Eye Movement Desensitization and Reprocessing), a psychotherapeutic process using eye movement rhythm to access the patient's inner experience. It is primarily for treating psychological trauma. It made me think about the similarity between ancient and modern methods of healing, as both used rhythm to change consciousness.

I also thought there was a collective rhythm in the culture related to mechanism. People were moving like machines as a way to survive in the culture and may have been in a collective trance to avoid underlying pain and suffering. Materialism was and is the antidote for spiritual emptiness, and not a very effective one.

I started writing this book in a traditional way, attempting to clearly conceptualize my ideas to tell people about the rigidity and alienation in our present-day culture. As I wrote, I began to realize this was also a story about my own journey and the feeling of alienation and loneliness within myself. The glue for the connecting links between various parts of this book are my own questions. Some are answered through experience, some through philosophical explanations, academically through description of what others have said about it, and other questions will be answered through my dreams, through my dances and through poetry. I am in search of myself and who I am. I am desperate to deal with the alienation in myself and in my culture. In 2002 when these initiating ideas were written, I said, "I am very worried about where we are today, particularly in America. I feel we are losing our health and our freedom." This is even more true today, 2025.

Those Who Supported My Writings, My story/Mythos Dance of Psyche: Rhythm of Consciousness

Anne Elizabeth Nelson

Anne Nelson PsyD, RN.

Anne and I have had a beautiful friendship, being there for each other for almost a lifetime. She was a good witness across time reflecting understanding the significance of past events, present situations and future hopes, able to resonate with my experiences on a deep level. I was there for her as well. She is now on the other side. She passed away on September 30th of 2023.

We met as Navy Nurses during the Viet Nam era. Both saw the wounds of war in the amputee ward — amputations, bungee stick wounds coated with agent orange, shrapnel wounds. I also worked in neurosurgery and met many marines who would not walk again. Support for each other was so important. We both remember a Captain who lost both of his legs. We both are wounded by toxic stress in the Navy. There was targeting of nurses because of the need of patriarchy to dominate over the feminine.

We met at the Officers Club when she first arrived and then both of us lived at the BOQ (Bachelor Officers Quarters) at Alameda Naval Air Station; she lived right next door to my suite. When we first met, we stayed up late talking about our lives and about why we were in the Navy. We both got our Doctoral degrees in Psychology and maintained our RN license across the years. Her husband was an EENT specialist — they met when we were all at Oak Knoll Naval Hospital. They had three children: Jenni, Beth, and Chris. I am their Auntie, and Beth is my Godchild. Jenni is a Naturopath Physician, Beth is a counselor, Chris went into the Navy for five years. So, the mutuality is in the next generation as well.

She always asked about my writing, and her comment I included in the first book (2003):

For over 30 years, I have deeply respected Dr. Campbell's passion for knowledge and insight, not only for herself, but for others and society at large. She is a healer, teacher, artist, and dancer, and one who has the courage to go "beneath the surface" in her role as a researcher seeking the collective links between illness and health. Dr. Campbell has orchestrated a remarkable and honest book about relationship and healing which emphasizes the unifying significance of music and dance. The reader is taken on a journey of thoughtful discovery.

I went to her memorial and shared the information that is here. There was so much love expressed for her. God bless you, dear friend on the other side, sending love to heaven.

Patti Szerlip RN now Retired

I met Patti, RN, at the time while working as a teacher at Dominican University. I was teaching Psychiatric Nursing at the time and had students at Psychiatric Emergency where Patti was working as an RN. We became a great team in giving students hands-on experience with patients. We became good friends then and after both of us retired. She was an incredible witness to who I am and awesome support, able to resonate with my experiences, especially as nurses in the field. She often asked me about my writing, and her insight and support went a long way to give me encouragement for writing this book; and also importantly to understand and resonate with the bullying in the health care/hospital systems and at the University. This is the power of the witness.

She was exceptional nurse with such compassion… so effective in calming delusional, psychotic, schizophrenic patients. There was one very delusional patient who came in, her hair matted, a football guard in her mouth, and very tense. Patti walked in to take her blood pressure and the tone of Patti's voice was so compassionate, the patient calmed right down.

She is also an artist painting beautiful nature, people, and the memories in her life. She appreciated my being there when her husband Sandy died; so, we were there for each other, and have continued this support to this day.

She has also written books and writes beautiful poetry. Her first book is titled: Meet Me Under the Bed, a love story about love and Mental Disability. The second one is now in the process of being written. It is about a young woman wanting to become a Mother without the complications of being with a man. It is based on a true story.

She was there for my performance of the Dances of Psyche at the Cruising Club sponsored by the City of Sausalito. She has offered to read this second book and give me feedback.

In summary, she has been there for me for support, acknowledgement of my work with students, and in writing this book. Her poetry is included here. She is a beautiful friend.

Saroj Chaman PHD : Professor of Fine Art & Mythology, Now Retired

I was writing the first book and talked to my friends at Avatar's Restaurant, an Indian restaurant in Sausalito. I told them about my writing related to rhythm and healing. They suggested I talk to their relative in Patiala, India. I started writing to her. She did her dissertation on the dancing God Shiva, from the paintings in the caves of the Himalayas. We communicated now over 20 years. I was invited to Patiala, India. I went there and visited Punjabi University, met her students and was introduced to Roma Gypsy scholars, and was treated like a Goddess; they were so generous. The full story of my visit is more thoroughly described later in the book

Kathy Hoare PHD, RN, now retired

Kathy and I met when we were teaching Nursing at San Francisco State. She taught Medical-Surgical Nursing and I taught Psychiatric/ Mental Health Nursing. We were then hired to teach Nursing Research at Stanford Medical Center. The purpose of the National grant was to teach Nurses on the front lines how to do research. We worked with seven hospitals in the Bay Area. Many nurses did very innovative work and spoke at national conferences. I became friends with her and her husband Tyler who was an artist. She came to the presentation of my first book at Bistro E with Gypsy Flavor Restaurant in San Francisco. She offered to read this book and give feedback.

Alicia Bright PhD, RN

We were both teaching at the University. She was very supportive when we were both dealing with toxic bosses. Her support was invaluable. She later left there and was hired at the College of Marin as their Director of Nursing. I was very happy for her. I will be going to visit her there. Many of the faculty we worked with were hired by the College. I have been invited to visit and look forward to seeing everyone.

Dr. Daniel Wong, DOC, Doctor of Oriental Medicine

I met Daniel, Dr. Wong when he was attending Five Branches Institute of Chinese Medicine. My brother, now Dr. Walter Allen Campbell, was attending there as well. He was open for more work, so I thought he could come into my practice. He did the acupuncture and herbs for patients, and I did the trauma work. So, we had an East/West Practice. He did acupuncture and herbs, and I did trauma psychotherapy. He had worked with the monks in Tibet. So, he told me to dream about an image, an image in nature and I had a series of dreams related to Tibetan medicine. The description of these dreams and a more detailed description of this process is in the chapter on Tibetan Medicine. This is one of those synchronous miracles, as my mother studied Tibetan Medicine and my brother now has a practice in Traditional Chinese Medicine. I am truly appreciative of this awesome journey. He is now teaching at a Chinese Medicine College in Florida.

Julia Peacock, Roma, Gypsy from Hungary

Julia supported my work by having a celebration of the first book at her restaurant, Bistro E Europe, with Gypsy Flavor in San Francisco, California. I performed the dances in the book, The Dances of Psyche, there. We invited friends, family, and those who were interested to this celebration. She was important as many of the dances and dreams that I performed were related to Roma Holocaust and persecution. Now in this second book as well, she was in one of my dreams of gold light. I was kneeling down and extended my hand that was filled with gold light to her.

Sani Rifati, President of Voice of Roma

In a miracle of coincidence, I met Shani at Papas restaurant when I decided to go Greek dancing. I was writing my first book and had dreams of the Roma Holocaust on the anniversary they were killed at Auschwitz concentration camps. He fled Kosovo from the bombings from our war planes. He fled to the US and started an activist group for Roma as they are still being persecuted. He gave me articles on the Roma Holocaust. He organizes presentations describing this persecution and prejudice that is still going on. He organizes festivals and events with presentations, Gypsy music and dance.

Every spring, he has the Herdelezi Festival. It is when the wagons would leave the forest and start to travel. There are presentations informing people about the Romani culture. I so appreciate having this knowledge and support across many years now. He was the one who brought me to Julia's Restaurant, Bistro E with Gypsy Flavor. It was a blessing in that I stayed connected and experienced the Romani Culture, and I continue to this day.

Jasmine Mabalatan: Dancer/Artist

I met Jasmine in a Middle Eastern dance class, and we became friends. We performed in many concerts throughout many years — in particular, Life Dance Theatre led by Lorna Zilba. We performed Bedouin, classical Persian, Egyptian, Tunisian dance, and Gypsy dance at many concerts in the Bay Area across many years. I took her to Julia's restaurant, Bistro E. with Gypsy Flavor, and we both became friends with the Roma Community as well as attending festivals through the Voice of Roma led by Sani Rifati, in particular, Herdelezi festival, the festival celebrating Spring. She also performed in my concerts, the Dances of Psyche, at Julia's restaurant and at the Cruising Club, organized by the City of Sausalito. It's been good to have her on this journey with me. She is also an artist, has done oil paintings that have Oriental themes.

Susan Morris: Former Recreation Director for the City of Sausalito

Susan took an interest in my work/my writing and offered to organize a concert at the Cruising Club in Sausalito. This is where I presented my first book, Dance of Psyche, and performed the dances in the book. She died a few years ago, but lives in my memories and I feel grateful for her contribution to make my work visible…. Sending gratitude to you in heaven.

Dannhae Maya Herrera: Counselor/ Dola/ Dancer/ Artist

Dannhae and I met at dance class. We performed together and became very good friends. She was going to college at the time and since then received her Bachelors's Degree. She is very committed to the care of pregnant mothers and birthing. She has become a Duala now. So, we share an interest in caring for mothers and babies. She was in the performance of my Dances of Psyche at the Cruising Club sponsored by the City of Sausalito. We also performed many dances together as well. including Middle Eastern, Persian, Tunisian, Egyptian dances. She was an incredible Middle Eastern dancer and did solo performances. We support each other's creative work which is so valuable, and I appreciate her so much.

Walter Allen Buck Campbell: DOM, Doctor of Oriental Medicine

He is my brother and has had a deep love for his sister throughout our lives. Our Brother/Sister bond has brought gatherings and adventures across a lifetime now. He was working for the airlines as in-flight supervisor and previously as flight attendant. As his sister, I was able to get free or low-cost flights to Europe and visit his friends there. I visited London, and then his friend Michelle took me all across Paris.

He was also a photographer at the time, and his photograph of the seagulls flying with the beautiful poetry introduced the book here. He then went to Five Branches Institute of Chinese Medicine and has a Traditional Chinese Medicine clinic in Florida. He is very innovative in treating conditions the medical system has not done very well with. He followed the tradition in healing from my mother who studied Tibetan Medicine and became a healer. My mother followed in her mother's path who studied with advanced healers in Italy. He is also an artist, teacher, healer as well.

Lisa Zazlove Ph.D., Psychologist

Lisa and I worked together at Sausalito Professional Clinic. It was a Mental Health clinic that treated dual diagnosis: Dual diagnosis meaning addiction plus a mental diagnosis, such as depression, anxiety and, also had underlying trauma. We are colleagues and friends, supporting each other in dealing with difficult patient dynamics. She has been supportive of my writing, and it was great that she attended book presentations and dance performances.

Jennifer Whitebauden, Phd: Psychologist

Jennifer and I met more recently. We both were credentialed in EMDR therapy for the treatment of trauma. She also worked as a nurse, so we had a lot to share about our experiences in both fields. So, it was very helpful to have her professional support and support of my writing. Her father was Native American, and I admired her ancestry. She moved to Portugal, but we still keep in touch.

Elsa Ng, LCSW: Licensed Clinical Social Worker

I worked with Elsa when I was on Psychiatric Emergency with students. She was a crisis counselor there. We also attended the same dance classes. We were colleagues and friends. She is supportive and resonates with what is happening in Gaza with the Israeli/Palestinian conflict. We support each other relating to the enormous suffering as a result of the war. She also supports what I have written here.

Mark Weiman of Regent Press: Publisher and Printer, Berkely, California

He was helpful in printing the first book and now helpful with this second book. I appreciated his caring and attentiveness and his ability to connect me with resources in editing, writing and printing my books. I also appreciated the artistic quality of the books he is printing and publishing.

Nona, My Italian Grandmother, Angelina Fragasso

I have a special feeling for my Nona, Grandmother on my mother's side. She studied with advanced healers in Italy. Her story is here. I want to honor the healing gifts that were handed down to my brother and me. Sending love to heaven.

My Mother: Rose Marie Fragasso Campbell

I am grateful to my mother as she studied Tibetan Medicine when we were kids. This influenced both my brother and I, who became healing practitioners. Sending love to heaven.

My Spiritual Team

My spiritual team on the other side that I pray to for guidance and support Includes; Archangel Uriel, Blessed Mother, Jesus, Mother and Father, Nona, and kitty, Boots and other kitties: Conyac and Coco.

Chapter 3

Professional Background / Purpose and Need Embracing the Dark to Find the Light, Acquiring Wisdom Across the Decades

MY INTENTION IN WRITING this book is to source my experience across a 50-year career as Trauma Psychologist, Nurse, and Healing Artist/Dancer to illuminate the traumatic effects of a society which prioritizes profit over the needs of people, and the values related to humanity become fractured. My life's work is dedicated to healing self, healing others, healing the personal and collective trauma we are all experiencing in an age of bully bosses, violence as solutions to problems, an epidemic of child emotional, physical and sexual abuse, inequality of minorities: African Americans, Native Americans, Latinos, Roma, Muslim, Gays; and now the Haitians; but also to inspire and share my spiritual experience with the light, the light of being.

The letter I wrote (2002) to the editor describing the first book, is relevant for this second book, a sequel to the first.

Experience and knowledge as a trauma psychologist, nurse, teacher, researcher, and dancer since 1968 helped me to write this book: Mythos: Dance of Psyche: Rhythm of Consciousness. As a trauma psychologist I was using eye movement rhythms (EMDR) to access the patients' inner experiences and dreams. As a dancer, I was shaping choreography from an inner rhythm that I was discovering was the lucid dream, and premonition for the nighttime dream. These were modern methods, but similar to the ancient philosophy of healing: knowledge of the creative unconscious acquired through the natural rhythms of the body. Rhythm can show the moods of humanity, and thus tell a personal but collective story about the society in which we live, and access ancestral trauma — a way to show a shift from the world as machine to one that is alive and united by rhythm, a vibrational force, energy, a cosmos connected by dance.

This is also a healer's story/Mythos created by dance/movement as reflection/symbol of the Psyche/soul tapping both the personal and collective trauma of our times. The emotional/spiritual conditions are described through rhythm. It is an intuitive way of knowing, as rhythm is portal to dreams, the creative unconscious. Unity through rhythm to deal with tyranny. Dreams and images as hope for survival. The story shaped by posture, rhythms, images and dreams.

Some of the main ideas that are explored in this book are:

The present-day hurry-up rhythm madness, the robotic rhythm, has consequences to health and freedom.

The robotic rhythm may be a collective trance to numb the pain of unresolved trauma.

The collective myth of the machine is that being perfect, productive and strong leads to the illusion that society can dominate over nature.

Trauma may predispose individuals and cultures to split themselves from the whole and become machine-like. The machine is the false self, the paradox of helplessness, the Nazi movement was the ultimate machine.

The most prevalent diseases of our time are related to mechanism, a robotic rhythm. Illness is thus a disorder of rhythm.

Healing through rhythm is an ancient idea but needed in the 21st century.

Rhythm is a way to acquire knowledge and a way to heal the split with ourselves, with the culture, nature, and the divine.

Rhythm can tap our dreams and show a way out of fear and a survival mentality.

In the last chapter of the first book, this healing artist demonstrates these ideas through her dances and dreams that show a shift from trauma to well-being, from moving robotically to dancing with life. It tells a story that heals fractured memories torn apart by stress/trauma and integrates the fragments into a whole authentic self. The dances then appear paranormal in that there is a trace of fire from the movements, shows the life force of the dance. Active imagination in rhythm/dance and movement shaped choreography representing a reflection of the psyche, showing the way through the personal and collective trauma in the American Society today. Ancient practice of trance, ancient healing ritual emerges now to inspire a new reality: love, and the light of being found in the dance, the dance of psyche, rhythm of consciousness — sourcing wisdom in an age of tyranny — Rhythm unites. Vocabulary for the dance came from dances from around the world experienced as ancient healing ritual: Greek, Persian, Arabic, Flamenco, Indian, Turkish, Gypsy, Tunisian. Images and dreams come alive through watercolor paintings and collages and show a way to a spiritual reality — the light appears. The story of healing through dreams and dance continues in the second book.

The conclusion is that human beings are more than flesh and blood: the fabric of our being is light, rhythm and vibration, and thus human beings are part of nature and the cosmos. Being human means to be alive. Dance helps us to be vibrant and to look being in the face. The light of being is discovered in the dance and in dreams.

Paradigm Shift

This is paradigm shift from a world conceptualized as a machine based on materialistic values with the emphasis on separation and classification to one that is vibrant, a system's view where there is unity in nature. I was inspired by Fritjof Capra, his book on the Tao of Physics (1975, 2010) emphasizing this shift. Thus, Predictions would no longer be made from a static reality but from the field or force behind how things move. The new physics was compared to Eastern Mysticism. Science was changing its way of knowing about nature, away from an objective to a subjective one. This was very significant information as I felt the body had the capacity to give us information about ourselves and explore our nature. Dance was a way to embody life and unite us to all living things.

Body Movement is significant as it is not only the physical reality, but it is the life force reflected in the movement revealing vitality and health. How people walk, talk and express themselves non-verbally when communicating with others, patterns of breath and other physiological rhythms reveal the unconscious dimensions of the psyche. Movement has symbolic significance reflecting intension toward life and death. Consequently, the study of body movement represents a shift from cognitive knowledge to one obtained through body experience, this is an intuitive way of knowing. It is experiential knowledge from moving like a machine, a robotic rhythm in trance state, separating us from ourselves and others to one that unites through vibrance. The effect of a robotic rhythm driven by values of efficiency and production disconnects us from the inner self/being. This is presently the dominant body politic. The hidden assumption in this body politic is that acknowledging the body/human need and suffering is not profitable. This disconnect from the body and emotions fuels the need for war; fuels the need for the bombing of the innocent. Numb and hollow, they do not understand the consequences of bombing innocent lives. If they would feel the devastation of bombing their own children burned alive by bombs, there might be more hope for change. The shift is to one that has the capacity to establish a feeling of life and wholeness and relationship to others, compassion for the suffering of others. Would we not accomplish more through humanitarian aid and diplomacy versus bombs?

There is a destructive effect of the profit machine on the personal and collective psyche. The Machine is the split-off part of the self, engrossed in materialism, bigger is better, more is better, numbs the body, mind and spirit and increases the propensity for violence. It embraces competition that values power and control over others, versus human need which encourages collaboration. Disconnected from the body, efficiency and production is trumped. The robotic rhythm, trance state fractures truth, creates false reality. There is disembodiment of human needs and feelings which threatened the bottom line. Talking heads justify exploitation and war. Many in the society move to this robotic rhythm draining energy, bankrupting the life force. My writing deals with this disembodiment that contributes to denial about consequences of violence including mass shootings, war, genocide and holocaust.

The denial of human needs also takes its toll on workers; many are denied a living wage, opportunity through education. Violence including in-school shootings and shootings in the street may become a means of restoring power which has hurt and devastated many lives.

Those at the top in Washington are addicted to money as an opiate... more money, never enough, splits them from themselves, empty and hollow, they are disconnected to the needs of others. There is no compassion. They suffer; people suffer more. The need for violence through the profit of war, sale of weapons, is now long term.

Movement is a reflection of the psyche, a way to break the isolation and a way to get clarity about a need to make a shift in values away from the machine to "being human." As I said in the first book as well, "We are here for each other and not to support the bottom line." There is a need to shift from the machine that separates mind, body and spirit — a robotic rhythm — which thus separates us from ourselves, others, nature and the divine. This is present-day trauma. In trauma one separates from the body, disconnects from self, and fractures memory, so the shift is from trauma to one that is alive and vibrant united by rhythm uniting us to others and all living things — mysticism. Rhythm is a unifying force in healing self, culture, nature and the divine.

Walk together for change in values.

Significant in acquiring knowledge and the ability to tap the unconscious through posture, rhythm, images and dreams.

Healing the split, giving us insight.

The capacity to experience what lies beneath the surface.

Consciousness

We seek to know.

Dance as a way to know by how the body shapes itself in time and space.

It is a way to travel from fast in time to sustained.

Opening to a new reality from outer to inner space; here is where the lucid dream occurs, taps the night-time dream.

This is the wisdom of the dancer... the mirror of beauty and love of another for cultural healing.

Experiencing the divine in trance in sacred ceremony.

Deepening heart.

Sacred light appears.

Shape shifting in being at one with all living things and ancestral spirits and kitties on the other side.

Playful and courageous, spontaneous shaping for survival in the face of life and death.

This is the dance of Psyche, the wisdom of consciousness.

Human Beings

We are nature, the rhythm and cycle of life and death.

We have mind, body and spirit, and can experience the life force in ourselves, others nature and the divine.

This will unite us versus fracture.

We have a body with needs and feelings.

We can look being in the face.

We can unite through the mirror of life and death.

Through vibration and rhythm.

The Sufi Message:

Movement is life and stillness is death; for in movement there is the significance of life and in stillness we see the signs of death.

Therefore, with regard to our physical health, movement is the principal thing, regulation of movement, of its rhythm in pulsation and the circulation of blood. The whole cause of death and decay can be traced to the lack of movement, all different aspects of disease are to be traced to congestion. Every decay is caused by congestion, and congestion is caused by lack of movement. (Khan, 1961, p. 22)

We destroy nature, we destroy ourselves.

Understanding the dynamics of trauma and healing is important to saving the earth. There is enormous powerlessness in the feelings underneath trauma with the protective mechanism to then want to dominate and control, to win, sometimes at all costs, or be victimized by the perpetrator — both are reenacting trauma. In trauma there is a split from the whole separating us from ourselves, others, nature and the divine. Healing the split for self will help heal society, heal the earth.

Thus, the major goal is healing self and culture from traumatic experience. This requires a shift in a way of knowing from "I think therefore I am to also including I feel and experience, therefore I understand more fully who I am, and then have logic and emotions, mind and body communicate with each other.

As I have said, Human Beings are more than flesh and blood; we are light, vibration, and energy that also helps us connect with ourselves, each other, nature and the divine.

The reality deepens as the light is love.

Thus, I can experience nature as alive versus just a physical reality, thus realize more fully that Nature has control; we depend on preserving nature for survival — to perceive her beauty and embody the rhythm of nature to unite with her will help us survive. We are the wind, fire, water, air, sky and earth.

Professional Experience: A Story of Healing and Resilience: Embracing the dark to find the light, acquiring wisdom across the decades.

My first nursing job after receiving my RN license was in Pediatrics at Shands Teaching Hospital, University of Florida, Gainesville. I worked one month of nights and one month of days with every third weekend off, often 7-8 nights in a row. There was an infant unit of 20 patients with congenital defects — liver disease, spina bifida, leukemia, cardiac anomalies, and other very serious diagnoses, which were also problems in the children's unit of 40 patients. There were often problems with patients admitted with either viral or bacterial encephalitis. I remember one child who was comatose from viral encephalitis which had no treatment at the time. I remember his small body which would likely never recover. I was turning him, giving him passive range of motion so that he would not acquire muscle contractions. I remember a child who was seizing through the night, being attentive to him, calling the physician who ordered phenobarbital for him; still remember the smell of it. I remember staying with a child who had a high fever and putting clothes on the body with water and alcohol to cool the body down through the night. The assignments were quite overwhelming. As I remember, I feel a sense of worth. However, at the time I often had feelings of "not good enough." Later, in acquiring expertise in dealing with trauma, I found that I was not alone. It is often felt by frontline nurses, physicians, and firefighters; especially that in spite of your efforts many do not make it contributing to feelings of helplessness and contributing to burnout. This is particularly true as a result of patients getting worse or dying, especially with children, and also a result of too many patients to care for and it's impossible to keep up with the demands of rapidly changing acuity. I remember a child who had leukemia. I established a rapport with him and was concerned how he was coping with his illness and how he was handling his poor prognosis, that he could die. However, at the time, the medical doctors did not tell patients about a poor prognosis which they felt might result in death. I remember enjoying the rapport I had with him and his family. He gave me a beautiful blue vase I have to this day, and I still think of him. He did die soon after this. This was the early seed of my later becoming a trauma psychologist — the concern about the potential of trauma or stress from illness, hospitalization, procedures and facing death.

I remember seeing a chaplain to deal with my feelings, but in looking back I did not have the insight to understand fully what I was experiencing as I do now. It was also a system that did not take into account reasonable assignments and, also, the trauma of dealing with illness, crisis and death were significant factors in the stress of staff.

On my days off I would teach synchronized swimming to kids at a nearby pool. I would encourage them to develop their own choreography. They were so excited, and they would call to me: "Christina, watch this." It was part of who I was to inspire self-determination and creativity in others. This would be the cornerstone of my teaching psychiatric nursing and psychology in the future — inspiring self-determination. This also inspired me, later in life, to develop my own dance from my deep internal feelings; dreams representing the personal and collective unconscious of our times.

I remember not having much of a social life. I did have a date to go tubbing down the Ichetucknee River. Worked all night and then was at the river all day, then went to work that night. The other nurses were very kind to me that shift and helped me out.

A solution to difficult working conditions: Becoming a Navy Nurse, Viet Nam era. I decided to go into the Navy as they had better working conditions/ schedules, so I thought, and benefits. It was the Viet Nam era and they needed nurses. I got my first choice of assignment which was at Oak Knoll Naval Hospital, Oakland, California in the San Francisco Bay Area.

Sargent Walter John Kolocauscous Campbell
MY DAD: WORLD WAR II VETERAN
Written up as a stellar Sergeant, Fort Hamilton, Brooklyn, NY

I grew up with a positive regard for the military as my father was in the Army during WWII. He was stationed at Fort Hamilton, Brooklyn, New York. There was so much pride about his service. He was written up in the newsletter at Fort Hamilton as stellar. The sketch of him from that newsletter was on the fireplace in our home. He would prepare the men to board the ships to go to Europe to fight. He was told to shoot the deserters if they jumped ship. Instead, he pulled them out of the water, put them back on the ship and gave them a shot of whiskey. So, he is a hero to me. I inherited being the rescuer. So, off I went into the military during the Viet Nam Era to be a Navy Nurse.

I worked different units. The first was the amputee ward. I remember a Captain who was a double amputee. I walked into his room; he was very handsome and virile, then I saw both legs amputated above the knee, flesh still raw. It took my breath away and I was speechless. Looking back, I was quite young 22, and was not experienced enough to know what to say. My friend, also a Navy Nurse, remembers him as well to this day, just over 50 years ago now.

I rehearse now what I wanted to do and say. I think I would compose myself, be calm and present for him, get to know him and be ready to listen to his story. I regret not being able to do this at the time. I remember others with shrapnel wounds, other amputees, patients with punji stick wounds that were covered with agent orange.

Today I hear about some vets who are dying of cancer years later, most likely from exposure to agent orange toxicity. I remember them.

Thinking back, I remember them being released to the outlying wards and hearing about many of them getting drunk. I felt, even as a young nurse in this instance, that they were medicating their traumas and needed more continuity of care. Today we would say they had PTSD and were medicating their pain with alcohol. PTSD was not a diagnosis at the time. Later in my career, I became a trauma psychologist and worked with dual diagnoses, addiction and mental disorders. As the addiction subsided, the trauma started to surface.

Navy Nurse Vietnam Era
Neurosurgery Unity Oak Knoll Naval Hospital

Portrait of the Author

I then worked in the Neurosurgery unit. I remember the paraplegic patients being turned on Stryker frames by the corpsmen. Stryker frames are designed for patients with spinal injuries so they can be turned without difficulty. These patients most likely would not walk again. I had strong feelings about this. One patient one evening asked me to put on music and massage his back ... which I did. He seemed to appreciate this so much ... remember it to this day. He was paraplegic.

I remember a Parkinson's patient who had problems with motor coordination. We developed a care plan with exercises. One was to string paperclips together to help hand coordination. He seemed to benefit greatly from this. Later, when I was working in the Pedi clinic, he came in to thank me and gave me his chain of paperclips. I appreciated this so much. The experience of working with the wounds of war, I do believe, helped to shape my writing. It broke the denial about the devastating effects of war, the carnage versus the patriotic idealization "for democracy" with the young men and women in sharp uniforms. No matter the great ideals, it did not justify this carnage. Perhaps in WWII, but later wars: Viet Nam, Afghanistan, Iraq and others were immoral wars for power and control of "our resources." I was later to find out.

It was in Psychiatric Nursing as Navy Nurse that I had my first experience with Bullying. At the time, I was not aware that it was epidemic in Nursing and also in the military. I kept being called out on the carpet for mistakes I was making. I was new and needed mentoring, so some were legitimate. I was very conscientious, however, and very kind, but had some insecurity. After many years, I know now these are characteristics that make you a target. I was also very feminine and beautiful, more of an artist, which did not help in the military. It was many years later I heard that "Nurses eat their young." I was labeled as a flirt and castrating bitch. This was due to the resentment that some masculine forces had for women in the Navy, the military. I say masculine forces because the administrators, whether men or women, often embodied a masculine mentality. I would say masculine mentality in extreme; the feminine, kindness and conscientiousness were often threatening. Many years later I was to find out that many of my Navy nurse friends were also targeted, and in one instance I found out one of the corpsmen raped one of the nurses. This bullying experience triggered a severe depression and suicidal crisis at the time. The experience was very damaging to my self-esteem as a nurse. It took enormous strength to pull out of it. There was much shame and a feeling of being defective or not good enough that drove the depression. One of the worst experiences during this time was attending a group meeting with other psychiatric nurses on the floor. I remember being attacked and criticized and that voice, saying how horrible it was. I had a soft voice. I left crying, took a few minutes to compose myself and returned to posture strong. It made its mark, however.

After several months, I felt more confident in my role as psychiatric nurse. It was then the Commander decided to take me off the unit and transfer me to the women's medical floor. The most devastating thing about this experience was not the toxic behavior of the Nurse Commander, but the lack of support and betrayal of the other nurses. In the military, or in health care, this is a very serious offense as it is a survival issue that your colleagues have your back. This, more than the toxic behavior of the nurse commander, brought me down and broke my sense of safety in my role as a nurse. I carried this with me throughout my career over several decades being on guard and lacked a sense of safety with other nurses and physicians. It has contributed to anxiety, depression, and self-esteem issues with roots in enormous losses in childhood. In looking back, if I had mentoring and support, I would not have had this scare. In knowing how important mentoring and support was, I became a good mentor when teaching psychiatric nursing and also psychology to students, especially during their clinical experiences with patients.

I then worked on a women's medical unit on nights. I remember talking to the women there, mostly wives of the service men. I saw a relationship of the timing of their illnesses to the men leaving for sea duty for six months at a time. The nurses were upset with me because the desk

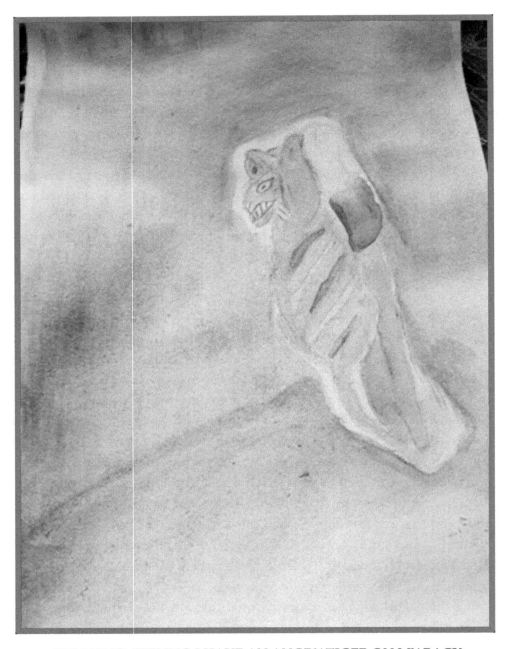

BULLYING: FEELING I HAVE AN ANGRY TIGER ON MY BACK
Later, from Chinese Medicine Perspective,
the Tiger was there for protection

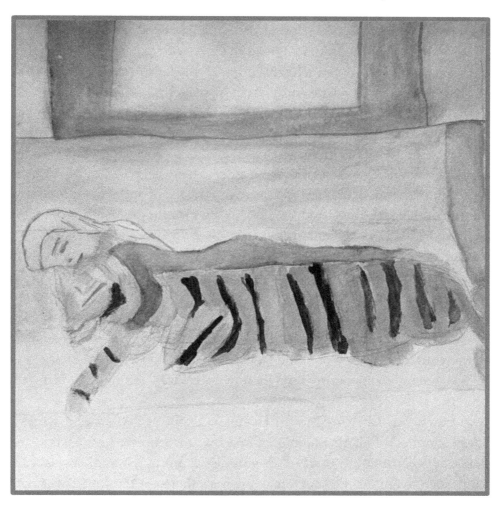

BEING AT PEACE WITH THE TIGER
Watercolor by Christina

was left messy. Really... after dealing with medical and emotional issues all night. It might have been threatening at that time to deal with the emotional issues on a medical floor which was a very medical model.

My next assignment was Pedi clinic and rotation to the med clinic and the Emergency Room. My supervisors were less rigid, and I developed a close rapport with the staff. I enjoyed the E.R. with experts from all different areas. I enjoyed very much working with the kids in the Pedi clinic and started Education programs for them in many areas.

I was working in the med clinic one day and remember this woman who came in with headaches. I asked her when they started, and she said that it started when her husband passed away. She was not crying. I felt the headache might have been repressed grief. This was a seed of my interest in mind/body medicine (1971). This was unheard of at the time. I remember the docs being bored and felt very excited for the challenge of patients who were "really sick" with serious diagnoses. I would estimate that about 80% or more of patients at the time had emotional issues or high levels of stress that manifested in physical symptoms. This was true for the ER as well. I left the Navy in good spirits with a positive send-off from the staff and honorable discharge. I did work in the reserves at Treasure Island, San Francisco, for another five years in the Medical Corp. However, they were not paying me like they paid the men. I was then honorably discharged in 1977. I wanted to spend my time more wisely. I was getting my Maste's in Nursing at the time.

I then was hired by Moffitt Hospital, UCSF, in Pediatrics. I worked seven months on nights, 7-8 nights in a row sometimes. I was exhausted and was ready to quit. I put in for a day position in the Pedi-special care unit. There were insider/outsider dynamics there. At the time I was considered an outsider and would be assigned the harder patients. Because of my experience in the Navy, I wanted to prove I was a good nurse. I was very conscientious which made me a target once again.

I did get assigned to the day position in Pedi-special care. The nurses there objected as they had chosen someone else. However, that nurse did not put in a written request to the supervisor, which was a requirement which I had fulfilled.

It was tough because I was once again an outsider. There was pressure, and feelings of being a potential target came up again. I went through the same thing again being the new nurse who was going to be "eaten." I made it through, however, getting support from the Head Nurse. I sat down with nurses and physicians and confronted them over their negative criticism. They often backed down. One nurse, who was going to be the Head Nurse, threatened me when I was late one day, "I will fire you." I said, "Go ahead," and stood up to her. I started to be part of the team after that. Many years later, I found out that many nurses had gone through this initiation. I was not alone... and, also, many nurses have noted the frequency of the insider/outsider dynamics. Perhaps, this is why many new nurses do not make it. The retention rate is very low, 30% drop out. Decades later, about five years ago, they started a mentoring program for nurses who are just starting out. There is also now continuing education on bullying for nurses.

Patients were very ill: kidney transplant patients who were on dialysis, cardiac congenital defects, who needed careful monitoring, liver disease, seizures and many other serious illnesses.

In particular, I remember this one child who came in with having ingested English Furniture polish that was in a coke bottle. He was having trouble breathing as the furniture polish was toxic to his lungs. If I remember correctly, the alveoli blew-up and he was in respiratory distress. I had just gotten on the shift and taken his vital signs. Something signaled danger to me, but his vital signs were the same. I called the physician on call right away anyway and said I thought he needed to come. He asked about the vital signs, and I said they were the same. He did not come. About five minutes later, the child arrested. I called him back and he came right away and did CPR. The child did not make it. He died. I remember comforting the mother, crying.

There was another incident when I sensed a patient was going to die.

It was on the psych unit. I called the physician to come in, wrote it in the chart. There were no significant physical changes, so he did not come in. The patient died that night.

When I was on the sixth floor prior to going to the Pedi Special Care unit, I noticed that the kids were not emotionally prepared for cardiac catheterization procedure. At the time, many kids had congenital heart defects — PDA, Aortic Stenosis, etc. We called them blue babies. They would go to the cardiac cath lab where the diagnosis was more refined. A catheter was put in the groin into the chambers of the heart, where O2 and CO2 levels were obtained. Also, angiogram dye was injected to see the blood flow through the heart and arteries.

I noticed that the kids were given Demerol the morning of the cath. They were wheeled upstairs to the cath lab — restraints put on, drapes put in front of the face, and told they could urinate on the table if they needed to go. So, on my days off, I worked with the Nursing professors to help develop a play preparation to prepare the children for the procedure. I came into their room the night before and had puppets and dolls and items that they would see, hear, and feel during the procedure the next day. Initially I would explain what was going to happen but then I realized that they would recreate their fears with these items on their own with support and guidance, gently correcting their fears with the reality of what would happen. I would walk in with these toys and items in the box with a bow and tell them I was here to tell them about their heart test tomorrow. They were curious and excited to take the ribbon off and see what was in the box. It did look like a present that begged to be opened.

In the box were betadine and alcohol swabs; there were miniature restraints they could put on the dolls; there were drapes to place in front of the doll's face. The syringes were a big hit as one of their big fears was shots. One child put a syringe in the doll's feet, head, legs. I would gently say, "You will only have two shots — one here — and I would point to the place on the thigh, before you go upstairs; and then another when you go upstairs. I pointed to the groin which was anesthetized before they put the catheter in. "It will hurt but if you count to ten, the pain will be over." One very expressive child was a Sarah Bernhardt. She picked up the doll and said to it, "Your heart is broken and needs to be fixed."

The purpose of the research was to prevent more serious trauma by providing emotional support. We had three groups: the traditional protocol, support with familiar person, and lastly an individualized preparation dealing with the child's unique needs and fears. Outcome measures on stress and coping were obtained. One measure was the behavior in the lab. The patients in the individualized group had the most significant difference, and the cardiologist was able to complete the procedure in less time because the child was calm and better behaved. This study was completed in the mid-70s. Better outcomes were obtained for those who had the preparation and support versus the control group.

This was one of the most satisfying experiences I have had as a nurse. I was given a grant from UCSF Department of Nursing Research to prepare the children, develop the grant, and was relieved from my Pedi special care duties for a period of six months with guarantee to return to the unit. I was just 24 at the time, and even back then I was dedicated to preventing and treating trauma. I saw that procedures, surgery, hospitalization, and illness were potentially traumatic experiences. I did become known for dealing with difficult behavioral problems and was called to help with emotionally difficult patients. I felt honored. Another patient has come to mind. I was on the night shift and the nurses were having a hard time with this one young boy. If I remember correctly, he had bone transplants and was very thin. He was given tube feedings every four hours. This young boy was acting out and angry and was throwing up on the nurses. I sensed that he felt a loss of control. So, I walked in bowed, and said, "You are the King, and I am your servant. Where would you like your blood pressure taken? Left arm, right arm? Would you like your feeding now or 10 minutes from now?" He smiled for the first time. I will never forget.

I was getting very burnt out dealing with serious illnesses and death of children, so after two years, I left there to take a break. I worked per diem at these Public Health clinics which were like urgent care today. They eventually were closed.

After this experience, I decided to go to graduate school and was accepted at San Jose State University in Community Health Nursing, focusing on Mental Health in Teaching and Research. I was hired as a psychiatric nurse on the adolescent unit at Langely Porter Psychiatric hospital, UCSF. My thesis was on the stress of the staff working in the unit. Some of my assumptions were that the stress of the staff affected quality of care. In staff meetings we would discuss how the patients' behavior affected staff response; what feelings patients stirred up in staff. A few of the important results were that there was more stress related to other staff members than to the patients and that there was stress related to concern about quality of patient care.

This research project contributed to my understanding of stress/ trauma in context of emotional climates of systems and how they affect health of the people working in those systems. I became acutely aware that maintaining integrity was important in preventing stress/trauma. Working there was also very valuable as it was based on psychoanalytical treatment. I learned about early development, parental attachment and its effect on behavior. I also was co-therapist doing family therapy and learned about family systems therapy. The Medical Director was very wise about emotional dynamics; I learned from him as well. He was Persian and reminded me of a Persian sage.

These experiences contributed to understanding the effect of stress and vulnerability on Hospice workers when I did my dissertation. The dissertation was on the outcome of Hospice objectives of reducing pain, anxiety, and depression, increasing quality of life, and assessing family coping. I also looked to see if the patient's stress/coping style may have contributed to the onset of cancer. There was denial of vulnerability and enormous underlying powerlessness. I observed that the staff's denial of these feelings of powerlessness reverberated in staff dynamics. Staff may have acted out these feelings by arguing about the correct treatment approach. I see this happening in medical units as well. Power and control as the antidote for traumatic experiences of death, illness, and suffering enormous vulnerability. The underlying feelings related to trauma are powerlessness, helplessness, negative feelings about the self, and feeling inadequate or guilty because you should have had control. "I am at fault, I am defective," with an underlying shame or disgust. "Something is very wrong with me." Extreme feelings: "I should be destroyed." Thus, the person may feel suicidal, to destroy the defective part of the self and to destroy the pain. Another way some attempt to rid these painful feelings is through homicide, to project them onto someone else, kill them in an attempt to destroy that part of themselves, the part that feels powerless, defective.

It is also the dynamic in genocide, holocaust and/or war in the greater society. One needs to be on guard in an unsafe environment triggering the stress response. This is a significant factor in burnout on the front lines. This was true in my case.

Treating Patients with Trauma: Understanding the Bully in the Workplace. I did have an interest in supporting and dealing with trauma throughout my career as can be seen in the above experience as a nurse through clinical practice, teaching and research. I became a psychologist in 1992 and trained in EMDR therapy the same year. The technical term is Eye Movement Desensitization Reprocessing. A comparatively new treatment, particularly good for treating trauma. My decision was to specialize in the treatment of trauma. Many patients came in with complaints of dealing with toxic bosses and environments as well as rape and childhood emotional, sexual, and physical abuse. So, my knowledge of the dynamics of trauma was expanded here. It did seem as if toxic environments were in many institutions and was epidemic. This included hospitals, banks, fire departments, schools and universities. Generally speaking, the present toxic situation touched off or restimulated past family trauma. One example was: a patient who had a bipolar mother who would fly into rages. This resulted in insecurity — "I'm not good enough." So, the person was not able to see clearly the toxic character of the authority figure. They were overwhelmed with negative feelings about the self. In treatment, they were able to identify the trigger going back in time, clear the negative feelings about the self, and then see clearly "It's not about me; it's the negative character of my boss/supervisor; and going back in time, my mother's illness."

The other devastating effect of bully boss experiences is the denial by co-workers. It is often difficult for co-workers to admit that someone is being targeted. There are several reasons for this. One is the conditioning in our culture for authority to not question it. In my own situation, it was: "Well, the department head supports her, so it must be OK." The other reason to look the other way is feared retaliation from the bully boss —. possible loss of job — especially when someone has a family to support. Retaliation and fear are two of the main tactics of bullies. They can sense insecurity/vulnerability in their employees and target them. It often is a distraction from their incompetent behaviors, and a way to take power and control.

Another tactic is to split the group — who gets privilege, and who doesn't? Praising one while ignoring another creates conflict/resentment in the group and they can start fighting with each other. It signals another opportunity to take power and control. Expressing the truth about what is happening could get you fired or put on the back burner for promotion, an example of retaliatory tactics. The denial of co-workers amounts to severe betrayal. This compounds the vulnerability of the person targeted.

Most of the people who have come into the practice are very conscientious. What has helped them the most is coming to grips with the truth, knowing they maintained their integrity. After this experience, they were more able to find a work environment that had integrity and was more fulfilling. One of the best ways to cope with toxicity, if possible, is to gather colleagues who can see through the manipulation. Once organized to have the group lay out what is happening and have it signed by the group versus a single person. This protects individuals from being targeted. Isolation compounds the traumatic experience, so an important part of helping people was to encourage them to get support.

The integration of good and bad. Another reason people have trouble is they cannot see that good people can do bad things. Discernment about this helps. Advanced existential ability is to be able to separate this out, to see the humanity in the bully, to see the root of his/her inhumanity. For brutal dictators, it is often a childhood in poverty, being disenfranchised, or one that was not included, a loner and not having a clear identity. In Hitler's case, he had an alcoholic father who beat him. One man said he was drawn to the Neo Nazis because it gave him an identity; so he joined an all-white Nationalist group. I heard about one Isis leader who grew up in poverty. In all these cases there is an underlying powerlessness, so gaining power becomes all important. So, for toxic bosses, there is underlying insecurity. The patient is helped when he/she can clear their own sense of powerlessness and then see clearly the insecurity in the bully.

Leaders in this area were our visionaries — Martin Luther King and Gandhi, for example. Rather than splitting, revenge, and disenfranchise, they united through respect and being inclusive; unity through acceptance. Martin Luther King led a non-violent revolution; unity expressed by walking hand-and-hand together with the message of peace and stated with such powerful words. The ability to bring unity to a group is the mark of a very gifted leader.

The ability to split and fragment through fear and violence is the hallmark of a Tyrant/Bully. This fractures trust. It is important to hold them accountable for their actions. Lack of accountability fuels the power of the tyrant. As I have said, unity of the group is the most desirable way to accomplish this. Continued lack of accountability increases distrust.

Trust and Safety. There is shock involved in bullying; it is traumatizing. It sometimes splits memory from the whole self, fracturing body from mind, from spirit and soul. The memories of traumatic events are also split from consciousness. A healing atmosphere of trust and safety allows the body to soften the tension; the breath opens. Full breath allows the grief to surface. The tears are in the lungs. In this relaxed state, the deep feelings of grief and sadness are brought to the surface. The person is then able to feel his/her emotions, tolerating gradually opening more fully across time. Memories of strength in the situation then surface; this strengthens the self. Another effect of trauma is an inability to feel positive emotions and another outcome of a more relaxed and trusting state is the recovered ability to feel positive emotions as well. Safety and trust in relationships allows the person to be more visible and have a voice. This is also a gradual process, but very important in healing.

Trauma Education for Firefighters. I was thinking about firefighters one day and thought perhaps they would benefit from Education about Trauma. So, I walked to the fire station down the street. I talked with the Battalion Chief, Vince Webster, and presented this idea. He was very open to it and suggested I teach the class to Sausalito Fire. As I talked about what I would teach, he decided to open it to all of southern Marin County. We decided that I would teach a class on PTSD (Post Traumatic Stress) as it related to Critical Incident Stress. We decided the CISD, (Critical Incident Stress Debriefing) would be taught by a firefighter trained in Debriefing for Firefighters and I would give information on post-traumatic stress, the symptoms to look for and options for treatment. This was applied to their traumatic experiences in the field.

Then, another Battalion Chief, Fred Bunker, retired from Sausalito Fire and was hired by the fire training school at Santa Rosa Junior College. He asked me to teach my trauma course there. I taught there for a few years. The class was cut, and I wondered why. I received word from him: "The class was well received by all our Fire Academy students. I imagine these classes have become very important for fire responders today with all the disasters they have recently encountered." We have had enormous wild-fires burning in Northern California and many accidents and shootings.

This class was taught to many other front-line professionals: Nurses, Physicians, Psychologists and Therapists across many decades.

Another "bully boss" experience came up later in my career when I was teaching Psychiatric Nursing at the University. This was at the end of my career approaching 50 years on the front lines. I was teaching/supervising students in Psychiatric Emergency, Inpatient Locked Psychiatric Unit and had students in the community at a hotel for the mentally ill. I loved teaching the importance of relationship to Nursing students whether it be in the hospital, community, pedi , medicine, or psych. I was working as Associate Professor at this time. Once again, I had a supervisor on my case.

I was objecting to rotating students too often as it was a safety issue. The students would not know what was going on in an environment where patients may be acting out with physical or verbal threats. They also would not be able to develop rapport with the staff and would be left just to observe, diminishing their ability to learn through experience. I let her know my reasoning. Evidently, they wanted to push more students through than was safe. Students needed guidance in judgement and safety.

I made some compromise, leaving most of the students there but rotating one student in to see what it was like in the other units. My colleague had the same concerns. Said he refused to rotate students in an unsafe manner. He was a very competent psychiatric nurse and teacher and had been at the university for several decades. He wanted to fail a student for not being accountable, which is very serious in Nursing taking care of sick and dying patients. He was told, "We have a no fail policy" by our supervisor. He was fired for speaking up. Students told me she was not showing up for clinical teaching as well. I reported this to tenure track faculty who looked the other way. The Chair, the head of the Nursing Department at the time, supported her. The message to me was, 'She is in charge of the Department, and this is her policy." So, the implication was that we had to honor the authority of the head of the department, the status quo. I suspected that this may have been tuition-driven, but when I heard that we had a no-fail policy, I was sure of it. Tuition was a priority over safety. At this time, board scores on National Nursing exams dropped to an all-time low. I was targeted for not going along with the status quo. Toward the end of the semester, I was feeling like leaving this toxic environment. I was exhausted. I was late for a memorial for a friend and was rushing, opened the door, and there was a step there I did not see. I stepped out as if it was flat and fell and hit the pavement, breaking my arm. It was an omen that I had to leave; it was an emotional fracture as well.

It took about a year to recover the movement of the arm. I started spiraling into a deep depression, and my nervous system was dysregulated, becoming hypersensitive to stimuli alternating with extreme exhaustion. I continued my practice for a while but decided to close, heal myself now. The factors that contributed to my vulnerability/susceptibility to this toxicity were complex. One was so many years on the front lines — 50 to be exact. The principle here is stress is cumulative; previous experience with toxic work environment in US Navy, now reoccurring in university environment, and childhood trauma, secondary trauma, listening to others' trauma across so many decades.

Physical trauma: accidents, fractures, surgeries, medical procedures may open the door to most all past traumas. It can be seen as an opportunity to heal and clear previous traumas. That's how I looked at it. The stress triggered in the present are doorways to the past, even past lives, as was the case with the near accident/near head-on collision 30 years ago, and more recently with arm fracture.

The emotional response to a trigger was hyper-arousal, exhaustion and then enormous grief. The grief was exacerbated by my kitty of 13 years disappearing. It was a sudden, unexpected loss. I was able to feel the enormous grief and let it pass through me, which has lasted five years now. It is still there now, but much less so.

Sudden losses: The unexpected sudden loss was a trigger for the arm fracture, which was sudden and unpredictable. The loss of kitty disappearing suddenly. Then also going back into the Navy. Being suddenly called on the carpet. My mother being suddenly taken out of my arms. Then unexpectantly taken by my aunties and physician, tranquilized, and taken against her will into a psychiatric hospital. My father's illness and death at age 9.

All of these events involved enormous grief. I was able to feel it and let it pass through me. The other major trigger was what I call finger pointing leadership, both in the Navy and the university. There were finger-pointing styles of retaliation for not going along with the status quo. There was enormous terror involved in speaking-up, going against the grain which appeared out of proportion to what the threat was. It felt life-threatening. In this insight, I was able to connect the finger-pointing to past life, see watercolor of the dream. Nazi finger-pointing, running down a hallway and ending-up in a shower where I was gassed. This dream occurred the first week of August, the anniversary of Romani (Gypsy) Holocaust (see watercolor painting of Holocaust dream page 114). So, finger-pointing for me was life threatening. This was the trigger in the Navy that led to suicidal crises, unknown at the time.

The gas leak; trauma reenactment of holocaust experience. Decades later, I had a gas leak in my wall heater. PG&E man had come to check it out as the carbon dioxide alarm went off. In attempting to check-out what was wrong, the gas pipe fell off and gas flowed into my place. He told me to call 911. I did not freeze, but mobilized, calling 911. Ran down the hall to go outside. The building needed to be evacuated. Fire trucks arrived. They had trouble turning off the main gas valve. I called the management company of the homeowners. She pointed the finger at me saying I was responsible and needed to pay for it. I told her that it was an emergency, and I did not want to talk about that then. I handed the phone to the PG&E person who explained what happened. The gas was secured in the building. The windows were opened, and a large fan cleared the gas from the building and my unit. The firefighters stopped the evacuations of my neighbors as it was safe to return to the building. A new gas valve was put in so that I would be able to turn off the gas. My neighbors were very supportive and validating that the leadership was very quick to blame. They gave me hugs and sat with me afterwards for comfort. Another neighbor said, "This could happen to any one of us." This went right into the holocaust experience of finger-pointing and possible death through gassing. See dream where I was running down the hallway into the showers where I was gassed. It was helpful reenactment of past holocaust. It was empowering and shored-up my feelings of survival, survivor versus victim. The ability to have a voice, to be able to move spontaneously, and having neighbors support lessened the traumatic impact.

Tyrants often have finger-pointing styles of leadership, and the most effective and healing approach is to unite and support each other, just as my neighbors did. The tyrant, with underlying insecurity, will sometimes back down with a unified approach from the community.

It did have consequences in my nervous system, however, in difficult sleep, hypersensitivity and exhaustion. A deeper clearing was done in EMDR therapy which I will describe later in this book when I talk more in depth about healing this personal trauma. The dance and dreams describing the depth of feeling related to these traumas come alive in present-day time. This is now very relevant to the collective trauma we have in society today with toxic environments and Bully bosses. One was in the White House and now 2025 is in the White House again. I have written about healing trauma, both for the individual and the collective society. I will continue this story. I feel it is important to heal the alienation and trauma in society today. Healing personal trauma reverberates in the collective and helps heal the culture. Identifying cultural values for profit over the human needs of people is also helpful in healing society. The machine, moving to a robotic rhythm, separates us from ourselves and others. Stories heal the split, the fracture, in self from violence, shootings, and war, and messages from bully bosses that we are not good enough. There is violence in the message that more is better; mind, body, spirit are fractured — split from one another. This is the effect of Trauma. Isolation from self, from another, is the killer; primary in causing illness. One way this happens is the commercialization of society. One becomes a number to be statistically counted for assessing production quotas and profit. This is a root to alienation. Holocaust victims had numbers tattooed on their arms.

So, knowledge of trauma and Bully boss experience came from enormous experience on the front lines — healing others, and also healing self, sharing this experience to now help others and society. Not only describing descriptions of what happened, but sharing the depth of the experience using the body and how it moves to reach this depth through posture, rhythm, images and dreams. Movement will help raise consciousness.

Survival in the nuclear age is dependent on judgement. The real danger is not only the bomb itself, but push-button mentality, robotic philosophy and an underlying sense of separation, fragmentation and alienation. Movement is thus viewed as a psychic metaphor for unconscious conflicts. It is the characteristic style, the compulsive repetition that is related to the underlying dynamics., the trauma.

Movement is thus the way we face the world. It is the use of inner and outer space, time, flow and strength. It is a reflection of oneself, of values of the culture in which we live. Movement is communication of our world view and an expression of our reality. Is robotic movement symptomatic of our mechanical culture with emphasis on linear thinking, quantitative outcomes, and denial of inner reality and consequent loss of spiritual reality?

What are our heart patients running from? What underlies the psychic numbing of aerobics classes? Loud noise in restaurants and public places? Is it stepping to the rhythm of external values ... looking good and dressing for success. Is the prize the mechanical heart... the underlying belief is invulnerability: "We will survive a nuclear holocaust. The holocaust did not happen; another one will never happen."

If robotic movement is a metaphor for mechanical mentality, dance would be the metaphor for "being" whole. When one is split from nature, one is internally preoccupied with thoughts, sometimes racing out of control, feeling controlled. This is the extreme of the robotic mentality. This is the ultimate split of mind and body. It is hard to feel the emotions. This is the talking head.

Dance is the psychic symbol of life, of culture and of health. The intent of dance is connection with oneself, others, nature and the divine ... to be in synchrony with the rhythm of life, the Tao. Perhaps, by learning to dance metaphorically speaking, we can learn how we connect with one another ... so that destruction and violence are no longer as threatening. There is a need to shift in consciousness, away from the robotic rhythm toward that which dances with life, toward harmony with nature and our environment. This shift is demonstrated through the metaphor of movement. It is an inquiry into the depth of the psyche through imagination in rhythm: poetry, music and dance as portal to the dream.

The study of the way the human body shapes itself in time and space from this internal psychic well, a kaleidoscope of emotions, is the ultimate paradigm of human inquiry. It can be described in terms of different colors, swirling like storms and tornadoes, peaceful like the smooth glass of a lake before sunrise. The best description of the internal states of humanity are mirrored in nature and the best way to explore our nature, which is one with it, is to imitate nature's rhythms.

I am the wind, the sun, and the sea. I am nature.
So that health is congruent with the images of nature.
Breath is the wind of life that unites us with each other.
Tears are the oceans well, the reservoirs of water,
Willing freshness from it's cleansing,
Flowing over cracks in one's psychic desert,
Softening the ground, making it ready for life,
The softness allowing the blossoming of flowers,
Soft, tender and beautiful.
A child in white gathers the flowers and takes them one by one,
Throwing them on the path of life, marking it clearly.
The innocence creating the bond of mind, body and nature,
When mind, body and soul unite.
This is being one with self.
The image, the body expression and the sound are congruent,
There is connection bringing forth the psychic reservoirs of water that whirl
*   us clean with our tears.*
This is health that allows the flow of life and creativity.
Expression is sustained in the psyche and brings forth love.
It is the wind of our breath/spirit.
The fragmentation of self, the splitting of mind, body,
Rejection of parts of the self shatters the psychic mirror, bringing darkness.
*   In physical illness, the expression of anger is directed toward the self,*
symbolically destroying the organs representing the rejected part of the self.

In psychiatric illness, the rejection of needs and feelings are projected out of the body onto hallucinations and delusions. This is the ultimate split of the psyche from the body. creating numbness. and third person mentality

Someone is chasing him or her... the paranoid ideation.
The mind is intrinsically preoccupied with thoughts, racing out of control.
The feeling is one of being controlled,
In a psychotic state, of having wires in one's head.
This is the ultimate split of mind and body.
It is outside of me, the cause external.
The solution is an internal journey.

I was attending Story and Symbol continuing education class based on Joseph Campbell's Mythology. Ann Bach gave us a writing exercise to engage in creative imagination. "Start outer story which takes you to the inner story," she said. The poetry/rhythm of visceral sensations calls forth the unconscious. It shapes facial expression, eyes turning toward a particular picture. Yes, it is the picture on the wall of the warrior woman and her sword with the life force coming forth... the journey toward the life force, whirling, there is energy pouring forth from my palms, serving others in this way. Energy healing, that is my direction:

The direction of my Psyche.
May it be a beacon shinning bright,
Like the gold light of angels within a tree, within me
Come to me, no, it is already in me, visualizing it, amplifying it,
Sourcing ancient and modern ritual that is the inheritance within across time.
Archeological find I am, the ancient, modern ritual within me.
The gold light shining bright.
Becoming the healing artist, I was meant to be for self and others, in me for them.
The Divine love within me as in them,
Imagination in rhythm: poetry, music, dance, is portal to the dream and the
   creative unconscious.

Anne Bach, LMFT, Jonathan Young, PhD. *Story and Symbol.*
Continuing education providers for health care professionals.

DANCE OF PSYCHE: RHYTHMS OF CONSCIOUSNESS

Movement is an authentic expression and thus, a way to raise consciousness about our nature. The dance of one's psyche, its rhythm, reflects the level of consciousness.

Movement in time and space shapes the reality of a person and that of one's culture.

Health is a union of mind, body and spirit. It is the acknowledgement of human needs and empathy for others. It is the capacity to feel and thus, have union with others.... to love self, to love others. It is the value for self and others that determines the capacity to love.

Women and Men are symbolic Beings. To be human is to create symbols and to communicate with these symbols. Body movement is thus a symbolic language.

The relationship between mind, body and spirit is thus symbolic.

This union with self and others is characterized by synchrony and harmony, and flows with life.

Disease is the splitting of various parts of the self from the whole. In particular, it is the denial of human needs, and it is the incapacity to feel. Thus, the capacity for compassion and union with others is damaged.

Disease is, thus, characterized by disharmony and disorganized movement and body rhythms. The flow of life is inhibited. It is disconnection.

When there is a relationship between mind, body and spirit, they are one.

Life force is a measure of intension toward life.

Life force is reflected in the style of movement and shapes perception.

Perception shapes movement. Movement shapes perception.

The psyche is like a kaleidoscope and continues to change.

Health is characterized by intension which is an expression of purpose and design.

Illness is characterized by stasis and by lack of intension or purpose.

Quality of movement reflects intension toward life and intension toward life is related to health. Quality of movement is a measure of health.

Dance is a metaphor for wholeness; it is unity of mind, body, and spirit. It is rhythm, harmony and synchrony. Dance is the psychic symbol of life, of culture, of health. The intension of dance is unity with self and others, to be in synchrony with the rhythm of life, to be in synchrony with nature and the divine.

Movement describes one's philosophy of life. It is the way we face the world; it is the use of inner and outer space. It is a reflection of oneself; of values, and the culture in which we live. Movement is communication of our world view and an expression of our reality.

Perception is shaped by an interaction between the culture and the person.

It is a symbolic interaction between external and internal reality. Health and illness are thus seen in the context of culture.

Cultural rhythms can shape our values and affect our life and our health.

Movement rhythms predict health and illness.

Patterns of movement are communication and should be assessed in context of culture.

Movement in this sense is a metaphor of self and of culture. It is a value statement about the meaning of life and reflects the continual birth and death process.

Consciousness means having life and being present, empathic, connected to all things

In this next section, I will present a speech I made in 1987, Nurses Week, to the Nurses at United Hospital. It ties together the values of the culture for production, competition and its relationship to health and illness; and articulates the need for a shift in values to more human values, a holistic philosophy. The title of the speech was: Human Values in the Health Care System: Visions for the future. This speech is as relevant today as it was over 30 years ago. Some of the concepts and ideas are also highlights of the first book which is a good review going into this second book.

Human Values in the Health Care System: Visions for the Future

The first step in creating a humane environment is to speak honestly about our condition. It's what's missing in many of our institutions today. The truth has suffered greatly, severely damaging our trust in each other. In telling you openly what I see, I am taking a risk, perhaps being imperfect, or rejected, these are fears of vulnerability. This keeps us from growing and may contribute to illness. In opening honest dialogue between us today, perhaps we can make some progress.

There is a need for human values in the health care system. It is what people are crying out for and it seems that the survival of the health care system will depend on their ability to become humanized. We can agree that human values are important. We agree that this is the ideal, so then on a practical level. What contributes to the dehumanization of health care? What does it take to ask the question? What is the real need, what is the human value?

I will first talk about contemporary values in America and relate problems in health care as a reflection of contemporary values, the need to shift from mechanistic values to human ones.

In recent years, it seems we have gone backwards rather than forward, and frankly I am very worried about what I see. A symptom of this backward slide is the nursing shortage. Nurses do not want to work in a dehumanized system.

The health care system is a reflection of contemporary values in America. Symptoms of this deterioration of values can be seen in the numbers of homeless, an epidemic of addiction, including bad relationships, drugs, the number of people addicted to cocaine is epidemic, eating disorder, sexual and physical abuse, an increase in the number of adolescent suicides and geriatric suicides. In the Medical and Nursing profession we have impaired nurses and physicians.

These problems I attribute to mechanistic values; the values for production and perfection. The false notion that bigger is better. The myth that technology will save us, leading us to believe that the more precise the measurement, the more predictable, the better the treatment and diagnosis. Dossey (1982) in his book, Space, Time Medicine called this "hurry-up illness." There is no time to hold someone's hand and feel their warmth. In imitating the rhythm of machines, it creates the false notion that we are invulnerable and perhaps immortal and leads to the insanity of believing that we can survive a nuclear war. We have a get-tough philosophy that leads to a denial of vulnerability — those who are vulnerable being left out; the homeless, women and children, immigrants to name just a few.

In the words of Martin Luther King (2018), (Martin Luther famous quotes by Mjhoy's whole timber):

Mammoth production facilities with computer minds, cities that engulf the landscape and pierce the clouds, planes that almost outrace time- these are awesome, but they cannot be spiritually inspiring. Nothing in our glittering technology can raise man to new heights because material growth has been made an end in itself, and in our glittering technology can raise man to new heights because material growth has been made an end in itself, and in the absence of moral purpose, man becomes smaller as the works of man become bigger.

Gargantuan industrial and government, woven into an intricate computerized mechanism leave the person outside. The sense of participation is lost. The feeling that ordinary individuals influence important decisions vanishes, and man becomes separate and diminished.

When an individual is no longer a true participant, when he no longer feels a sense of responsibility for his society, the content of democracy is emptied.

When culture is degraded and vulgarity enthroned, when the social system does not build security but induces perils, inexorably, the individual is impelled to pull away from a soulless society. This process produces alienation-perhaps the most persuasive and insidious development in contemporary society.

The content of our hearts will keep health care from becoming a vast tech-driven dehumanized society.

I will compare medical model/mechanistic with holistic model to show risks and benefits of each, the outcome of this being that we need both models. The question is, what model for what purpose?

I will compare the assumptions of mechanism reflected in the medical model and compare it with holistic care; talk about the differences between them and then give examples. The idea is that they are complementary. We need both. The medical model uses science, a linear model, if x then y. It is hierarchical and the major way of knowing is through categorization through separation of parts. This is the model we primarily work with in our health care system since we place importance on specialization. Mental health separate from physical health; we have Medical care and Psychiatric care, specialization of Cardiac care, Infectious Diseases, Gynecology, Urology, Oncology etc.

In recent years, many have acknowledged our need to change, to shift our way of thinking. Many in the field talk about this in terms of paradigm shift. Simply, this means a shift away from mechanism to more holistic/ human values. Despite our efforts to shift to more human values, we continue to build more bombs, and our addictive fast-paced values and illnesses escalate.

Like an alcoholic who keeps drinking and it is not until death does the person get a glimmer of a need to act in a different way. Perhaps, it is our cognitive philosophy that leads to the deadening of our spirit. In the course of everyday life; school health care, driving a car, television, theatre, entertainment, the primary mode of communication is head to mouth, the nonverbal metaphor for "I think therefore I am" philosophy. This kind of communication splits the head from the rest of the body; one becomes the talking head. An example is the newscaster. Information is given one fragment after another, bits of disconnected information. In one breath we are talking about the Easter parade and in another 5,000 people are being killed. History and context are abandoned. Does this kind of talking head communication, with expression silenced, contribute to the deadening of purpose and loss of morals? (Campbell, C., 2003, p 11)

Even in the education system, the primary mode of communication was mechanical. Communication was talked about as input and output information. The assumption here is that one doesn't have a body or emotions, which is the crux of understanding human beings. Another example of mechanism is in the concepts we use. The popularity of the concept of stress. Stress was adapted from the engineering term to mean a force and the resistance opposed to that force. The term is so popular; perhaps we feel like machines. Could stress be a coverup term for masking emotion? Could stress be a term that comes from not being permitted to express anger, pain, tears in most everyday life? We maintain that cool distant, planned objective reality known as rational. When there is so much repression underneath, this calm objective lifeless position is far from rational. These are examples of static materialistic philosophy. (Campbell, C. 2003, p. 11)

In the health care system, the focus is on pathology. The emphasis has been on what went wrong. The focus is on the diseased part. In medicine, the psychological is neglected and in psychiatry, the physical is neglected. The mind and body are split.

The shift in philosophy that needs to take place is from mechanism to one that has life. This comes from the expression of human emotion which necessitates having a body. To not talk from just our heads but to feel from our hearts; love and pain, tears from our eyes, power from our pelvis, grounding from having our feet anchored and stability through a balanced life. This is connection to self which is necessary requisite to health. This internal connection gives us power.... Without this emotional clarity through expression, we have men and women held captive through addiction, drugs, alcohol incestuous relationships, overeating, anorexia, physical illness and violence. This is the essence of powerlessness. It is disconnection.

It is the feminine principle that is held captive by our culture — the value for nurturance, touch, and open expression. I am not talking about the devaluation of the masculine mentality, however, when it is pushed to extreme as mechanism, moving like machines to keep up, to the exclusion of the feminine principle, we are a fragmented people lacking a soul. When it becomes a way of life, a way of not being, it produces sickness. Could it be that the psychodynamics of the most prevalent diseases of our time are symptomatic of mechanistic values? I have observed a denial of vulnerability and a type of internal isolation with heart disease as the lonely heart, cancer as the protected heart, and eating disorders as the empty heart. (Campbell, C., 2003, p.12)

The major difference in the models is in one we deny our vulnerability and in the other we are able to feel our vulnerability. So, if we are moving fast in time under pressure, human needs and values are repressed and we have rigid structures. When it is adapted as a lifestyle, it leads to illness. The result of this denial is the feminine voice is not heard because there is no connection of the head to the rest of the body. It is the difference between talking about something versus experiencing it. Perhaps this is why nurses are not being heard around the country. Scapegoating may be the result of this pressure. Vulnerability is not tolerated or dealt with and, thus, one sets up the most vulnerable in the group to take the flack. This happens to nurses because they are at the bottom of the hierarchy, and then they may turn on each other and scapegoat.

We have pushed the extreme of the masculine model in all our institutions. However, change is occurring on the outside and numerous books, programs, and in the life of the artists come the value for the feminine — the need to respect life of oneself and the life of the earth. There is an increase in feminine consciousness. I'm afraid that in institutions we are clinging to old models that are competitive rather than complimentary and collaborative. In the process of change, there is great fear. Some try and cling to the old, and thus rigidify structures. Others let go and look and sense the emerging new forms. They let go and create new structures. The survival of old institutions will be dependent on their ability to feel and sense new directions. This will be based on being sensitive to real needs and values. Clinging and holding onto old ways will likely assure their demise and these rigid structures will crumble.

Nurses can play a primary role in bringing human needs and values to the health care system by uniting and having a strong voice. Here are some of the needs now:

1. Recognizing that health care workers need to be healthy. It is only when you are healthy can you be sensitive to your own needs and then able to more clearly assess patients' needs. Being production oriented and wearing out the nurses and physicians runs contrary to this goal.

2. CCU and ICU and ER are very stressful and potentially traumatic. There is a need for R and R particularly for these nurses — and also for nurses on the units.

3. The education of Nurses and Physicians needs to be more humane.

4. Understand that often health care nurses and physicians come with their own emotional wounds. So there needs to be education available and therapy to deal with stressful traumatic triggers.

5. Therefore, there needs to be a process of communication that deals with the dynamics between the healer and patient.

6. Working in the medical system is potentially traumatic re: accidents, hospitalizations, procedures and surgery. They have teams that are trained in critical incident stress debriefing. CISD is a process that helps front line deal with an incident/situation that can be potentially traumatic. It includes saying what happened, what was the difficult part — and, on reflection, what they did learn.

7. This means that some on the team are trauma informed. Trauma on the front lines that often triggered include: the death of a child, disasters with many injured or killed, issues of bullying, scapegoating, cumulative time on the front lines, shortage of staff, overwork as stress is cumulative.

8. Have education on the symptoms of stress and post-traumatic stress, so they can head off more serious symptoms, and have therapists available for referral.

9. Have mentoring for new nurses.

10. In order to have health care, one needs to understand the psychophysiological relationship between health and illness.

11. Psychology would be an integral part of medical care.

12. Critical thinking is needed to examine the relationship between the

mission statement, what is done and outcome. Often in evaluating programs, I find holistic goals, being people oriented, but then what happens is production.

One important way to keep staff healthy is to have reasonable patient assignments.

The cost of health care is enormous. It will pay to keep people healthy.

Nurses are well suited to create programs based on holistic care including touch, open expression and nurturance.

A shift is needed out of a profit system to one that serves needs.

Chapter 4

The Destructive Effects of the Profit Machine Profit over the Human Needs of People

MANY DECADES AGO, in the late 70's I thought society would be in deep trouble with a profit motive over the needs of people. There was a potential for fascism. It is now 2025 and has become more of a reality. Violence and alienation are epidemic. The society is fractured by classism, racism, materialism, and corporatism. The values for strength and control over others reign supreme. It is white supremacy. Our wars in the Middle East continue.

Here is my perspective writing with an understanding of collective trauma, the soul of America at stake.

The war in Afghanistan was one of the longest wars in our history. This began with an illegal war in Iraq and now other Middle Eastern countries and contributed to the development of Isis. The gap between the haves and have-nots has widened even more with most of the profit going to the top .1%. The disenfranchised are angry and often full of rage. They have found a leader in our former president, now president (2025) who speaks out for them but incites violence and breaks his promises and gives power to white rich guys. He speaks to and for the profit system which gave him control.

The vulnerable suffer. Violence has increased toward blacks, Muslims, the mentally ill, and now immigrants. They are targeted and scapegoated in this era of exploitation. The militarization of police is on the rise and has contributed to this scapegoating. Hospitals have cut budgets for the mentally ill and many are homeless and on the street. Lobbyists have taken Washington with Citizens United giving corporations the rights of citizens. The priority of profit has pushed deregulation of corporations which has affected the safety of food and water and safety of workers. This profit motive pushing increased production for workers and is contributing to burnout and illness. The profit motive has fractured society and has split us from ourselves increasing alienation and contributing to violence. The Glass Steagall Act which regulated banks was voted down and led to the 2008 meltdown.

These are just a few examples of the devastation from the profit motive. The profit motive has fractured society and split us from ourselves, increasing alienation and contributing to violence.

Since I wrote the first edition, I was drawn to many events taking place in society related to prioritizing greed. Profit over people has invaded every sector of the society; most every institution: the banks, the military industrial complex, health care, pharmacies, insurance companies, the prisons, the schools and universities, the criminal justice system, food and water, the media, and the immigration system and in Washington, our politicians.

The Banks

The economy collapsed in 2008 because of recklessness in large banks such as J.P. Morgan and Goldman Sacks. They were betting on high-risk mortgages called credit default swaps. Many people lost their homes, mortgages were underwater, many were bankrupted. Quick sales became common for these properties. Banks profited on the misfortune of the people, particularly the poor and black communities. Robert Reich says it well:

The moral Crisis for our ages has nothing to do with Gay Marriage or abortion; it's insider trading, obscene CEO pay, wage theft from ordinary workers, Wall Street's continued gambling addiction, corporate payoffs to friendly politicians and the Billionaire takeover of our Democracy.

These banking institutions were not held accountable for their fraud. In fact, they were rewarded with huge bailouts.

I read *Confessions of an Economic Hit Man* by John Perkins (2004) who was working for Chase T Main in Boston. He would work mostly in poor countries and offer infrastructure; set up an energy grid, build a dam, etc. When this small country could not pay for it, the bank would lend them money. They would give up their resources. He would pursue poor countries with rich resources and cheap labor. Money would be funneled from the World Bank and United States Aides to US corporations there. The people would not benefit, just the upper class. They would be left indebted and American companies would benefit from their resources. The local environment would be destroyed. They would be left in debt by these large loans and contribute to bankruptcy. Thus, big money hijacked these small countries leaving the common person in poverty; just the wealthy, the upper crust of the society, benefited and so did U.S. corporations.

At the time of this economic crisis in the U.S., 60 Minutes (November 27, 2011) reported that there were 16 million homeless children; one in four construction workers were homeless, particularly in Florida. Kids felt unsafe and would stay up all night and watch Mom. One-fourth of these homeless families were living in the street. Kids were fearful living in crisis.

War

Both men and women from disadvantaged backgrounds get pulled into the military as they may have little opportunity elsewhere. On both sides of the conflict, the disadvantaged get caught in fighting for a cause and will give up their lives as there may be little opportunity otherwise. The oligarchy once again profits from the poor, taking advantage of the vulnerable. It also provides an identity which is otherwise missing in childhood development. The military industrial conflict is one of the biggest funded priorities in Washington reflective of get-tough values. Once again, the vulnerable suffer.

Politics

The passing of Citizens United gave corporations the rights of people to accept money for political reasons. Donations to Washington/ Congress increased. Thus, the corporate world gained a stronghold through contributions and now gained increased power in Washington.

Noam Chomsky (2017) in his new book, *Requiem of the American Dream, The 10 Principles of Wealth and Power,* clarifies the American political and economic system:

Through excessive lobbying by banks in Washington, the banks and lobbyists are actually writing the laws of financial regulation. Corporations rigged from top to bottom to insure corporations always win through regulatory control. He calls it regulatory capture.

He gave the example of Glass Steagall Act passed in 1933 which separated commercial from investment banks. Commercial banks were given Federal insurance, whereas investment banks were given no guarantee. However, this rule was reversed in 1999 by President Clinton. The government then guaranteed bail out for the investment banks. Mortgages were then sold to those who could not afford them as they had mortgage-backed securities. When this came crashing down, the government bailed them out. This led to the crash of 2008.

He continues: This led to the concentration of power, "too big to fail." There was no accountability of those responsible — only when their actions affect other businesses are they held accountable. The economic climate was characterized by no consequences to others. Risk to self, calculated with no assessment of systemic risk. Rewards self-perpetuation versus service. There is a bipartisan imperative when money is made — no one takes a stand.

He also noted the incestuous relationship between big banks and lobbyists. He gives the example of Robert Ruban who became part of President Obama's economic team; then became Director of City Group team. Legislature to lobbyist is common to a position in corporations. It becomes a revolving door contributing to their wealth and control by corporations. This is corporatocracy. There is triple the amount of money to Lobbying. This is notable for insurance companies and pharmaceuticals.

Chomsky continues and gives a clear description of Neoliberal policy. Let the market control. Take government out. Cutback healthcare, social security, which are regularly framed as entitlements. Let the market run everything except for the powerful; the state will bail you out. One set of rules for the rich and one for the poor. Market forces for the poor; bail outs for the rich. "Market forces are already being shaped by government policies that are structuring the market in ways that ensure that income flares upwards."

Bill Moyers (2013) interviews Mark Leibovich on his book, *This Town*; it is about how crony capitalism has become pervasive in the nation's capital. Public services have become a major source for profit; he raises the question, "Why is America falling apart rotting from within?" It is a town where money rules the day, and status is determined by who you know and what they can do for you. They are disconnected to every-day people; "out of touch." There is a get-rich culture, wealth culture, with the language of selling; it rewards self-perpetuation versus service. The rewards go to the status quo, the cowards, not to those who take a stand.

He gives an example of the BP spill, how disasters get managed. There is a "too close for comfort" relationship between media, government officials and business interests. Through media spin, BP was able to reduce compensation to victims by questioning the science behind water quality.

Jane Meyers (2016) book titled *Dark Money, The Hidden History of the Billionaires behind the Rise of the Radical Right* is a nonfiction book; she writes as an American investigative journalist. She notes the Koch brothers were threatened by Obama's policies and free market. They started the movement of the conservative right with gaining enormous funding for Libertarian views; reduce government for free market but, in reality, it was control of markets. They discouraged paper trail and became secret. She says that "media spin contributes to lack of accountability as upper-class crime is not part of the news."

The Media. George Orwell comes alive now in present day times. Double-speak is in media and politics — "It is — No it isn't." The truth is fractured. History and context continue, absent in how the news is delivered. Newscasters have pressured speech and reporting one event after another: murders, accidents, war, bombings said in rapid fire without pauses. Emotional hype and sensationalism reigns supreme. The weather and sports can occupy a large segment of the news. Emphasis is placed on those victimized without a balance in reporting about the pushback including those speaking out for justice and the laws pertinent for accountability. People's protests do not get as much coverage. Double-speak has been common in the news coming from Washington. The spin distracts and the truth slides under the shock and chaos of the delivery. This chaos allows for take-over and control of the population. Melanie Klien's (2001) shock and awe says it well.

Repetition of false information over and over conditions people to think this is the truth. Critical thinking is needed. Carl Sagan, an astrophysicist, perfectly diagnosed American Society in an article, Media Matters (2014).

The dumbing down of America is most evident in the slow decay of substantive content in the enormously influential media, the 30-second sound bites (now down to 10 seconds or less) is the lowest common denominator programming, credulous presentations on pseudoscience and superstition, but especially a kind of celebration of ignorance.

President Obama in a speech noted, "It is speed over depth." Media made money in presenting Trump as glittering entertainment.

In my experience, the news declined when the content presented was based on ratings. Ratings and profit trumps human needs and values.

When sensationalism fractures truth, our democracy is in peril.

Also, the question is: "What is being left out of the news?"

I would say once again, "Modern Man moving fast in time, where are you going, where is your heart?"

The business model has become all powerful for many of our institutions. I have witnessed the detrimental effects particularly in the health care and education; but it has also jeopardized safety of products, the lives of workers, and most basic of life-giving resources, such as food and water. Lobbyists control Congress and the Senate, so unsafe products often pass.

Health Care.

I share my experiences now in the front lines of health care and education. I have witnessed first-hand the detrimental effects of the business model providing care to patients and in teaching at universities.

Patients are no longer patients; they are consumers who need to be satisfied. Objective health care outcomes take second place to satisfaction. Health Care then is a product.

Doctors lose their power, they become "providers" versus "doctors." Insurance companies have control over reimbursement, and reimbursement rates have not kept up with market rates/inflation; and thus, many general practitioners, mental health doctors, psychotherapists have lost their practices. Nurses are often overworked, with unreasonable staff/patient ratios jeopardizing patient safety and leading to burnout. Suicides among both doctors and nurses have increased. Many hospitals with non-profit status have cut indigent care, mostly Mental Health as it is not profitable.

POC (Physicians Organizing Committee), an activist group representing Physicians, held them accountable for their non-profit status. Non-profit status requires them to care for indigent patients; so, if they don't, they lose their non -profit status. POC has been successful in holding them accountable, thus keeping beds available for the mentally ill. But it is an uphill battle, holding them accountable.

Pharmaceutical Drugs.

Costs of drugs are beyond affordable for the average person. The government picks up the tab for those in Medi-cal. One anti-psychotic could cost up to $800 to $1,600 per month. Some patients are on 5-15 medications. It makes me ask the question: "Is the pharmaceutical company in bed with the government?"

This was the case for Epi-pen, an emergency drug for allergic reactions which is of life-saving importance. Mylan, maker of the drug, raised the price up from $100 in 2007 to $600 in 2016 (New York Times Op-Ed, Sept 21, 2016). This was unaffordable for the average family and/or person. The price of brand name prescription drugs jumped 164% according to Express Scrips, a pharmaceutical prescription service offered by Walgreens and Tricare (Tricare is an insurance company for optional service for Veterans). According to a study by the AMA (American Medical Association), a person spent $800 versus $400 in other industrial countries. Congress has prohibited Medicare to negotiate prices and granted patent monopolies to drug companies keeping prices high.

School Shootings

School Shootings have become epidemic, and they are reflective of the profit motive in that the gun lobbies power has blocked gun control. Later, it was revealed there was underlying greed. Frontline, March ,25, 2020.

Analysis of school shootings in schools and universities is tracked by Everytown, an independent organization whose mission is dedicated to understanding and reducing gun violence in America. Between 2013 and 2015, there were 160 incidents across 38 states, including fatal and non-fatal assaults, suicides and unintentional shootings — 59 deaths and 124 non-fatal gunshot injuries. For those in primary and secondary school, half the kids obtained the gun from home; adults did not store it locked and unloaded. One in six, 24 shootings, occurred after a verbal argument intensified, because of the presence of a gun, rather than in spite of it.

In 2018, Everytown report showed that in half the mass shootings, the shooter showed warning signs before the shootings. In 2017 there were 173 mass shootings tracked by Everytown between 2009-2017. 2017 was the deadliest year on record for mass shootings than the previous eight years. The Las Vegas shooting caused a spike in fatalities. In 2021, it was 83 percent higher than the previous year. Gun violence kills 40,000 people a year. In February 2023, there have been 39 mass shootings as of this date. As of January 24, 2023, there has been tragedy upon tragedy. Why so many mass shootings? (The Guardian.com)

My experience in my community is that students are pressured for performance and are often lacking in emotional support. There was a program in the county to provide this support and grades and performance went up naturally. Once again, values for proficiency and performance over human needs effects Mental Health and may lead to violence through school shootings and suicide.

At the University level, banks earn profit from school loans. The privatizing of universities has caused tuition to rise to unbearable amounts for most students, thus threatening democracy as mostly the rich can afford tuition. Many students are indebted "for life." This is profiting by banks over the needs of students.

In summary, profit motive has contributed to inequality and has deprived most of our society of safety and security, and thus contributes to stress and trauma, including violence. There is a need to provide for equality in our economy, improve our health care by taking out the business model, and provide for regulation of institutions so that there is equal distribution of resources. This will provide for the needs of all people and contribute to health and quality of life; and maintain our Democratic values, our human values.

Inspiring Quotes by Joseph Stiglitz, Nobel Laureate in Economics who wrote: *The Price of Inequality: How Today's Divided Society Endangers our Future.* (Goodreads, 10/11/2022)

These quotes by Joseph Stiglitz give us inspiration about reshaping our lives with values for human needs versus the profit machine. He states:

Development is about transforming the lives of people, not just transforming economics. He comments on the present structure in countries that affect the poor.

Any society has to regulate the responsibility to maintain certain kinds of order.

Enforcing regulations, making sure people stop at stoplights etc. We cannot function in a society without rules and regulations. These free-market economists are also more inclined to believe that markets by themselves, without government intervention, are efficient and the best way to help the poor is simply to let the economy to grow — and, somehow, the benefits will trickle down to the poor. Interestingly, such beliefs have persisted, even as economic research has undermined their intellectual foundations.

He continues, *It is not globalization per se by industrial countries, but it is the management of it within them that have a set of rules that are based on self-interest.*

He continues, *The way globalization has been managed has taken away much of the developing countries' sovereignty and their ability to make decisions themselves in key areas that affected their wellbeing and undermined democracy.*

41.6 percent of the world lives in poverty. The head of the World Bank, the international institution charged with oversight of the global financial system states that a single country, the U.S., has effective veto.

It is bit a question of "One country, one vote, one man, one vote... dollars vote."

On a more positive note: In 1965, there was a meeting of Independent countries to have 18 percent of the poorest countries write off their debt — mostly in Africa.

In 2013, Icelanders overthrow government and rewrite constitution after banking fraud, an inspirational event for citizens to take control over a country's greed. Liberty Voice, boldly inclusive Icelanders, a group of randomly chosen citizens rewrote the constitution to include measures that banned corporate fraud. They forced their entire government to resign after a banking fraud scandal; overthrew the ruling party and created citizens tasked with writing a new constitution that offered a solution to prevent corporate greed from destroying the country. They were sourcing input from social media. The fraud had been going on since 2008. No U.S. media covered this story. A documentary was made called *Pots, Pans and Other*

Solutions. Banks inflated their value and led to bankruptcy in 2008. The bubble burst. Citizens took to the street by the thousands, banging pots and pans in what is now called "Pots and Pans Revolution." Unscrupulous bankers were arrested and prosecuted. Icelander's citizens also refused to pay for the sins of the bankers and rejected any measure of taxation to bail them out. (https//m. utube.com, uploaded by Miguel Marques, posted June 20, 2012) and in the *Independent News* article by Phillips, England's, Ireland's Pots and Pans Revolution: Lessons from a Nation that Peoples' Power helped to Emerge from its 2008 Crisis all Stronger).

In the U.S. the government bailed out the bankers and there were no arrests.

Hopefully, this story inspires action. Noam Chomsky states:

As long as the general population is passive, apathetic, diverted to consumerism or hatred of the vulnerable, then the powerful can do as they please and those who survive will be left to contemplate the outcome. (2015)-

Another quote by Noam Chomsky:

Neoliberal Democracy:

Instead of citizens, it produces consumers. Instead of communities, it produces shopping malls. The net result is an itemized society of disengaged individuals who feel demoralized and socially powerless. (Quote in Goodreads)

A quote by Henry A. Wallace from *The Danger of Fascism (1944)* is relevant here:

A fascist is one whose lust for money or power is combined with such an intensity of intolerance toward those of other races, parties. classes. religions. cultures, regions or nations as to make him ruthless in his use of deceit or violence to attain his ends.

And, lastly, a quote by Pope Francis (1988):

Greed for money is a subtle dictatorship that condones and enslaves men and women.

Austerity programs:

Not to yield to an economic model which is idolatrous which needs to sacrifice human lives on the altar of money and profit.

The Emotional Dynamics of the Epidemic of Bullying:
Materialism — Man as Machine

There is an epidemic of Bullying now in this profit-making machine. There needs to be a task master to orchestrate systems that push for efficiency, production, and bottom-line outcome. The tyrant is in politics, in university systems, in health care, in schools, in the justice system, and in law. The bully has become the gatekeeper of the profit motive. It has devastated our democratic way of life and has affected our health. Masculine power remains dominant. The feminine with values for tenderness, nurturance, and care is oppressed.

The assumptions that guide this mentality are that power and control and dominance through profit are more important than the human needs of people. The masculine dominates the feminine. Violence becomes the solution; war, the military becomes all powerful. This may include dominance over women and destroying Mother Nature which fuels climate change. Might is right. Thus, the bully has trouble with vulnerability, the body, and death is the ultimate vulnerability.

This fuels the desire of profit through war. The fuel for wealth is behind wars, conflicts. The Pope says: "Unbridled greed for wealth and possessions is a sickness that is driving force behind wars and conflicts in the World." The National Catholic report (https:www.ncronline.org>vatican, August, 2022).

Persecutors, dictators, are shut off from their bodies and, thus. have no empathy. They are shut off from their own internal suffering and horror and switch into monsters. The darkness within their own suffering and pain is projected onto others. A victim is chosen; usually a person or population that is vulnerable: the poor, the handicapped, the elderly, the mentally ill, homosexuals, transexuals, minorities: including Blacks, Jews, Asian, Latinos, Muslims, immigrants and now Palestinians, and now, in the latest rant, Haitians. The vulnerable are targets because of the Bullies' internal powerlessness and helplessness. Conditioning in childhood to not show weakness so he denies vulnerability and postures strong; and once again, because the Bully does not accept the vulnerable part of himself, he projects it onto those that represent this disowned part. He sees them as week. He may then try to destroy them and may cause genocide or holocaust.

Dominance and control over the vulnerable inflate the ego, puffs him up: he presents as arrogant and entitled, posturing power and strength. What is underneath is a scared little boy. Important to see the fear and vulnerability when dealing with bullies/tyrants, hold him firm and stare into his monstrous face. I had a dream of Hitler, and he was there; I was scared. Then I had my hands around his neck, he was scared, and dropped him down a stairwell from five floors up. He hit the ground and turned into a little boy and ran into a women's arms. Dictators and tyrants may be talking heads or all instinct with no access to the frontal lobe/reason.

Control and Power through Bombing the Innocent

Bombs exploding... the sense of destruction through explosions... fear and terror... total destruction.

Power over death Destroying the Fear Within

 Destroying the hated vulnerable part of self.

Total obliteration, The power within soothing the fearful little boy. The power over death to make others afraid

This is the little boy Tyrant.

The dead body becomes something to control,

Soldiers' caskets out of sight.

Carnage minimized.

The persecution and oppression out of sight.

The body becomes a threat to profit. People need to eat, go to the bathroom, have a living wage, have a roof over their head.

Time out from the machine to take care of the body threatens the bottom line. Breast-feeding babies becomes controversial.

This is the incentive to deny the body and one becomes the talking head.

Moving fast in time for efficiency also numbs the body.

Modern Man moving fast in time
>*Where are you going?*
>*Where is your heart?*
>*Beating to external rhythms*
>*Believing bigger is better*
>*More is better*
>*Precise, explicit, splits you into parts*
>*Each moving precisely*
>*Splits you into parts*
>*Separating you from yourself and others*
>*Win the mechanical heart, survive nuclear war,*
>*Build more bombs to create peace.*
>*Could this be behind the killing of the innocent?*

American Television / Death Denial

Could this be behind the killing of the innocent in American television? Death. denial and objectification of it can be seen in many TV series. CIS Miami, CIS New York, CIS Louisiana, CIS LA, Blood and Bones, Criminal Minds, to name a few. They almost always start out with an announcement of a murder. Talking-head detectives examine the dead body as an inanimate object. Talented coroners also objectify and find additional evidence in the dead body. Is this power and control over death?

Opening scenes often have corpses hanging from ceilings, bodies found in graves on roadsides. Carnage is less so in the news, but much focus on accidents and fires. Carnage is more prevalent in TV series programs. Less carnage and death shown with war and caskets of soldiers. Does this give us some false sense of security by finding out who did the shooting or poisoning or hanging which is actually epidemic in real life now? Does it give us some sense of control in a violent society?

The insecure need to control the body through profit, through denial of needs, through control of the vulnerable, the poor, those who are different through violence, bombing, power over vulnerability, power over death. The body represents vulnerability as it represents death, the ultimate vulnerability. Arrogance and superiority protect against feelings of insecurity and powerlessness. This is the external circumstances in the Society. The solution is an internal journey through dance and dreams to source the personal and collective trauma that lies underneath. This is the *Dance of Psyche: the Rhythm of Consciousness.*

Chapter 5

The Internal Journey Continues / The Dance of Psyche: Rhythm of Consciousness

THE WARNING/PREMONITIONS in the dreams and dances in the first book that represented the traumatic effects of profit over people mentality, a hurry-up rhythm has now become a reality. It has affected our health and our freedom: democracy in peril with the rise of fascism, health care and health compromised, violence in the society ever present with school shootings, shootings on the street and black lives, immigrants, minorities, and the poor more affected. Dance/ dreams continue to be used in the second book as symbols of the psyche. The story continues tapping the creative unconscious through, posture, rhythm, and dreams, an intuitive way through the personal and collective trauma.

In this chapter I will review the dances, images and dreams from the first book and describe how they are even more relevant today. The dreams and dances were premonitions of our times now and sourced the underlying moods in society. The images and dreams were sourced through imagination in rhythm: poetry, music and dance. Imagination in rhythm taps the lucid dream and is related to the nighttime dream. I will add more recent dreams and describe the relevance to what is happening more currently. It represents a shift from trauma to wellbeing, from war/violence to peace, from moving like a machine to dancing with life. After the darkness of trauma, sacred light appears.

There is a dance that is internal: it has a rhythm and shapes itself in different postures to bring to life the waking dream. Underneath the fabric of everyday reality is a dreamscape containing images, colors, and textures. Archetypes surface, mythology is created; a story is told, both personal and collective. In this chapter I describe the creative process used to develop choreography from my imagination. I was drawn to a rhythm, an image of a posture, a vision of the costume including the colors and textures. What arose was a personal but collective story describing a shift, an internal process, from the fight against being the machine to being human, from being traumatized to wellbeing. The dances and dreams are described: Guernica: the Nazi and the Roma (Gypsy), Dance of Gentle Sorrow, Dance of Wind and Fire, Venus: Goddess of Love and peace. The symbols in the dance would be related to my dreams, and, also, the collective imagery that would emerge in the events in the future... which is now occurring. Both the personal and collective symbolism is interpreted after the description is given. The images, dreams and dances are personal and collective symbols of the psyche. The dreams also taped ancestral trauma.

Guernica: The Nazi and the Roma

It was 1985 and I was thinking one day of the differences between Western and technological rhythm of the machine and contrasting it with Eastern rhythm. I found a musical piece by Avatar, a busy energetic rhythm. It contrasted a frenetic continuous rhythm with a Karsilimas beat. I made a costume that was Spanish. I found rayon with flames all over it and made a full flowing skirt. I also made a scarf. I put the music on and started moving to this music. It was mechanical and I moved robotically and then would rage against the rigidity, with the Karsilimas, a rhythm incorporating Flamenco postures. I saw broken angles in the floor and thought of "Guernica." Out of the rhythm surfaced the postures of the Robot, the Nazi, and the clock time. There were violent sections to the music, and I thought about all the violence in society which often focuses on materialistic, bottom-line mentality. The robot is a symbol of moving in rigidly defined ways, solely for the purpose of production. The Nazi is the extreme expression of the machine. I thought about the scene in Treblinka; Hitler ordered the SS soldiers to get a few hundred Jews, Roma, disabled, mentally ill and homosexuals into the gas chamber every ten minutes. The SS soldiers were busy looking at their watches, oblivious to the horror/holocaust that was taking place. I feared that the Reagan era with its bottom-line mentality had the potential for ushering in a new Neo-Nazi movement. This would come true, as there is a new generation of Neo-Nazis in the United States and Europe. I was afraid there would be another Holocaust. (See page 101, Collage of Hate Crimes)

The message here is that we are oblivious to the needs of human beings when there is an obsession with the bottom line. The new corporate model has the potential to be Fascistic. Could it be because of the demands on postal workers to handle so many letters without regard for their needs that contributed to the violence that occurred? Going Postal takes on meaning. Present dehumanization occurs when migrant workers are not allowed to go to the bathroom, when corporations are more concerned with profit, and the medical industrial complex ushers in managed care; again profits over people. (See also Chomsky, N., 1999)

I thought about the Roma and the Holocaust. There were many Roma persecuted in the Holocaust which is less known. Roma represents the passion, the intuitive life that is killed by the machine. Guernica was a painting that represented the destructiveness of war in the modern era. The painting was done to express Picasso's outrage at the bombing of innocent people.

Similarly, Flamenco is a dance of pride and passion, an attitude that expresses rage against rejection, destruction, and oppression. I feel a similar feeling with the Karsilimas rhythm (Turkish Gypsy dance). Eight years after the dance was created, the clock emerged in the commercials as symbols of production (see pages 100 & 101).

Collage of Clocks

Collage of Hate Crimes

PRINT OF GUERNICA' PAINTING BY PICASSO
Painting expressing outrage at man's inhumanity to man
Courtesy of Picasso Estate, 2003 Estate of Pablo Picasso/Artists Right's Society
(ARS)

Guernica's History

According to an online Picasso project regarding the ancient Basque Village Guernica on April 26,1937, one-third of the population was sense-lessly slaughtered or wounded in little more than three hours. The unpro-voked attack began at 4:30, the busiest hour of the market day. The streets were jammed with townspeople and peasants from the countryside. Never before in modern warfare had non-combatants been slaughtered in such numbers, and by such means. (Wertenbaker,1967), quoted in(http://www.tamu.edu/mod/picasso/study/history.html)

The bombing took place during the Spanish Civil War. Franco's army was often assisted by Germany. The Nazi General Goering's policy was to use the Spanish Civil War as an arena for trying out the airmen and planes of the new Lufwaffe, the German Airforce. Wolfram Von Righthoffen, a cousin of the mythical Red Baron of the First World War, headed the attack.

The goal of the assault was hitting a bridge near an important road junction that could be used in the future by Republican forces. (http//www.tamu.edu/mocl/ picasso/study/history.html)

Kosovo: In 1992, our bombers flew over Kosovo to bomb bridges, and destroy the infrastructure. The new B56 bomber was being tested. The notion was that the bombers' technological accuracy could hit military tar-gets and would minimize hurting innocent people. Our aim was to break Milosevic. Once again, innocent people were killed; hospitals, schools, homes and infrastructure were destroyed. The Roma were burned out of their homes and fled to Italy.

When I heard a speech by Sani Rifati, a Roma activist, I was struck by several parallels between the bombing of the town of Guernica in the 1930's and of Kosovo in the 90's. Both were new bombers and were targeting bridges. Both were inaccurate in their targeting and killed innocent people. There was a pervasive denial that people were wounded and killed.

Von Richthofen wrote in his diary that "the concentrated attack of Guernica was the greatest success." During the Kosovo bombing, millions of Americans watched on their TV sets. The predominate image was a green sanitized target viewed from the sky with the bombs falling. There were no bodies and no blood witnessed. Hitting targets and winning was more important than the killing of innocent people.

Picasso's Guernica depicts the experience of terror when the bombs fell, and the horror of people and animals being killed and blown to pieces. The people have their mouths held open, their necks back, looking at the sky with an expression of primal fear. Animals and people are twisted in grotesque postures. According to Wertenbaker (p. 126), "Guernica is a monumental outcry of human grief at its most anguished." (See p. 102)

Guernica in Present-day Time. Guernica, the symbol of man's inhumanity to man, and the loss of innocent lives by bombing continues in present day times. This symbol has gained more significance now as countries bomb without feeling the consequences of children and families being maimed for life or killed. The war in the Middle East has spread: Syria, Yemen, Lebanon, Iraq and Syria now threats of war from North Korea and Iran... and now 2024 Russia's bombing of Ukraine and the genocide of Israel bombing of Palestine by Russian leader Netanyahu.

Heisenberger (2004, p. 1) described the powerful symbolism of Guernica:

Guernica's position in history to the status of world art elevated as it has become to the status of moral exemplar, a universal icon warning that unless we studied its lessons, history was doomed to repeat itself.

Quoting from Heisenberger:

It is a rallying cry in paint for anti-fascist cause. Chopped up fragmentary treatment of form makes the image more startling and makes the image convey more violence.

Guernica, the picture of all bombed cities.

In 2003, after the Twin Towers tragedy, a blue shroud was ignominiously thrown over the Picasso tapestry to hide it from public view by UN officials; the spot is where diplomats and others make statements to the press. Officials thought it would be inappropriate for Colin Powel to speak about the war in Iraq with the 20th century most iconic protest against the inhumanity of war as his backdrop. (Cohen, 2003) The Picasso painting was too much opposition to the war drums being played for the illegal

Iraq war. Talking heads touted smart bombs and fear mongering saying Iraq had weapons of mass destruction, which turned out to be a lie. The media coverage of the bombing on TV looked like fireworks; described as "shock and awe." I think of Naomi Kline who wrote, "The Shock Doctrine, the Rise of Capitalism, here creates chaos to then take power and control."

I would like to quote Amy Goodman on Democracy Now (November 29, 2015 @ 9:00 p.m.):

"I really do think that if for one week in the U.S. we saw peoples' limbs sheared off, we saw kids blown apart, for one week, war would be eradicated. Instead, what we see in the U.S. media is the video war game."

We have the Ukraine/Russian war with billions spent on weapons. No matter what the reasons, the innocent die.

Now we have the bombing of the innocent in Israel by Hamas. 125 hostages abducted. 1,200 Israeli deaths. Reportedly, there were many rapes and sexual assaults as well. This has resulted in enormous suffering and death. It is present-day holocaust. What was less visible in the press was the repression of the Palestinians across many decades. The revenge by Netanyahu was the worst atrocity since the holocaust. 40,000 Palestinians killed, most of them women and children, 1 million sought refuge from the war, hospitals destroyed, 80,000 injured, 19,000 orphaned, 75 percent displaced. Food and medicine trucks blocked. The innocent not seen, heard or felt. Retaliation by Israel, the Palestinian people not seen, heard or felt, yes, present day holocaust. Guernica alive, the bombing of the innocent. Golda Meir's quote as relevant today: "When we love our children more than we hate our enemies, we will have peace."

What spoke more of the horror and suffering were the children's cries. With enormous tears and anguish in his face, a young boy screams out the horror of seeing his friend's head blown apart, now a lifetime trauma; and a little girl cries out, "Mama, Mama," in tears as bombs explode close by. A Palestinian child went to hug his mother in her tent: both were burned alive by the bombs exploding. A father picked up his child; his head was decapitated. Many were bombed, their tents in Rafah, and were burned alive. Fifty killed.

Although Biden disapproved and wanted a cease fire, Israeli's used bombs made by the U.S., and the one that hit Rafah was a U.S. bomb. I think of this as trauma reenactment; not as victims of holocaust but as perpetrated by Netanyahu. The extent of the suffering can be felt by a child crying alone amongst the rubble. This says more than the statistics about the pain and grief of the experience. I recall the naked child running from the bombing during the Viet Nam War. This child's image ended the war. So, then I am recalling a Palestinian mother with her dead child wrapped in a white sheet held by a mother in the grips of enormous grief.

The killing of the innocent is wrong on both sides. More press was given to the Israelis. Less acknowledgement of the suffering of the Palestinian people who have been oppressed for decades by the Israelis.

My thought is that there was experience of the holocaust by Netanyahu's extreme right wing people; and could it be that this is trauma reenactment, not as victims but as aggressors, perpetrators, power through violence cleansing the horror and helplessness of being a victim? Now billions of dollars for war given to the Israelis and Ukraine and Taiwan. Thus, the military industrial complex benefits. Is it profit over the needs of people? Does profit trump the needs of people for food, water and medical supplies? Diplomacy and communication.. where is it?

According to the Council on Foreign Relations, Micahzenko reported the bombing of six countries from January 7 to March 15, 2015:

In 2015, during the Obama administration, 20,000 bombs were dropped in Muslim countries according to the CFR Council on Foreign Relations; Iraq, Syria, Afghanistan, Pakistan, and Somali, noted by Micah Zenko, Senior Fellow, CFR.

Total 23,144 Bombs

22,110 Iraq and Syria

947 Afghanistan

58 Yemen

18 Somalia

11 Pakistan

In July 2017, during Trumps's presidency, more civilians were killed in six months versus the entire presidency of Obama. Trump stated, "I'm going to bomb the shit out of them. I don't care." These are primitive emotions without logic or understanding of consequences, evidence of disassociating from the suffering of the innocent. Another talking head quote described by Amnesty International, "The most precise targeting in the history of warfare... the best job to avoid civilian casualties." This quote does not hold up to the truth of the devastation suffered. It is as Amy Goodmen (2015) said, "It is described as a war game."

So, what happens that there is not more outrage over the killing of the innocent by those that are in charge? As I was thinking of this, I heard about the film, The Zone of Interest, a film by Jonathan Glazer. It is a harrowing and disturbing drama that explains the lives of the Nazi commander of Auschwitz (Rubolt Hoss) and his wife Hedwig, who live in a house and garden next to the camp.

Hoss, a devoted Nazi leader, wrote in his own diary of his pride in running "the greatest human destructive machine of all time." It was no idle boast. This is the inflated ego, entitled authoritarian that drives the killing machine which numbs his humanity... no feeling for the killing of the innocent.

Killing of innocent children in school shootings. The symbolism of Guernica is relevant to innocent children being killed by school shootings. It is the loss of innocent lives. The image that represents this was the 14,000 shoes on the lawn of the White House; each pair representing a child or adolescent that was killed in these shootings.

The first devastating school shooting was at Columbine High School. There also was an attempted bombing April 20th, 1999 (en.m. wikipedia. org), in addition to the shooting; the attack involved homemade bombs. Two were placed in the cafeteria. Fortunately, they failed to detonate. Harris and Klebold hoped the massacre would cause the most deaths in US history, exceeding the Oklahoma City bombing, "planned as grand." They would often cite the Oklahoma City bombing as an inspiration and as a goal to surpass the bombing's casualties. The perpetrators (12th grade seniors, Eric Harris and Dylan Klebold) murdered 12 students and one teacher. Ten students were killed in the school library where the pair subsequently committed suicide; 21 were injured by gunfire. It was the deadliest shooting in US history. The crime has been known as the Columbine effect and has become a symbol for mass shootings.

Some of the emotional issues raised by this were the issues of being an outcast, high school cliques, teenage use of antidepressants, the internet and violence in video games and movies. In searching for the background of these two students, I found out that they were frequent targets of bullying, however had some status with other students.

They were arrested for stealing equipment from a van and arrested. Since that time, they meticulously built explosives. In a journal entry describing a shooting in 1997, the date was the same as Hitler's birthday speculating that they may have been inspired by Nazism. Other causes may have been poor parenting, bullying once again, reactions to anti-depressant medication, violence in the media; but the cause at this time is undetermined.

Sandy Hook Elementary Shooting

The next shooting I would like to talk about is Sandy Hook Elementary School Shooting on December 14, 2012 (Wikipedia). Twenty children between 6-7 were shot. I chose this one because of these very young innocent lives that were lost. 154 rounds in five minutes by an AR15. In all 28 were killed, two injured

The question raised is: "What was the motivation for the shooter to do this?" A topic presented in CBS News on December 10. 2018. The title of the presentation was, "Documents Shed Light on Sandy Hook Shooter Adam Lanza." The shooter was 16 when father and mother divorced. His mother was a gun enthusiast and would take him to the shooting range rather than leaving him alone. He was described as fidgety, deeply troubled; had a tortured mind. He had anger and scorn for other people and deep social isolation, a scorn for humanity. He states, "I have been desperate to feel anything positive for someone for my entire life." A Connecticut child advocate said, "His preoccupation with violence and access to his mother's weapons proved a recipe for mass murder." He spent long hours playing violent video games. School records show he has autism spectrum, anxious, and was obsessive/compulsive. On the anniversary of the shooting, there were bomb threats.

Orlando Shooting

The targets for the Orlando shooter were LGBQ and Latinos. A case of terror and Hate," said Obama (2012). 49 dead and 53 wounded. According to CNN (06/12/2016), "The shooter pledged allegiance to Isis. Witnesses described it as 'a timeline of terror, a deadly Oakland nightclub shooting.'" The New York Times (June 17, 2016) described the Orlando massacre turned sanctuary of fantasy and escape into a sobering scene all too familiar in America. What is the root of this young man's motivation for killing? Some of the possible contributing factors to his violence were described.

He came from a culture where his Afghan roots and Muslim faith were fractured and there is male privilege in his Muslim faith. He was verbally abusive in school; disciplined 30 times. Sought attention through noise, disruption; he made a sound of a plane exploding soon after 9/11 attacks ... off-putting employee ... made jokes about killing those who offended him. Made sounds like a motor, then made an explosive sound before taking his seat in school bus. Was suspended for fighting in school. Was ridiculed for being flabby. Then lifted weights and became very muscular. Incensed by two men kissing.

May have been on steroids. He became a security guard but was fired. When he was a security guard at a gate his behavior was described as follows:

When I would go grab my ID from his hands, he would hover over my car window, lean in, breathe leaning, teeth clenched, jaw muscles stretching out.

It was like I was staring into the eyes of Ted Bundy husband said. I was irate, but he was completely detached.

He married but isolated his wife and beat her.

In this article by NYTimes they describe the killer Omar Mateen as *"always agitated, always mad, forever not at peace, forever out of step."* According to another article by the NY Times (2016) a few days later, the Attorney General said police failed to anticipate his actions. Red flag warnings were that he boasted about his ties to terrorist groups, boasted that he would carry out a suicide bomb in Syria. The Department was reflecting on what they did.

This was of interest to the Dance of Psyche, Rhythm of Consciousness. He was described as out of step in his native Afghan dance, Atton.

Atton is a dance of synchronized turns and moves which create an almost trancelike state creating a sense of oneness.

He was clumsy, out of sync, head down, dressed in black following his own rhythm.

Pulse nightclub, where hundreds of people were drinking, dancing and celebrating life the way families do at weddings; and following his own rhythm, he began to shoot.

His wife avoided clues that he was getting radicalized. Sixty-four percent of cases, relatives and family, were aware of intent to commit terrorism. (NYTimes, 2016).

The Parkland Students: Stoneman Douglas High School Shooting February 14, 2018 (Wikipedia, cn.m.wikipedia.a.org). "Nikolas Cruz, shooter, opened fire with semi-automatic rifle at Marjory Stoneman Douglas High School in Parkland, Florida. killing 17 people and injuring 17 others. His motive was unknown. It was the deadliest shooting greater than Columbine that killed 15.

He had a pattern of disciplinary issues, unnerving behaviors and threatening behaviors, but got past the loopholes in the law. He posted a message in 2017 about becoming a school shooter. This was reported to the FBI, but it did not get to the local office. The Parkland students became passionately involved in preventing violence through shooting from ever happening again. The survivors were upset at inaction of the Republican-dominated legislature. Governor Rick Scott proposed legislation for waiting periods in purchasing guns, background checks, and raising the age to 21. This was pushed by a growing movement led by teenage survivors. This became the "Never Again Movement."

Then Governor Matt Bevern stated, *"The things (guns), being put in the hands of young people. Video games desensitized people to the value of human life."* Governor Rick Scott backs raising age for rifle purchases to 21 (Washington Post, Democracy Dies in Darkness, February 23, 2018) and supports a ban on assault weapons. Brian Mast, a Republican from Florida, wrote an op-ed in the NY Times February 28, 2018. He supported a ban on the sale of a civilian version of the military rifle. He stated:

"I cannot support the primary weapon I used to defend our people, used to kill innocent children I swore to defend."

This represented a dramatic shift in position for the state's Republican leaders, who spent decades easing the regulation of guns and giving legal protection to those who use firearms in self-defense. (Scherer, 2018)

Collective Trauma Surfaces in Experience and Dream

The dance was fortelling of the dreams.

Two years after the dance was completed. I developed a traumatic response to an accident. An 82-year-old man got on the highway going the wrong way. He did not see me. I got out of his way, but he hit me on the left rear tire. My car became airborn over four lanes and landed upside down in the shoulder lane. The glass blew out of the car, which was crushed, totaled. I felt as if I would be OK, and it was not a big deal. I remember thinking he hit me — OK, I'm upside-down, no problem. I remember feeling sadness that there was no one there for me. It was a subtle feeling.

I developed a severe stress response to this accident. I felt terrified during the night, and I had the following dream. I was running and being chased by two SS soldiers. There were the oven and the fire in the background. I was a young girl running naked down the hallways, trying to escape. I was feeling terror that I would be killed. I eventually ran into a shower to hide and wrapped myself up in clear plastic. The feeling was that I was transparent and would be caught. There was a showerhead dripping just a few drops of water. It was clear the SS soldiers would find me. I felt so much fear in my body. Several years would pass before I would connect the shower to the gas chamber. The concentration camp victims thought they were going to take showers, but instead they were killed by the gas that was piped into the showers (see watercolor page 114).

I debated whether to include this watercolor because it looks like a child did it. However, I heard that some adult survivors of the holocaust told their stories in a child's voice, so I kept the paintings in the book.

Does the dream have significance to the collective consciousness? The Nazis were the ultimate war machine. When we devalue life for the sake of production, do we not create a situation where there is danger of another Holocaust? In terms of the personal unconscious, the Nazi represents the internal critical voice that can turn inward and destroy oneself. The Nazis externalized their hate onto the Jews and the Roma, mentally ill, the handicapped, the gays, and destroyed them. They were the vulnerable in this process; they destroyed the part of themselves that represented life.

Because of the intensity of the dream, I sometimes thought that this might have been a past life reality. I had not taken the concept of past life as seriously prior to this experience. In an EMDR therapy session, I regressed back in time to the last lifetime. It felt real. There was a feeling of being separated from "my people" and then reexperiencing the dream provided relief from the terror. After this session, the experience seemed more likely a past life reality because of the attraction to and use of Romani rhythm.

The extreme loneliness I felt may have been due to being exterminated in isolation. In my experience with trauma victims, suffering trauma in isolation is where the devastation occurs. It was hard to account for the extreme loneliness. I could also explain the dream from childhood experiences in terms of the paranoid rages of my mother. The fear was that I would be completely rejected or destroyed if I were to disagree with her or were to be myself. The fear was that if I was to come out, I would be destroyed, for not being perfect, for any irrational reason whatever.

The traumatic response would last 10 years. I thought I was over the major part of it when Princess Diana was killed in a car crash in Paris. This may have triggered a trauma reenactment of my devastating car crash. The following dream occurred after the announcement on TV and scenes of her crash were shown.

I was in Germany, and I was running from the Nazis. There were people ice skating on frozen lakes. There was a grate in the sidewalk to an underneath cavern. I decided not to go with the two other men. They were caught and there were large hot electric coils that people were burned alive on. The two men were put on the hot coils and burned alive. I kept running and escaped into an orphanage where there were children. They looked pale and sickly. The SS soldiers came to the door, but then left. I was safe. The dream ended.

In thinking about the dream, I felt that if you come out, you could get killed. Diana was in her prime when she died, so to shine, to develop fully — to come out means to get killed, to be burned alive. Perhaps if one embodies human or activist, there is greater danger in being destroyed.

I also know that other women have fears and dreams of being burned when they start coming out with their power. Women healers whom I know cite the witch burnings that occurred just 300 years ago. It has been history that those who are intuitive healers, witches, Roma have been persecuted, burned at the stake, or subjected to holocaust.

Historical Facts About the Romani/Sinti People Killed in the Holocaust
The following historical facts corroborate details in the dream.

There were 500,000 to 600,000 Romani/Sinti people exterminated by the Nazis, most of them gassed in Auschwitz. (p.1 on gypsies, http//
www.remember.org/witness//wit.vic.gyp.htm).

At Auschwitz-Birkenau, officials set up a separate "Gypsy family camp." From the wooden barracks, the gas chambers were clearly visible. Many were killed by gassing. In the summer of 1942, German and Polish gypsies imprisoned in the Warsaw ghetto were deported to Treblinka

HOLOCAUST DREAM: WATERCOLOR PAINTING BY CHRISTINA
Holocaust Dream: Painted soon after Accident, August, 1988

where they were gassed. Authorities took many Sinti and Romani children from their families and brought them to special homes for children as wards of the state (p.4 of 7, Sinti and Roma (Gypsies), victims of the Nazi era. (http//www.holocaust.trc.org/sinti.htm)

Guernica: The Nazi and the Roma; now 2020, it's the Nazis and African Americans, Muslims, Mexicans, Native Americans, Immigrants and now again the Roma in Europe...and now, 2024, Haitian Americans.

The premonitions in the dance; the Nazi, the Robot, and the clock and dreams of holocaust, are now more of a reality, as is the bombing of the innocent in wars.

The Nazi. The rise of white supremacy has become ever stronger. Fascism and authoritarianism are stronger threats to our Democratic values. This is fueled by the takeover of greed in our corporations and in the White House. The lobbyist control Washington. NRA money influences the push back against gun control so that the killing of the innocent students in school shootings with weapons designed to kill many at once does not get through to Washington; greed is the opiate for them, numbs them and kills their soul and they become incapable of compassion. School shootings continue, bombings in the Middle East continued, Guernica alive; Fascism amplified. The rhetoric coming from the past President, "I would knock the hell out of Isis, you have to take out their families." Ross, (2015)

White Nationalists, head of Brietbart Organization leader was advisor to the President. Rhetoric demeaned handicapped, immigrants, blacks, the poor, Mexicans, Muslims, the vulnerable became scapegoats. The KKK is not openly rejected. Militancy has taken over many police encounters with African Americans; excessive force becomes epidemic. In many police departments, it's a matter of numbers of tickets or arrests, not for the sake of justice, e.g. stop and frisk. Thus, the images on pages 100 and 101 become more of a reality, crime or quota. A disproportionate number of black men are arrested and are in prison. Fascism and extreme Right are also prevalent in Europe. Roma once again are discriminated against; their children separated from their parents; their camp set on fire where a beautiful little girl lost her life. In the U.S., immigrants are demeaned: Mexicans as Rapist. Cruelty at the border as immigrants cross over. Once again, children separated from their parents and put in cages. The conditions there are inhumane. I want to acknowledge Native Americans who were also separated from their families and put in schools of indoctrination, deprived of their language and culture. Racism is driven by a sense of superiority and entitlement. One of dreams I had was that the Roma children were separated from their parents and put in an orphanage by the Nazis.

Innocent Black Lives Lost; Honoring; Black Lives Matter. As I was writing about the Black women and men who lost their lives, a video of Daniel Prude, 31, from Rochester, N.Y. was shown on the news. As with other Black people who lost their lives, the situation seemed innocent with excessive force by police. According to an article in the NY Times (2020) titled "What we Knew about Daniel Prude's Case" by Colosseum T. and Gold M., referenced extensively here, he had mental health problems; ran into the street without clothes. Truck driver called 911, said he was breaking into a car. Police put a spit hood and pressed him into the ground for two minutes. Coroner later said he died of asphyxia in the setting of physical restraint. He died March 31 after life support was removed. Family showed video footage from police officer video cameras. (T. Closson and Shanahan, 2020). In hearing about this after writing about the other Black Lives lost, I thought this is epidemic; it is not stopping. This was right after the George Floyd lost his life and protests erupted all over the United States and in Europe. "Enough!" people were saying.

The visceral sensation of seeing George Floyd pinned to the ground with the policeman's knee on his neck and saying, "I can"t breathe" was a powerful symbol of oppression. A whole nation response to perhaps feeling a body felt sense of mirroring his experience of suffocation and oppression, being held to the ground and not being able to breathe. I remember seeing a post by the American Women's group with the Statue of Liberty with a mask on her face, and I put a caption underneath that image. The Statue of Liberty saying, "I can't breathe," symbolizing the loss of Democracy in America.

Brianna Taylor, 26, from Louisville, Kentucky. She was innocently sleeping at home. Police barged into her apartment with a search warrant in a drug case. Her boyfriend thought it was a break-in and fired a gun. Police shot Brianna eight times.

Alatiana Jefferson, 28, Miami, Florida, was shot and killed through the window of her home in the presence of her eight-year-old nephew. Police were responding to a call from a neighbor who reported that Jefferson's front door had been open. Officer Dean resigned and was indicted for murder. This eight-year-old will likely suffer the pain of this traumatic event for his lifetime.

Aura Rossier, 40, 2014, from Ann Arbor, Michigan (2018). Boyfriend called 911 due to an argument. Had a knife in hand and refused to drop it. Police fired one shot that killed her. There were no charges over her death. Reforms using cameras for police implemented.

Stephen Clark, 22, from Sacramento, California. He was standing in his grandmother's yard holding a mobile phone which was perceived as a gun by Police. District Attorney did not file charges. Family reached a $2.4 million settlement with the City of Sacramento.

Botham Jean, 26, from Dallas Texas (2018). He was seated on his sofa at home eating ice cream. He was shot by off-duty officers as she entered his apartment thinking it was hers. He was shot as she thought he was an intruder by officer Amber Greiger. She was found guilty of murder, sentenced to 10 years in jail. Jean's brother hugged her to forgive her. This shows great emotional strength to forgive the violence related to a loved one.

I vividly remember this shooting of Philando Castille, 32, in Falcon Heights, Minnesota when the Dash Cam video was shown on TV. Police made a traffic stop. He reported he had a firearm. Police started shooting seconds later. His girlfriend was in the car with her four-year-old daughter. It was captured on Facebook live. Police were acquitted of second-degree manslaughter. A $3 million dollar settlement was made with Castille's mother. Money does not replace a loved one. I think about the mother and child who witnessed this shooting. This is lifetime trauma and loss of innocence through violence.

Allen Sterling, 37, Baton Rouge, Louisiana. He was confronted by two officers in front of a shop. He was tasered and pinned to the ground. He was threatened by Officer Salmomi that he would shout; he was shot six times, allegedly reaching for a loaded handgun in his pants pocket. He was reportedly selling CDs and used a gun to threaten a man outside a convenience store. The owner of the CD store stated that, "He was not the one causing trouble." Officer Salmomi called him a stupid xxxxx after shooting him. Shooting was recorded by multiple bystanders. Attorney General Landry would not file charges against the officers stating that they "acted in a reasonable and justifiable manner." An investigation into the shooting would be opened by the State of Louisiana once the Department of Justice released the physical evidence. Lawsuit against the officers is pending. On July 5th, 100 protestors shouted, "No justice, no peace." Flowers and messages left at the place of his death. A candlelight vigil a day later calling for justice. After peaceful protest, Micah Xavier opened fire in an ambush and killed five police officers and wounding 11 others, including two civilians. He fled inside a building on the campus of El Centro College. Police followed him there. Guernica alive here; Johnson was killed by a bomb attached to a remote control bomb disposal robot. This was the first tie U.S. law enforcement had used a robot to kill a suspect. Who was Johnson? He was an Army Reserve Afghan War veteran and was angry over police shootings of black men. He said he wanted to kill white people, especially white police officers. Obama stated, "Americans should feel outraged at episodes of police brutality since they're rooted in long-simmering racial discord."

The Bahamian citizens received a travel warning to the U.S. due to racial tensions and advised young men to use "extreme caution" when interacting with police.

Similar advisories were issued by the governments of United Arab Emirates and Bahrain, days later. The United Nations Working Group of Experts on People of African Descent issued a statement strongly condemning Sterling and Castile's killings. The current Chair said that the killings demonstrate "a high level of structural and institutional racism."

United States is far from recognizing the rights of all its citizens. Existing measures to address racist crimes motivated by prejudice are insufficient and have failed to stop the killings.

Michelle Cassenx, 50, Phoenix, Arizona (2015). Police arrived for a transport to Mental Health facility. They removed her security door perhaps after an exchange. She lunged toward them with a hammer. Sergeant Perry Deepra fired a single shot. He was demoted.

Frederick Gray, 23, (2015). He was arrested and put in a police van. He was tossed around, and his spine was almost severed. Hands and feet were shackled, and he was without a seatbelt. Officers were charged; three were acquitted. A $6.4 million settlement was made.

Jacob Black, Kenosha, Wisconsin. On the news August 27, 2020. A video showing him leaning into his car and was shot seven times by police officer, Rusten Sheskey. He was paralyzed from the waist down. Family witnessed the shooting. This case is now under investigation for a breach in civil rights. There was a reason to suspect him as dangerous with an alleged history of having a gun and threatening others with it. There is uncertainty that this was him, as someone else had his name and lived close by according to National Pulse. These charges were dismissed and the only other charge that came up was for not having a driver's license.

In an article written in the Guardian by David Johnson titled "In America Black Deaths" are not a flaw in the System. They are the System. (January 20, 2020)

Police violence, poor medical care, or simply trying to breathe; we suffer from the underlying condition: racism. There was an image there, a black woman with a mask saying, "I can't breathe" quotes by them:

We die driving our cars. We die playing outside. We die babysitting. We die eating ice cream. We die sleeping in our own beds. We die and die at the hands of police, who are sworn to serve and protect us.

Even when we are not dying, we die giving birth. We die trying to breathe. We die when doctors under treat our heart attacks and dismiss our calls for help.

We die because we are overrepresented where it hurts, such as poverty and prisons, and underrepresented where it helps, such as higher education, elected office and the federal judiciary. We die from many causes; this is racism. This is the voice of the innocent Black lives suffering

Cobolt Red. More recently I read *How the Blood of the Congo Powers our Lives* by Sidarthra Kara (2023). An investigation revealed the human rights abuse behind cobalt mining operation and the moral implications that affect us all. Cobalt Red is the searing, the first ever expose of the immense toll taken on the people and environment of the Democratic Republic of the Congo by cobalt mining as told by the Congolese people themselves activist and researcher traveled deep into cobalt territory to document the testimonials of the people, living, working and dying for cobalt.

Cobalt is an essential component to every lithium-ion rechargeable battery made. To uncover the truth about brutal mining practices, Kara investigated militia-controlled mining areas, traced the supply chain of the child mined cobalt.

Today, the batteries that power our smart phones, tablets, laptops, and electric vehicles, laptops and electric vehicles. Roughly 75% of the world's supply of cobalt is mined by the Congo, often by peasants and children in sub-human conditions. Billions of people in the world cannot conduct their daily lives without participating in human right and environmental catastrophe in the Congo. In this stark and crucial book, Kara argues that we must all care about what is happening in the Congo because we are all implicated. This implies the need to be able to feel the suffering of the innocent, the children, Guernica alive.

The machine separates us from body and soul, from each other... fracturing society for power and control; winning versus justice is characteristic of authoritarian rule.

The Nazi in the Collective Psyche

Hitler comes alive; Swastikas and Nazi salutes are in former president rallies. These large rallies enhance the denial in the populace. The supporters, many who have lost their jobs, identify with the power and wealth they perceive in the leader. He appeals to their emotional needs, but then betrays their trust. They remain in denial entranced by him. The emotional rhetoric solidifies and unites his base.

Quoting from the first book (2003):

Synchronous sound, breath and movement are primal ways of relating and connecting. Rhythm is an expression of relationship in family, community, and culture. Leaders may use these principles to unconsciously or consciously restrict freedom. It is possible to use mirroring of movement, posture, and rhythm for political control as Hitler did. His base fell into trance states fracturing reality.

These techniques are also used in commercials to hook us through hypnotic suggestion. Perhaps rhythm and posture go right into the amygdala, the primitive area of the brain? Inducing trance states becomes possible in large political rallies as people synchronize to each other's rhythm and mirror postures, such as the Nazi salute. Thus, it is human nature to imitate the rhythm of the people and things in our life that we want to know and become part of. In the 21st century, there is the imitation of the machine because the god is technology.

Rhythm of the Machine. Collective Response to Trauma. The push to go fast in time to synchronize to the rhythm of the machine might be a collective trance to numb the pain of trauma. There is a pervasive denial of abuse and neglect of children as reflected by child-rearing practice, the shape of our school systems, the salaries of teachers, and refusal to provide mental health care to people. deMause, (1997), who has been a scholar in tracing the history of child rearing practices and the trauma of children states:

Massive denial of the origins of humanity's problems in the traumatic abuse of children is then one and the same as the massive denial of the psychological origin of behavior. Both are rooted in the fact that our deepest fears are stored in a separate brain system that remains largely unexplained by science and that is the source of restaging early traumas in social events in history. (deMause, 1997, p. 91)

Thus, the collective values for mechanism are a way to split off aspects of the self, splitting the body, mind, and spirit. People move like robots, act like Nazis to numb pain. Disconnected from the body and numbed by their experiences, a collective denial of human needs and spiritual emptiness occurs. The culture becomes sterile, a bigger house, an important job, compensate for spiritual emptiness. The machine is the split off part of the collective self, deadened and numb, the culture reacts-violence and war cleanse feelings of hate and pain.

In 2020, almost 20 years later in the Trump era, Adams writes an article titled *"Trump and the Social Trance."* In the section Repetition, it's form of mesmerization, he writes, *"Trump is a master of intoxicating voters, reviving up followers in raucous crowds with chants and slogans.* He states, *"Emotions are contagious in crowds. He uses repetition as a virtual drumbeat to syncopate the rhythm of collective responsiveness to the leader's version of reality."* (Adams, K. A., 2018, p.282)

I would say he taps into the underlying rage of the disenfranchised, many who have lost their livelihoods. They feel they have been beaten up. His scapegoating and demeaning of others, seeing them beaten up like they have been beaten up is relief from the underlying rage. His rallies are filled with violent rhetoric by him: "Let's bomb the hell out of Isis, let's kill their families, water boarding is OK, let's increase the torture. Anti-immigration sentiment has increased, "I am going to build a wall."

Bullies become popular when there is chaos and insecurity as it is an opportunity for power and control as someone has the answers for the disenfranchised. But evil lurks when it is about what I want versus what the people need. His statement that the system is corrupt rings true and is popular but is likely manipulative. Immigrants were put in camps; children separated from their parents and can be seen in cages. It brings to mind the internment camps of Japanese during World War II. There was a program on Democracy Now (June 24, 2019) on the Japanese internment camps as there was palpable fear and concern of a resurgence of hate and increasing fascism. In the holocaust, as I have described, Roma (Gypsies) parents were separated from their children and put in an orphanage. Native American children were separated from their families and put in separate schools to indoctrinate them into American ways; they were deprived of their language and culture. This is one of the most cruel tortures in racism and white supremacy. Underlying this is a sense of entitlement and superiority with underlying inadequacy and powerlessness.

This rage also stems from a traumatic fundamentalist childhood: the terrorization of children through religious dogma and corporal punishment. It was argued that fundamentalist parents traumatized their children, making them susceptible to trance induction, obedience to authority and defense against anxiety switching into social altars. Further he says that: "Trump and followers share a sense of victimhood." (Adams, 2020, p. 238) He also described that attraction and perceived hyper-masculinity was a reaction to rejecting women in authority — Hillary as President elect. Women in fundamentalist religion were conditioned to be subservient.

Marsha Gissen on Democracy Now (2017) quoted philosopher Carl Schmitt from the 1930's. He wrote a blueprint for the likes of Donald Trump and Vladimir Putin. He noted the Mystical connection between the leader and the masses. The leader articulates the internal emotions of the crowd. He articulates deepest fears and desires. The bluster and bravado articulate anger at the elites, divides between us and them; denying the external enemies creates enemies within. She also noted that Liberals ignored working class and the displaced and marginalized people. Both Hitler and Trump played their marginalization, built them up rallying for them. This was true of Franco and Mussolini as well.

Timothy McVeigh (see image on p. 101) and White Nationalism come alive today. In an incident on a train, a white Nationalist, Joseph A Christian, targeted two Muslim women. Two men on the train stood up to the attackers to protect the women. These men were stabbed. This white Nationalists' hero was Timothy McVeigh. He was a 35-year-old white supremacist with a criminal record; was arrested in the connection with the stabbing deaths of two white men on a light rail in Portland, Oregon. One who intervened when he began to hurl anti-Muslim epitaph at two women, one who was wearing a head scarf, hijab police reported... with Nazi salute he ranted, *"Muslims should die, Die Muslims. "* This white supremacist was arrested for the fatal stabbing death of these two white men. (Schmid, 2017).

In an article written by Nazaryan (2017) titled *Timothy McVeigh, Extremists New Hero,* he writes, *"Extremists are embracing Timothy McVeigh as patriot and hero ignoring his mass act of murder in Oklahoma City bombing April 21, 1995, the worst act of domestic terrorism in U.S. history."* The 1995 bombing took the lives of 168 innocent children according to the Southern Poverty Law Center new report, The New Extremist. Trend by Morlin. He notes Jeremy Christian praised the bomber in a Facebook post, *"May all the Gods bless Timothy McVeigh, a true Patriot."*

In 2017, the Gypsy/Roma travelers and Muslims said, "Wake-up, we will be persecuted worse than the Jews." This was said when far right march held in Poland was calling for "White Europe." On May 6, 2019, the Agence France Press reported, "Vandals scrawled Nazi Swastikas" and words "Gas Them" on Germany's memorial to the half million Roma and Sinti murdered by the Nazis; the foundation behind the monument. We Newmaker, head of the foundation, said it was,"an aggressive anti- Roma act." A Roma activist stated, *"Our people still experience exclusion and discrimination in Germany on a daily basis."*

The Robot. The robot is a significant symbol today as many corporations more and more require compliance; don't think, don't feel, just focus more on efficiency and performance. Workers are asked to be machine-like. This is the case for Amazon assemble line to get products out in record speed. Facebook employees checking posts are asked to do so every few seconds. Facebook employees in an interview with Business Insider (2015) revealed 22 awful things about working at Facebook; lack of focus on teamwork, more focused on outcome/ running 24/7 responsibility for engineers, to name just a few. It is growing so quickly, becoming so large it has lost focus. Fellow employees are rude. Instructions confusing with no feedback; some in the company described as *"holier than thou, overhyped."* Crowded tables, the chant is: *"Code, code, code, ship, ship, ship — I get tired just thinking about it. Can never really leave work."* The fast pace takes out the humanity; autonomy is threatened, and so is the health and safety of workers. Profit trumps needs and values of workers. In many institutions, whistle-blowers, those speaking out against the breeches in safety, are retaliated against and lose their jobs or are imprisoned. School children are subjected to pressure for performance without support and/or subjected to bullying become suicidal.

The computer, digitalized lifestyle where there is limited face-to-face contact, no mirroring of posture, gesture, and voice, tone and rhythm effects the health of the brain. This mirroring is necessary for health. Preoccupation with cell phones cuts down human interaction and may contribute to isolation — perhaps alienation as well.

Email, although positive in many regards, pushes employees to be responsible 24/7, so employees compromise downtime.

Robots and machines more and more are replacing workers. Robots unload cargo, collect tolls, issue traffic tickets, collect your money at the gas pump... you can even replace the grocery clerk with a machine to tally and pay for your groceries; you can pay your bills on-line with on-line banking; you can shop on line.

So, what are the risks and benefits of machines taking over? One risk is loss of community, loss of jobs for workers and perhaps, loss of health and freedom.

Robot warfare. Robot warfare was prevalent in the Middle East. There was a human disconnect when the enemy was targeted, like in digital war games. The carnage is not seen. However, the drone pilots still developed PTSD documented in an NPR report, The War may be Over, but the Trauma is Real (Common B.M., 2017).

Human experience versus computerized solutions. The Hudson River landing of flight 1549, USA Airlines on January 15, 2009 by Captain Chesly (Sully) Sullenberger landed in the Hudson River. He saved 155 passengers. He immediately lowered the nose of the plane after a flock of geese at low altitude caused both engines of the plane to lose thrust. The option was to land at La Guardia Airport or Teterboro Airport, New Jersey. This is what the computerized program recommended. He said, *"We are going to land in the Hudson."* He was blamed; they said he risked the lives of passengers according to computer analysis. The enormous experience of Sully was pitted against the assumption that computer's assessment was more accurate.

It was the teamwork of aircrew, traffic controllers, the aircraft designers, trainers, and so on that helped make this incident a safe landing. Good chance that the experience of the pilot was the factor that helped make this landing a safe one as well.

The age of computers calls into question the over-reliance on computers versus the experience of professionals across time.

In health care, computerized checklists are used to evaluate patient condition. An experienced nurse or physician may be better at assessing the patient's condition in a note versus a checklist, and better targets the patient's condition. Further, physicians and nurses are busy on computers documenting almost every word spoken. Face-to-face interaction time is jeopardized by the computer. Moreover, reliance on test results from machines versus hands-on assessment of the patient. In the book, Confessions of a Medical Man, many decades ago, a physician over-relied on lab results. His decision was to recommend an abortion. He recalls his experience of pulling out a live fetus ... so he wrote about the lost art of medicine. (Mendelson, R.S., 1979)

I also worry about time on computers in the classroom, taking away time in developing relationships as there is more brain health, memory and learning through attachment, relationship than sole learning with a computer.

Does this split us from ourselves ... from the feeling and sensation that make us human beings ... from meaning? Whole person fractured separating us from self, other, nature and the divine. Does this lead us to superiority, entitlement, more dominance and control over others?

The Clock. The clock speed is all important; this is the rhythm of the machine, the robotic rhythm.

The doomsday clock becomes all important as we build more bombs. According to Chomsky, now the U.S., China and Russia are building smaller nuclear bombs, pushing the hands of the doomsday clock closer to 12. The biggest threats are global warming and nuclear holocaust.

Healing Past Life Holocaust

My personal story of healing comes alive through past dreams of holocaust and the dreams involving separation of children from their families. This also includes images in my dance of the Nazi; the robot and the clock time continue relevant in my own healing 20 years later. Healing from personal trauma lends insight for us, healing the collective trauma we are experiencing now — the personal dynamics, but also how it represents the collective dynamics of our time. My purpose is to give understanding to those who have similar toxic experiences. It is very relevant now with Bully bosses as gatekeepers for the profit motive.

The holocaust dream was terrifying, and it gave me deep empathy for holocaust survivors and those who are under threat from bullies: in work and home and through authoritarian leadership; threats to their lives and their livelihoods ... and therefore enabled me to write about toxic environments as they related to others' experiences. Working as a nurse initially, and also as a trauma psychologist across 50 years, also contributed to this understanding. Many patients came in with Bully boss experiences; bullying is very toxic to the self. Consider kids who are bullied at school. Some commit suicide; a person bullied at work cannot sleep after five years. So now I will share the wisdom and insight from my own healing and healing others once again. Clarity in wisdom heals. (See also Campbell, C., 2003) Now, 2021, the bullying of Megan Markle by the UK Royal Institution became suicidal as a result of this bullying experience. When she asked human resources for help, they refused. I would say that not having protection and security is a huge trigger for depression and suicide.

I had bully boss experiences starting with sexual harassment in the United States Navy as Navy nurse. This led to a suicidal crisis. This remained with me over my entire career. My competence was attacked, so I lived in fear that I would be attacked again. This led to cumulative stress across this lifetime and perhaps the terror involved with past life holocaust contributed to the fear. The holocaust dream can be interpreted in this way. See image of holocaust dream, p 102. Notice the two SS soldiers are pointing their fingers at me as I run down a hallway into the showers where I was gassed. So, to be targeted by a boss or friend felt life-threatening at times; definitely frightening. It contributed to enormous stress response and depression at times in my life when I was targeted. However, each time I recovered. I was resilient. I most often spoke up, but that in itself, was a stress trigger. I will describe the whys behind this in this description coming up soon. Cumulative insight across time told me that being kind is considered weak in a get tough, might is right, environment and thus you are likely to be a target of a bully boss. In addition, speaking up, truth in an atmosphere of fraud, also makes you a target.

When traumatized, one embodies the experience of trauma which poisons the self. I become the hate, the shame, the guilt of the experience. My self-esteem plummets. I am aware that it is not the objective reality of who I am. In trauma, the part of the brain, the amygdala, where the emotional intensity of the trauma is cut off from the part of the brain where the objective reality is interpreted. You may have an intellectual understanding, but not a unity of deep-felt sense and objective reality of who I am. The unity of body and mind fractured. So, what is the way out? The way out is to feel the pain of it all; feel them, let them pass through you. These feelings need to be carefully titrated across time with someone with whom you feel trust and safety; a therapist is helpful here and/or a sensitive friend who is a witness across time. When the feelings pass through you, the light appears, and a brighter mood. Sometimes it is a long time; the pendulum swings back and forth, light and dark, until the light becomes stronger. This is the pendulum in healing. It is a non-linear process. Feeling worse, then feeling better for a time, going back a little, just a little, catapulting forward, then going back a lot, then moving forward. This is the pendulum in healing.

Situations, Triggers that stimulate hyper-arousal,
moods related to the Trauma

Situations in present-day life were symbols of the psyche. The Nazi represented bullying situations; the robot and the clock represented the push for performance without human needs or feelings, particularly a sense of safety; and, lastly, the value for profit over people which is the predominant work environment today. Because of the holocaust dreams and experiences with toxic environments, I experienced them as stressful. My initial experiences with Nursing were Robotic with emphasis on task orientation. Caring seemed to be second to procedures and surgery. That's why I became innovative in preparing patients for procedures and surgery and decided to become a trauma psychologist to deal with patients in a caring way. I also felt I wanted to separate from the predominant masculine model and developed a more intuitive way of knowing in treatment versus only analytical. I also enjoyed teaching psychology and nursing students about caring relationships in healing. The depth of feeling was related to present-day collective trauma. My personal trauma helped me understand the depth of others' pain. I feel that healing is done by chopping off the head, the chatter of thoughts, the ego, and entering the body and the deep-felt sense of darkness; the fear, the grief, letting the feeling in, allowing it to pass through you, paying attention to the imagery that spontaneously arises as they are clues to the past trauma. There are then associations to the way in which this trauma has affected the self. The internal feeling — I am not OK, defective, powerless, helpless. I thought, "Trauma is emotional poison poured over you and affects how one feels about the self."

I had a dream related to this. A woman was on my deck outside and she was about to pour gasoline on herself and light a match. I was stunned, wondering whether to call 911. The dream ended. Toxic communication, bullying by another, is like having gasoline poured on you. In a positive frame, metaphorically speaking, fire cleanses this toxicity for a new start.

The pendulum continues; healing is not linear. The pendulum continues to swing from dark to light and light to dark.

When the triggers are identified and the dark mood appears, one can identify the trigger/situation that goes back to the original trauma.

A second major trigger for trauma, grief, and sadness occurred when I was approaching 50 years on the front lines. I had another toxic boss at the university which triggered Navy Nurse toxic commander, sexual harassment, then back to holocaust. I was exhausted and fell and broke my arm. These cumulative traumas across time led to a dark night of the soul across the next eight years. On reflection, the triggers in present-day, going back in time, were related to sudden loss; suddenly falling and breaking my arm; my kitty of 11 years suddenly disappearing; being suddenly called on the carpet by a toxic boss at work. And then back to childhood with my father's illness and death and soon after, my mother suddenly taken out of my arms, tranquilized and taken to a psychiatric hospital against her will. She had a break and lived in fear that her relatives would do this again. I was nine at the time. Her rage would last a lifetime. All involved very enormous grief. Similar to my mother, I also lived in fear that I would be attacked again. Part of this was related to taking on this inherited trauma from my family. I was able to feel it, and let it pass through me.

The other major trigger was finger-pointing leadership (see holocaust dream p.114). The two SS finger-pointing as I ran down the hallway into the showers where I was gassed. So, finger pointing for me was life threatening. This was the trigger in the Navy that contributed to suicidal crisis, unknown at the time, and then also at the university recently. There was enormous terror involved in speaking up, going against the grain, which appeared out of proportion to what the threat was. It felt life-threatening. In this insight, I was able to connect the finger-pointing to past life.

I was triggered by a gas leak in my condo which went back to the holocaust dream of being gassed in the showers, running down the hall with SS chasing me. I would then use the dream, the image, the mood, in EMDR therapy. Much cleansing had already been done in therapy across many years. The first thing I did was bring in my support system: my ancestors on the other side — my Nona, my Archangel Uriel, my wise persons, to support me through the journey. I brought in Nona as nurturing figure; she was a healer in Italy; my kitties, now on the other side, my Archangel Uriel for protection — he holds the sword of truth, and healing fire in his hands. This created a safe place supported by ancestors, angels, and friends who love. This provided a sense of trust and safety needed to go through the trauma. Interestingly enough, when I was triggered by the gas leak going back to holocaust dream, it shifted more quickly than it did from when I dealt with it years ago. I assumed from this a stronger place I was in because it shifted more quickly. Here is a quote from my journal describing the EMDR session about the gas leak.

I recalled the memory of the gas leak from the wall heater. PG&E was fixing the heater when the pipe broke. He told me to call 911 and to evacuate neighbors. I ran down the hallway to warn neighbors and evacuate. This was symbolic of the hallway in the Holocaust dream. I was near the back gate talking to the condo manager. She was toxic in her communication saying I was to blame and would be held responsible. I was strong in my words to her. I said, "We are in the middle of an emergency, talk to PG&E"; the phone was passed to him. An image of a cobra appeared in the back of me as I spoke to her. It quickly shifted to a feeling of Love. I felt my feet on the ground and love in my hands. My hands were by my hips, with energy pouring out of my hands shifting bilaterally in a sustained movement. The feeling and strength of love was very strong.

On reflection, it was reassuring that love versus holocaust trauma was the primary focus. Positive light and love were over darkness. The cobra represented the power of spiritual energy, kundalini energy, love.

In my sacred dance afterwards, the movements to express this love were infinity movements: firstly, with feet, then knees, hips and chest, and then head. It is no wonder that asclepias, two snakes winding up a staff, is a symbol of healing. In the Yoga community, it is known as kundalini energy. The quality of movement, like a snake, is sustained in time alternating with quick movements, and definitely has flow. The energy is curled up at the base of the spine; the spine, the symbolic staff, rises with the serpentine movements. I went into a trance state, and the room lit up in green/gold light and also rose/pink light. I interpret these colors as heart energy. So, it indicated to me that these movements, movements inspired by love, stimulated energy.

Grief. Grief often follows feelings of love as it brings up the loss of love one did not have from childhood and from relationships throughout life. Grief may also follow the feelings of threat and hyper-arousal. In my own experience, it is the feeling of being alone; grief follows. This may be true in others who have had abuse in childhood as they are often alone in the threat. From the deep feelings of grief, the dance of sorrow was created.

When I picked a soulful song sung in Greek by Irene Pappas, I saw black veils. I dressed in black and began to move with slow weighted steps that one would see in a funeral procession. I moved forward as if going toward a casket, circling the casket, and then saying good-by to a loved one. I grieved the loss of child, the loss of love, and the loss of life. I retreated from the casket and in the middle of the floor spiraled inward to say a prayer, to make an offering to God. I knelt, opening my chest, raising my arms, stretching them to the heavens. I retreated, spiraling inward again, taking off my black veil; and when again I entered the center of the spiral, I slowly covered my face once again with the black veil of sorrow. The dance ended.

The dance of gentle sorrow is dedicated to the children who are starving from embargoes, killed or maimed by land mines, subjected to poverty, killed by bombing, and separated from their families due to ethnic and racial hatred. The image of children at the border in cages comes to mind. And, more recently, the discovery of the remains of Native American children in Canada who were separated from their families and put in schools for indoctrination. Many were abused and/or died. Many families lost their jobs during the covid epidemic, and many children were going hungry. Now, I carry and rock in my arms Palestinian children wrapped in white cloth. Again, I think of the quote by Golda Meir, "When we love our children more than we hate our enemies, we will have peace."

DANCE OF GENTLE SORROW
Christina, Dancer
Photograph by John Edward Culp

Dream of Father's Casket

In this dream, I was in my father's grave. It was black and as I grew closer to his casket, the blacker it got and the closer to death I felt. On the side of the casket were the stations of the cross. As I came closer to the casket, I felt increasing terror that I was going to die. Just as I was about to touch my father's casket, the dream ended. I felt extreme terror throughout my body, I woke up, it was 4:00 a.m.

The dream symbolized that I felt close to death, after the accident, but also as a child when my father died. The stations of the cross symbolize suffering, most likely from devastating loss and perhaps inheriting the sins of my father, his dysfunctional patterns of survival, which meant inheriting his suffering. (See watercolor of dream, p. 136.) Collectively, we have inherited the loss of fathers through the work machine, through alcohol, and in war. We are making progress in fatherhood but have a way to go to bring the men home.

The significance of this dream continued over many years. The dream of father's casket is a clue to the deep feelings of sorrow. The spirit coming close to death in approaching is faceless. The traumas and grief are related to not being seen, heard or felt. This is the case for children who are neglected or abused. They are not seen, heard or felt. There is no witness across time which helps children know who they are and to feel safe and supported. The witness can also remember important events, experiences across time and connect the dots.

This wise person understands the present as it relates to past experiences; not the analysis of it, but the deep-felt emotions of it. This wise person understands the present as it relates to the past experience of not being taken into account. This is the mark of an experienced therapist. This creates a narrative story that helps define the self; and one can also tell their stories through talks, through memoirs, through writing, through art: painting, dance theatre... not just talking about it but the experience of it. I am doing it through gesture, posture, images and dreams. I am connecting the dots as well.

DREAM OF FATHER'S CASKET
Watercolor by Christina
Feeling close to death in a dream after the accident, August 1988

It reminds me of a movie, *Dr. Zhivago.* It was on television lately. He lived in a time of war and revolution, and there were many threats to his safety. He was a Doctor, Healer and Artist. a mythological story of life and death, and the depth of feeling, living at that time. He lived and loved and wrote poetry, and you could see him experiencing the beauty of nature. at that time. The music score of lightness and depth of sorrow enhanced the story. It inspires me to live fully, to look to the beauty of nature for comfort, to continue to write my poetry, the story of our times now, for poetry is truth, much needed now.

Personal Healing: Secure Relationships as Medicine for Healing. The key to healing the fracture of trauma. A trusting safe relationship is important for healing; someone who is capable of validating the experience, validation of the pain and suffering. The need for people who really understand. In society today, there is a tendency to judge because you are not "happy," a victim. It is the expectation in society to be the energizer bunny, busy and upbeat, the hurry-up sickness. But it is compassion, understanding, acceptance/witnessing that heals. The one who can witness, help connect the dots across time, and understand the past and how it is resonating in the present.

In review, as I have just explained, identifying the triggers is important. This entails an understanding of what triggers the extreme sensitivity. This is done, as I have explained, by reflection of the over stimulation of the adrenalin surges or depression, and what is driving it helps with insight and some measure of control over the symptoms. In my own example, finger-pointing leadership and sudden unexpected loss were the other triggers. For finger-pointing leadership, there was a feeling of terror and later more clarity about feeling I would be killed, going back to holocaust. For sudden unexpected loss, there was enormous grief — for both triggered a feeling of negative self-worth, not good enough, not taken into account and a feeling of wanting to leave this life.

However, I realized that this was the experience of trauma and not the objective reality of it. My colleague was safe and secure and kept reminding me of facts about how I held students accountable, knew what was going on, helped staff, and this helped students learn. This was the objective reality. The toxic boss/bully fractures the integrity of the self and is extremely destructive. As I have said before, it poisons the self. In fact, failures are amplified, and you are unable to feel successful. They are split off from reality. This is why kids bullied on the internet or at school may end up in psychiatric emergency; bullying fractures the self. The experiences of the trauma are internalized.

The power of the witness who can help you track the triggers across time and connect the dots with great compassion is invaluable because you feel that someone has your back. This is the power of the witness. This is so critical when working on the front lines. I did start feeling some successes. An experience with a student came to mind. I recalled helping a student who was triggered by the report of a patient's suicide. Her father had committed suicide, which she had observed. I was able to be present in the moment. She was able to share her story. I stayed present for her, and she was able to return to the unit and work with the patients. There were many I helped across time; this positive sense is now growing stronger.

EMDR (Eye Movement Rhythm). I also brought in my support system in my EMDR therapy sessions. I started with accessing a felt sense of the body through going into a deep relaxed state, feeling myself breathe, breathing low into the abdomen versus high in the chest, feeling my feet on the floor, my back against the chair, going back to feeling the breathing. I called my Nona, healer on the other side, my Archangel Uriel, angels, Jesus as healer, Mom and Dad, my Russian Roma Grandfather on the other side, and Italian Grandfather Vincenzo, also on the other side to be with me as I went through the trauma.

I would then go to the traumatic event, the identified trigger related to the trauma: the finger-pointing, the loss — and feel where the tension was in the body or the pain; then shape my posture from that feeling — the posture of grief, fear, and also emotional strength, and love. I found this posture would go straight to the traumatic event. Through eye movements, the pain, grief and fear, anger of it would be processed and then it would shift to a brighter mood, a positive feeling about the self. I am OK; the person who was toxic is not OK, thus allowing more capacity for love.

I felt trauma is a fracture of the psyche. Healing is a way to unite aspects of the self torn apart by the trauma. On reflection, the experiences in my life that fractured were: the terminal illness of my father starting at age four and his death at age nine. Right afterwards, the loss of mother through her trauma of losing her husband, my father, her sisters, my Auntie's toxicity, putting her in a mental hospital against her will, her consequent rage at them across many years, my inability to have a voice with her about it, moving from my home in Jersey away from cousins whom I loved to Florida. I remember them coming to visit and I felt numb, the feelings of closeness were gone, the loss of many boyfriends who left for another woman.

For me, I do have the ability to embrace these very dark moods and let it pass through me. I know that feeling it, not obsessing about it, not trying to push it down, was helpful in healing... just letting it be. The moods often lifted to a brighter, more authentic positive mood a few days later — I would wake to a brighter day — and also knowing I had support was key to healing.

The posture of sadness... head down, arms crossed over chest, heaviness in the body, sustained movement was the dance of sorrow.

Healing through sacred dance helped in assessing moods and experiencing the loss more deeply. The music I used was sacred/trancelike inspiring a sense of calm and kindness. I was able to release the deeper felt sadness. It also assessed the powerful events in my life that were related to this deep-felt grief: sudden Nazi arrest in past life, a feeling of separation from my people, sudden loss of father and then mother, sudden unexpected trauma of breaking my arm, sudden loss of my kitty, sudden accident on freeway several decades ago. It felt like several lifetimes of sorrow and has lasted several decades now. As I have said, the rhythm of grief is heavy, embodied, slow and soulful. Breath is full which assesses the tears. The posture is bent over with arms crossed over the chest and heart. I am repeating myself here about the triggers; repetition of the trauma for healing is helpful.

Then, the body's response to toxic experiences. In finger-pointing experience where you are accused, the posture is one of tension in the body; it is bound flow. This is a great threat to safety, the body goes into fight or flight response, sympathetic arousal. This is particularly true when you cannot have a voice for fear of total rejection. As a child, this is life threatening. This fear comes up later in life in many of your relationships, especially in toxic situations which I found often in many institutions where I had worked for over 50 years now. In these situations where I was targeted, I would often speak up. It was partly reaction formation over being deprived of a voice earlier in life. Often, I was pointing out unethical behavior. I became the scapegoat to distract from the unethical behavior, often rejected for speaking the truth; and sometimes lost a job. I felt enormous rejection in spite of the circumstances. When there is consistent fear response across many years, it develops into post-traumatic stress. This was true for me. A posture of power, as in a Flamenco dance with the stamping of the feet, was a release from rejection and oppression. I also used the expression of the cobra strike to release the toxicity. I used serpentine movements from the feet, up the knees, hips and chest and then head. I put my arms above my head, hands coming together, and then would release with a strike. The cobra strike was a way to release the anger. The expression of anger was also in my dreams as the primitive power of the rattlesnake, a visceral sensation of reverence, embodying the power to protect self. This was a power within through the visceral sensation of moving on the earth, acquiring knowledge from the earth. Anger was also expressed by mimicking and ridiculing the corporate walk — moving fast, looking at the watch and the march turning into the Nazi march. This was anger about toxic rigid corporate systems that pushed for *"more is better;"* production and efficiency over human needs and values.

Expression of grief, fear and anger through posture and rhythm is a powerful way to connect with oneself and unite the fragmented, fractured pieces split apart by trauma... into a united whole, one's story, Mythos.

The rhythm of healing trauma is like a stone thrown in the water. Trauma ripples across time. Sometimes the trigger is present and clearly identified; sometimes it is not, and the painful wave comes in any case.

And through one's own depth of feeling reflected in images and dreams, one can connect the dots across lifetimes and with the collective unconscious in one's culture, to another, to nature and to the divine. This strengthens the belief that we are all connected and connected to all things.

Chapter 6

Healing Others in My Trauma Psychology Practice

MY EXPERIENCE IN HEALING SELF and healing others combined to acquire knowledge of healing trauma; and of course years of education and training by other professionals in the field. I did integrate somatic methods; EMDR therapy, an eye movement rhythm or tapping, and when patients were receptive, I used authentic movement, a Jungian method that uses active imagination in movement. I used the body in psychotherapy by integrating posture, rhythm, images and dreams into these sessions. I have described these methods in previous sections and in the first book, *Dance of Psyche: Rhythm of Consciousness,* (2003). The first important thing is to establish safety and trust and as therapist being fully present for them. Attentiveness and calmness create presence. Paying attention to the deep feelings that arise and what gets stirred-up in me that mirror these feelings was important. Attention to non-verbal expressions noting facial expression, body posture, gesture and rhythm, the cadence in speech and movement were also important. This helped in the deep sense of being seen, heard and felt by another, witnessed. This helped establish the trust which is necessary for going deeper. When trust and safety were established, I would then begin more in-depth work integrating somatic methods, EMDR, authentic movement. Often to be seen in a hostile environment means to be retaliated against, demeaned, or beaten up, so withdrawal may be one mechanism to protect the self. To be seen, heard and felt by another in safety heals. This underscores the importance of the witness who can track the nonverbal and help the person connect the dots present with past and future hopes. This assists the person in the deep sense of being felt by another human being.

We then bring in a situation of recently triggered anxiety or depression related to the trauma/stressful situation. It was sometimes helpful to bring in music that represented the rhythm/mood in the situation that helps resonate, amplify, the underlying feelings. I would also ask if there was a dream that represents the recent trigger/situation reflecting the trauma. Dreams were helpful because they embodied the visceral sensation of trauma and the depth of emotions. Triggers in present time were doorways into past trauma.

The trauma — rape, violence, abuse, accidents, deprivation, emotional toxicity —comes up in stressful situations in the present. In tracking these triggers across time, one can identify the past traumatic events that stimulated anxiety or depression in the present. For a woman who was raped in a parking lot, the trigger of fear would come up in parking lots and you would connect the symptoms of anxiety with the original trauma — the rape. Often the triggers would be sensations; smells, surroundings, circumstances that were related to the original trauma. For a mom who just gave birth, her difficulty in nurturing her child in the present could be traced to the lack of nurturing from her own mother. For a firefighter on the front lines who had conflict with an ego-ridden supervisor, it took him back to a father who was absent and out of touch with him.

In the session, I would start with a somatic exercise to relax, open the breath, and feel the body. Tell them to be in their body as much as possible: "Feel yourself breathe, breathe low into the abdomen, versus high in the chest, breathe fully, extend the exhalation. Take your mind into a safe place in nature, feel the sights, the sounds, the smells; allow yourself to be there. Now bring in the people or beings, spirits on the other side that support you, those who nurture you, protect you or provide wisdom. Be there with them. Feel their presence." (Attachment protocol of Dr. Laurel Parnell, expert in trauma treatment).

Patients would be in a trance state. I discovered that this helped them be more receptive to change. Then, I would ask them where they felt the tension, pain, in their body and they would say, for instance, "In my chest." Then I would ask them to shape their body around this feeling. The body would often be one of contraction and tension. Head down, chest compressed, restricting breathing. This shaped the posture that was related to the experience of the trauma. I would ask them to put into words the underlying belief about the self. The underlying feeling was related to the belief about the self: "I'm not OK, I am a terrible person, I am at fault." Then I would ask them how they would like to feel. They would say: "I am OK, I deserve love, I deserve success." The posture would immediately open, shoulders back, chest up, breathing fuller. I would use authentic movement for those who were receptive. Authentic movement is a process where the patient moves spontaneously through their imagination of a felt sense of where to move. It brought up images and feelings related to their experience, and then we would go back to the eye movement rhythm or tapping. It helped deepen their experience and visceral sensations, shaped the rhythm, the image that is reflective of mood and inner self. It was the waking dream. This waking dream or night-time dream and related imagery represented the visceral feeling, emotion, connected to the trauma. They would bring forward the situation or dream that represented the trauma.

We would then go into the situation or dream related to the trauma with the posture shaped by the experience of it and start eye movement rhythm or tapping. The eye movements followed the therapist's fingers moving left and right or bilateral tapping near the knees. This is similar to saccadic eye movements in sleep, or dream state.

The negative feelings of fear/grief would come to the surface, and after processing these feelings, it would often shift to a positive self-belief: "I am OK, the toxic person who abused me, demeaned me, threatened me, raped me, ignored me, put me in the shadows is not OK. I am not at fault. I do deserve happiness, love, success."

Deeper issues of abuse by parents, emotional deprivation, wounds in development are more difficult, and time and repetition in clearing trauma was necessary to heal. More time to establish trust. More time to release the fear, guilt, grief related to the original trauma or multiple traumas across time; the trauma feels as if it is occurring now. When a person heals, the experience of the trauma is no longer as activated in present time — the present insight is understood as originating in the past and brings alive future hopes.

Healing Trauma; Current Clinical Practice and Research

The purpose of this section is to summarize what was healing in the experience of trauma in self and others, and culture, both in what I have written here and also quote from the first book; then relate it to the current clinical practice and research in the trauma field. In my experience, the use of the body and body movement through gesture, posture, rhythm, images and dreams deepens the process of healing, helps reach the unconscious memory in psychotherapy. Firstly, current practice also acknowledges the importance of safety and trust, and now body movement and experience are considered important to reach the unconscious, the denial involved in traumatic response. This is a change from the more analytical process or just talking about it that has been used. So, this validates the use of posture, rhythm, (music and dance), images and dreams as they are body felt experiences. They connect with the visceral sensations in the body and help reach the unconscious parts of the psyche split off by trauma. The dances, dreams and images were also related to the collective culture and ancestral trauma. Dreams source emotional depth and provide clarity about the severity of the trauma and thus provide insight. The fragments were united through story, which is now considered important for healing. So, in my experience, the use of the body and body movement through posture, rhythm, images and dreams deepens the process of healing in psychotherapy and helps reach the unconscious memory: personal, collective and ancestral memory.

Movement has symbolic significance reflecting an intention toward life and death. Consequently, the study of body movement represents the shift away from cognitive knowledge to knowledge obtained through body experience. (C. Campbell, 2003, p.2). So, it is important to include experiential knowledge through the body and body movement, now current clinical practice and research.

Vanderkolk, B., who wrote *The Body Keeps the Score* (2014), states: *"Healing depends on experiential knowledge. You can be fully in charge of your life only if you acknowledge the reality of your body in all of it's dimensions."*

Trauma fractures... parts are split off from the self: body separated from mind, mind separated from body... separated from spirit and soul. Then it is difficult to connect with self; self to a great extent remains unknown. It is hidden from consciousness, memory fractured.

Vanderkolk also states:

Traumatic experiences are organized not as coherent narratives but in fragmented sensory and emotional trace images, sounds, and physical sensations These memory traces are activated through sensation. This underlies the importance of the body in healing trauma. (p. 178)

He quotes Catie Carson: *"Our bodies are the text that carry the memories and therefore remembering is no less than reincarnation."* (p. 186)

The goal in healing is wholeness: the unity of mind, body, spirit and soul, the art and science of healing. The Dance of Psyche is the movement of the body in rhythm; the rhythm, posture, images and dreams that help us access the hidden knowledge within and unite with our true self. We are nature — its rhythm, its music. Rhythm is a unifying force. This deepens the process of healing. unites self, other, nature and the divine.

In 2003, I wrote:

Dance and movement are ways to expand our awareness and our knowledge. There are many ways in which we can understand ourselves and many ways the body can heal. Dance and movement had not been commonly considered, however, because of the emphasis on more cognitive scientific ways of knowing. Human beings have both conscious and unconscious ways of knowing. Dance and movement can serve to expand awareness of both. The way we move in time and space, the use of our weight, and whether our movements are bound or free can describe our world view. Our use of time and space is the statement of our values. It reveals our vitality and our state of health, reflects our moods, beliefs, and attitudes. Dance and movement are reflections of the psyche. (p. 1)

Rhythm stimulates imagination, memory, dreams and rhyme. Rhythm in movement accesses the personal and collective unconscious and is a way to portray our mythology. It tells a personal story and a story about the culture in which we live. The body and how it moves in time and space, its rhythm, gesture, posture, the way people walk, talk and express themselves, make the moods of humanity visible. Thus, rhythm and posture can be used to acquire knowledge of self, culture, nature and the divine. Because one can observe the opposites between the internal feeling and the external expression with dance and movement, the paradoxical nature of the unconscious can be revealed. (Campbell, C., 2003)

So, what I have just written here in the second book was to expand my personal story that reflected the collective unconscious of our times. The dreams of Holocaust made me sensitive to the uprising of the Neo Nazi movement, most pronounced in the events of Charlottesville and now the Insurrection.

Story helped to connect the present with past experiences, release the trauma for the ability to have future hopes. And now, story is recognized as a way to integrate memory fractured by trauma and is a way to unite these fractured parts of the self into a united whole. Vanderkolk, B. (2014) highlights the importance of story:

The autobiography of self creates connections among experiences and assembles them into a coherent story. Not just talking about it, but deepening experience held in the body.

He quotes Kate Carson (p.186):

"Our bodies are the texts that carry the memories and therefore remembering is no less than reincarnation."

So, healing through the body sources the unconscious through posture, rhythm, images and dreams. Also, through my own experience with trauma, both self and others, trust and safety was powerfully demonstrated by a deep resonance in what is being felt. The ability to connect the dots, present triggers of grief, overwhelm, abandonment with past memory of enormous losses. The ability to pick up on facial expression, voice tones, posture, voice and movement cadence. This way one feels seen, heard and felt, a caring presence, compassion. This is the power of the witness.

"This healing process is only possible in the context of relationship, safety and emotional resonance." (Vanderkolk, B., p. 112) *This resonance is through the witnessing of non-verbal micro tracking. There is power in being witnessed, seen and validated.* (Vanderkolk, B., p. 289). Trauma is thus defined as not being witnessed or taken into account. This underscores the power of the witness in psychotherapy.

Traumatized human beings recover in context of relationship, safety and emotional resonance. The ability to resonate without judgment or shame in order to process trauma... being in tune with others. (Vanderkolk B., p. 218)

With trust and safety, the breath opens more fully. This then brings the intense pain and grief to the surface to be able to express. As I have said, this pain and grief needs to be carefully titrated across time. This is bringing the body on board for healing. Feeling the emotions of grief, pain and fear allows them to pass through you. Being able to feel deeply is related to healing; feel the enormous grief, pain, and let it pass through you, feel the fear and let it pass through you.

Pennebaker's research quoted in Vanderkolk 2014, (p. 242)

Those who allowed themselves to feel their emotions showed significant physiological changes both immediate and long term. This included blood pressure and heart rate and other autonomous functions.

The Integration of Body and Mind is Reflected in Brain Function.

In trauma, different parts of the brain are split from one another. The healthy brain is one where different parts of the brain communicate with each other. It receives sensation from the body, as well as feelings and thoughts, then the ability to reflect on this process to attribute meaning. This is self-awareness.

Vanderkolk, states:

"Self-awareness is based in physical sensation, feeling safe and not rushed, we can find words to communicate that experience." (2015, p. 238) Certainly this validates the critique of hurry-up illness in society presented in my writing here and in the first book, Dance of Psyche: Rhythm of Consciousness, 2003.

"Being able to perceive visceral sensations is the very foundation in emotional awareness." (Vanderkolk, 2015, p. 240)

Stephen Levine states:

It is only through building a refined awareness and allowing muscles and viscera spontaneous expression that we can dissolve the "neurotic" and traumatic split off part of ourselves and lay claim to a deeper, more authentic self. (Quoted in Vanderkolk, 2015, p. 295)

This validates authentic movement, a dance therapy process where the patient moves spontaneously from their inner experience. It brings up feelings, images and can tap the night-time dream. There is a witness and the mover. The witness tracks the mover's experience and gives feedback — definitely tracks the non-verbal expression. This was the case when I developed the dance Guernica: the Nazi and the Roma. (p. 98) It was developed through spontaneous movement. It brought up images of the Nazi, the robot, and clock time. I did the corporate walk, and it turned into the Nazi March. Later, after being in a horrendous accident, I had dreams of holocaust. See fuller description previously on page 130.

Vanderkolk describes the power of the witness (p. 289)

This underscores the tracking of non-verbal communication. Helps in being seen — stimulates the right side of the brain (p. 300), the more intuitive side. Creates nurturing, caring parent versus critical, judgmental one. (p. 305)

Bessel Vanderkolk's book was titled appropriately: *"The Body Keeps the Score, Brain, Mind and Body in Healing Trauma."*

He summarized the latest research in trauma including brain chemistry. The significant outcome of this research is that including the body is important for healing traumatic experience; the interaction of the body with the mind which in today's vernacular is called mindfulness is critical in healing.

He notes that the Insula, the part of the brain believed to process convergent information to produce an emotionally relevant context for sensory experience, integrates and interprets the input from the internal organs, muscles and joints, balance proprioceptor system to generate a sense of being embodied. It gives you a sense of who you are. (Vanderkolk, p. 249). The signals of danger from organs and muscles are sent to the amygdala which is the part of the brain that is the alarm system; it triggers flight, fight or freeze response.

The flight or fight nervous system, called the sympathetic nervous system, is activated in situations that are threatening including life threatening; hit by a car, auto accidents, shootings, bombings ... also lack of nurturing, lack of attachment in infancy and childhood is life-threatening. The mother's trauma may be transferred to the fetus. In society today, as I have mentioned here, bullying is often toxic to the self and very threatening. This automatic nervous system prepares us to deal with emergency. The heart rate goes up, respirations increase. The energy goes into these vital organs; more nonessential organs such as the digestive system shut down to give more energy to deal with the threat. In normal response after the threat is over, the nervous system returns to normal. Digestive functions return. Pulse rate goes down, respirations are fuller and reduced. When stress and overwhelm are ongoing for a long time, one may continue the stress response even though the threat has passed. This is post-traumatic stress. The nervous system becomes hypersensitive to stimuli, such as loud noise, triggering fight, flight, or freeze. It is also triggered by stimuli that represent the original trauma. In my own situation, it was not being taken into account with finger-pointing leadership. Not being taken into account was represented by the woman in a black veil who was faceless feeling death as she came closer to my father's casket; death was not feeling seen, heard or felt. This exemplifies the trauma of not being taken into account. Finger-pointing leadership was the other major trauma. This was triggered by Bully bosses across the years. The dream that represented this was the SS soldiers pointing their fingers at me as I was running down a hallway into the showers where I would be gassed. The dreams sourced the depth of the threat as life threatening. The dreams helped give insight that Bully boss behavior was life threatening for me across the decades on the front lines. After being triggered, this is followed by exhaustion.

In PTSD the overwhelm/stress stays stuck in the amygdala and cannot communicate with the cortex, the higher thinking areas of the brain. Further, this frontal lobe shuts down so that the person cannot put feeling into words. The thalamus also shuts down which integrates raw data of incoming sensations (Vanderkolk 2015, p. 178), so that:

"The imprints of traumatic experience are organized not as coherent logical narratives but in fragmented, sensory and emotional trace images, sounds, and physical sensations." This gives credence to the use of story which pulls physical sensations, imagery, memories into a unified whole.

In summary the body is important in uniting sensation, gesture, posture, images and dreams; and, thus, connects with the unconscious. In trauma, it is connecting with forgotten memory of the trauma. In particular, the experience of it, the pain, shame, the enormous grief of it.

The Vagus nerve has been given a lot of attention in recent presentations on trauma. It is a long nerve that is afferent meaning it supplies parasympathetic information to the brain. Parasympathetic nervous system is the autonomic nervous system which controls bodily functions when a person is at rest — stimulates digestion, activates metabolism and urinary systems. It is also important in control of the heart rate, bronchial constriction, and helping the body relax according to Stephen Porges. It is primary in social interaction as well (NICBM presentation, 2020). Levine, S.

(1991) describes the vagus nerve as a sensory nerve to the gut, an efferent nerve from brain to gut. It is also the enteric brain from the gut: having gall, heavy hearted, open hearted, swell with pride. He notes that in threat, sympathetic arousal, the gut shuts down. He notes that muscular and visceral states color our perceptions and intensions of others. (p. 121-124)

Posture and Rhythm in Attachment, Trauma, Health and Illness

I would like to review the significance of gesture, posture, rhythm and images in attachment, trauma and health and illness from the first book. This would be helpful in validating the current thinking and understanding of the body and body experience in healing.

Posture and rhythm in attachment. When we feel close to another, we mirror their facial expression, body posture, gestures, and the cadence, rhythm of their voice and movement; this starts in utero... the origin of the dance of psyche. Someone asked Isadora Duncan where she learned to dance. She said, *"I learned to dance in my mother's womb."* The idea therefore occurred to me that the origins were in Utero. Dance in this sense is the primal source of relationship. I was further surprised when I read the fetal studies of high-speed sound revealed patterning and design between the movements of the fetus and the mother, many years ago. For instance, fetuses were noted to move their left elbow in synchrony to the infant mother's pronouncement of the vowel k. These movements proved consistent; the infant made the same movement to the sound or sequence of sounds. (Condon and Sander, 1974, cited in Pearce, p. 49.) This implied that relationship between mother and child and patterning of movement and sound begins in utero.

Stanton (1983) presented to Nurse Researchers at Stanford Medical Center an active research study titled *Origins of Attachment, Culture and Cue Sensitivity.* She observed patterns of communication at birth between mother and child. Mothers out of synchrony with predicted cue patterns were questioned about their feelings and the nurse investigator was able to pick up emotional dysfunction early, enabling preventive emotional care and allaying more serious problems with bonding later on. The study was successful in other ways. Since patients and staff alike were active in hypothesis formation, they began to observe the differences in bonding between mother and child of mothers who were allowed to be with their child and those who were separated at birth. These studies revealed that synchrony of sound, breath, and movement patterns and attachment are related.

Just as little ducklings follow their mothers and pattern their movements, so do human beings learn by modeling the movements of their significant others, and the people in their culture. Many authors have stated that we are moral movers before the age of one. (Birdwhisle, p. 170)

If one observes closely, one can see father and son or mother and daughter walking hand and hand and notice that their pelvis is tilted in exactly the same way as the same sex parent. (Birdwhisle, p. 170) Body posture and expression mirror one another, meaning that they express themselves gesturally and posturally, and speak in similar patterns.

Dance therapists use this concept of mirroring in their work. A well-known dance therapy film demonstrates the power of this process in entering another person's world.

The film, *Looking for Me* by Janet Adler (1970) tells a story of a dance therapist's work with an autistic child. Janet's way of entering this child's estranged world was to mirror her sounds and her unique gestures. This was successful, for as the child began to trust she began to have eye contact and allow herself to be held for short periods, increasing contact over time. As the trust increased, so did the synchrony of their movements, and at the end of the treatment, the dance therapist and child held hands and were skipping together in harmony. It truly is one of the most beautiful films.

Birdwhistle (1970) studied the patterns of nonverbal communication between therapists and families in therapy. The whole course of psychotherapy could be predicted from the microanalysis of the first five minutes of filmed interaction between patient and therapist. He checked the linguist's micro record of the vocal strain with an equally detailed and informative notation of the accompanying body movements of the families.

Predictions of positive outcomes were made from the assessment of the synchrony between patterns of the therapist's voice and movements of the families. He described the synchrony as similar to that of a Corps de Ballet dance. His assumptions concur with mine:

Like other events in nature, the body movement or expression is without meaning in the context in which it appears. Thus, body motion behaviors are patterned by social and cultural experience.

A series of tapes recording family behavior revealed., "each family member appeared to have learned his lines, knew his cues and synchronized in the family drama". (Birdwhistle, p.183)

The significance of these studies implied that our body motion behavior is conditioned by our culture, that expression is culturally structured. Just as language shapes our perceptions and meaning, so does the structure of body movement expressions. Leaders throughout the centuries have been aware of the power of nonverbal language to teach morals and would prescribe certain movement exercises for their people to do daily; this was true for the ancient Chinese emperors. The goose-step conditioned fascist values. The Greek warrior prepared for war by using a dance that required strength and balance. (Redens,1978)

Values of cultures become apparent in observing the use of space and time; dance/movement demonstrates a people's relationship to nature, to one another, and to the divine. Perhaps the people of India move more slowly demonstrating their values for a more spiritual philosophy and value for internal versus external space.

Synchronicity of breath and movement can be used by a group to create an image. Imgard Bartenioff, a colleague of Laban, asked a workshop group to create the image of the wind by taking a breath of air and exhaling it like we were the wind blowing across the room. Our movements mirrored the patterns of breath. As we did the exercise over and over again, we became synchronous in our movements and expressed clearly the image of the wind.

A fast-paced life can contribute to shallow breathing and, consequently, affect our health. It is the work of many expressive therapies to open the breath so that it is full to allow for freedom of expression and liberate the body. This was the purpose of Reichian therapy, primal therapy and expressive arts therapies. Full breath increases expression and quality of life. In many spiritual philosophies breath is equated with the life force.

Synchronicity, rhythm in sound, and movement are primal ways of relating and connecting. Rhythm is expression of relationship in family, community and culture. Leaders may use these principles to unconsciously or consciously restrict freedom. It is possible to use mirroring of movement, posture, gesture and rhythm for political control as Hitler did and as a former president did and is doing again (2025) as well. These techniques are also used in commercials to hook us through hypnotic suggestion. Perhaps posture and rhythm go right into the amygdala, the primitive area of the brain? Inducing trance states becomes possible in large political rallies as people synchronize to each other's rhythm and mirror postures such as the Nazi salute. Thus, it is human nature to imitate the rhythm of the people and things in our life that we want to know and become part of. In this twenty-first century, there is the imitation of the machine because the god is technology.

There is power and significance to our health, our psyche, and our culture in the understanding of movement and breath. It is the understanding of how our responses are conditioned that helps us make decisions to be more free.

Posture and Rhythm in Trauma; the Rhythm of the Machine: Collective Response to Trauma. The push too fast in time, to synchronize to the rhythm of the machine, might be a collective trance to numb the pain of trauma. There is a pervasive denial of abuse and neglect of children as reflected by child rearing practices, the shape of our school system, the salaries of teachers, and refusal to provide mental health care to people.

deMause (1997) who has been a scholar in tracing the history of child rearing practices and the trauma of children states:

"Massive denial of the origins of humanity's problems in the traumatic abuse of children is then, one and the same as the massive denial of the psychological

origins of behavior. Both are rooted in our deepest fears are stored in a separate brain system that remains largely unexplained by science and that is the source of restaging early traumas in social events." (deMause, 1997, p. 125)

He further describes that disassociation is a method of coping with inescapable stress, allowing infants to enter into trance states and to ignore current sensory input. It is these early trance states that are responses to trauma that are captured in the social trances of history. (deMause, 1997, p. 91)

Thus, the collective value for Mechanism is a way to split off aspects of the self, splitting the body, mind and spirit. People move like robots, act like Nazis to numb pain. Disconnected from the body and numbed by their experience, a collective denial of human needs and spiritual emptiness occurs. The culture becomes sterile. A bigger house, an important job, compensates for spiritual emptiness. The machine is the split off part of the collective self; deadened and numb, the culture reacts — violence and war cleanse feelings of hate and pain.

> *Modern Man moving fast in time*
> *Where are you going?*
> *Where is your heart?*
> *Beating to external rhythms*
> *Believing bigger is better,*
> *More is better,*
> *Precise, explicit, splits you into parts*
> *Each moving precisely*
> *Separating you from yourself and others*
> *Win the mechanical heart, survive nuclear war*
> *Build more bombs to create peace* (Christina Campbell, 1982)

Thomas Moore in his book, *Care of the Soul* states:

We live in a world that has lost its body and therefore individuality. If we let the quality-of-life fade in the name of speed and efficiency, our bodies reflect or participate in the world's body. Our own body will feel the effects. (Moore, 1992, p. 171)

Further, the modern body is an efficient machine that needs to be kept in shape so that its organs will function smoothly and for as long as possible. If something goes wrong with any part, it can be replaced with a mechanical substitute because that is the way we picture the body as a machine, an ensouled body takes its life from the worlds body. The world lives and breathes and/or draws its spirit into us. (Moore, 1992 p. 171)

When we relate to our bodies as having soul, we attend to their beauty, their poetry and their expressiveness. Our very habit of treating the body as a machine whose muscles are like pulleys and its organs engines, forces its poetry underground, so we experience the body as an instrument and see its poetics only as illness. (Moore, 1992, p. 172)

Rhythm and Healing in Modern Times

In Modern times psychologists are using eye movement rhythms to access unconscious material. The technical term is eye movement desensitization and reprocessing. Francine Shapiro was the psychologist who developed EMDR process.

One day she was walking in the park feeling upset. She noticed that her eyes were moving back and forth and afterwards she felt less upset. She decided to integrate eye movements into a protocol to use in psychotherapy. She tried it out with patients who had been traumatized by rape or war in a research study. She found significant results; patients who had been treated by EMDR felt less disturbed compared with a control group (Shapiro, 1989). Since that time, over 40,000 therapists were trained in the use of EMDR.

As I have previously mentioned, EMDR was a powerful tool in the psychotherapeutic process in accessing images, dreams, underlying beliefs and attitudes about the self. Patients often reported spiritual experiences accessing spirit guides or animals and taped a rich imaginative landscape of archetypes and dreams. The process feels similar to Jung's process of active imagination in movement, and both incorporate principles of ancient healing that use posture and rhythm to access the unconscious.

EMDR is used for many disorders, but its origins and focus are in treating trauma. The theory has suggested that eye movement stimulates the brain bilaterally. It is known that traumatic material is stored in the part of the brain known as the amygdala; the emotional, motor area of the brain. The traumatic material appears to get compartmentalized in this area of the brain. The patient may feel the feelings, have a motor and sensory memory of the event that is felt and acted out in the body, but the patient does not have a conscious memory of the trauma. Instead, the trauma is unconsciously symbolically acted out through compulsive repetition of thought, emotion, behavior, and dreams. So, in this sense, rhythm heals the fracture of communication between different parts of the brain.

Patients unconsciously reenact trauma. It's as if the conscious memory of the trauma is somehow blocked and the motor memory, feeling and sensation keeps unconsciously repeating. de Mause, in 1997, theorized the outpouring of epinephrine and noradrenaline around the amygdala prevents the information from getting to the hypocampus where the more objective, conscious memory is operative. (p. 128)

Bilateral stimulation of the brain through eye movements, acoustic stimulation, or sensory tapping appears to help the transfer of traumatic experience to the other side of the brain. It is easy to see, in this way, that drumming or rattles of the Shaman may have served a similar purpose.

The transfer of information from the sensory, motor, emotional side of the brain to the more objective is what we see in therapy with bilateral stimulation through eye movement, acoustic stimulation, or bilateral touch. The bilateral stimulation appears to help the transfer of the traumatic experience to the more objective side of the brain. The person who was raped embodies the emotional experience of the rape. The underlying feeling is, "*I am a terrible person. I am ashamed. I was at fault.*" When the person *processes these negative emotions and feelings about the self through eye movement rhythm; the cognition about the self shifts to: "*I'm OK. He should be ashamed'. He is a terrible person for raping me. I had no control over what happened. There was nothing I could have done differently. I am a survivor.*"

This is the objective reality of the situation.

When the person does not work through the trauma, the repetition continues through behavior, thoughts, dreams, and feelings. There is emotional, motor memory repeats the trauma through posture and rhythm.

Posture and Rhythm in Trauma

Lloyd de Mause (1997) writes of a girl traumatized by sexual molestation by pornographers when she was five years old. She was disassociated from any conscious memories of the events, but accurately repeated being penetrated by an erect penis the same way she had been in the pornographic films. DeMause states, *"The accuracy of her body memories is amazing enough, but what was most astonishing was what she said as she staged the rape scene: "Who is this? My doll. She's lying on my bed naked. She is bad. You bad thing."* Thus, the trauma was repeated through shameful, guilty feelings about the self and repeating trauma through the exact posture.

In a 1995 article on the Personality of the Fetus deMause says the fetus is capable of sensing and feeling. He states that, *"At full term, there is already a human being in the womb, one that is capable of having experienced and accumulating body memories and even of organizing defensive measures to deal with trauma."* deMause quotes Winnecott who helped children work through fetal memories, which were stored in terms of posture and rhythm.

The boy who was then five spent a month or two of his analysis testing out my ability to accept his approaches. Eventually he came to sit on my lap. He would get inside my coat and turn upside down and slide down to the ground between my legs. This he repeated over and over again. After this experience I was prepared to believe that memory traces of birth can persist of course, the same thing in play has turned up in many analyses. (Winnecott, 1988, p. 149)

de Mause (1997) described another client who repeatedly fell off the couch. Another example of birth repetition was also accompanied by breathing changes, constriction of the body, severe pressure on the head, convulsive movements, and fears of annihilation. (Winnicott 1988, pp. 249-250 quoted in deMause, 1995, p. 3) deMause (1997) notes that studies confirm that types of suicide were correlated with kinds of perinatal traumas; asphyxia during birth, leading to more suicides through strangulation, hanging and drowning, mechanical traumas during birth correlated with mechanical suicidal elements, drug given during birth correlated to suicide by drugs. One example of obstetrical traumas that was cited was an umbilical cord around the baby's neck correlated with early childhood behavior of wrapping ropes, strings, and curtain cords around her head and neck. (p. 8)

The mother's emotional life, her anxiety, her drug and alcohol use, is communicated through the fetus; there is acceleration in heartbeat and alternations in neurotransmitters. The fetus acceleration of the heartbeat follows the mother's increase in heartbeat. If she feels fear, within 50 seconds the fetus feels fear. Threats of fear can also cause severe asphyxiation. Changes include alterations in adrenaline, plasma epinephrine and norepinephrine, levels of hydroozycortico-steroids, hyperventilation. The fetus thrashes around and kicks in pain during hypoxia and other conditions. Maternal distress related to spousal abuse, domestic violence, spousal death has been related to child morbidity, neurological dysfunction, developmental lags and behavioral disturbance. (deMause, 1995, p. 7)

The rhythm conveys fear. The heartbeat is central to life and survival. It is clear from these cases that although there is no conscious memory, the fears and defenses are recaptured through body memories including posture and rhythm.

Rhythm and Memory. Posture and rhythm may be gateways to memory and the unconscious. In an article entitled, *"Sitting on Memories Lap,"* Hale (1990) illustrated how personal dreams, childhood memories, family dynamics, and the source of memories, can be brought to the surface and dealt with through expressive therapy. In guided imagery and music GIM0, music is the stimulus for awakening, the imaginal realm and is played to match the client's mood and rhythm. She theorized that music's ability to stimulate specific images comes from the overlapping of the auditory cortes with the part of the visual context that deals with visual cortex that deals with visual associations. Starr (1992) noted that before the written word, rhythm was a means to memorize directions across distances, fields, and rivers.

One idea that EMDR therapists had was that EMDR was similar to rapid eye movement that occurs in sleep, thus helping the client to reorder and make sense out of emotional material. REM (Rapid Eye Movement) does reorder chaotic material during dreams, so that the process helps us learn and survive. Starr (1992) notes that this scanning process goes on in sleep matches recent events with past events, and links together mental contents that only share a similar feeling, but which may not be related in any other way. (p. 104)

The dream attempts to make order, sense out of this hodgepodge by trying to impose order of a story line to try to understand the world and order in it and in so doing can reach new and better adaptations (Starr, 1992 p. 105). He also notes that music may have originated from the expressive vocal sounds that are important in maintaining an intimate relationship between infant and mother, the psychoanalytic theory that music represents non-verbal or pre-verbal form of communication related to music as a way to take the person back to primary period when maternal voice conveyed assurance. It was interpreted as regression to earliest communication with mother and infant (Starr, 1992, pp 92-93). This provides another possible explanation why EMDR works: it can be understood as a mirroring between the therapist and client that is similar to the mirroring that occurs in utero. It is clear that playing a rhythm accesses memory. This could also apply to past life experience.

Present day acknowledgement of Healing Trauma.

It is now 2021 and there is a collective acknowledgement of the importance of healing trauma not only for the individual but for the Society at large. Many leaders in the field have organized summits to discuss this important topic. Gabor Mate came out with a film called *The Wisdom of Trauma* (November 4, 2024). He worked with many people who had addictions and were homeless. He noted that the addiction should not be labeled in a negative way but to understand that it was a way to cope with underlying Trauma ... that compassion was needed. The tone of his voice was very compassionate; it was very powerful and drew many people. It became a collective phenomena. This may be a strong driving force in changing our mindset from pathologizing addiction and mental illness to a more positive and hopeful way to address it. There were many talks as well from Native Americans and African Americans telling their stories of coping and resilience; this is progress with diversity. Another large gathering of presentations was titled *The Collective Trauma Summit* (2023) organized by Thomas Hubl. He noted that we need to have new methods for healing collective trauma to help us resolve wounds from the past and activate the evolutionary intelligence of humanity. His book is also titled, *Healing Collective Trauma*. He shares the importance of understanding individual and collective, ancestral, and historical trauma from both a scientific and mystical approach.

This resonated with many and 100,000 people attended this summit.

A recent conference held by Laurel Parnell, an EMDR therapist, author and presenter, included not only present trauma but past life trauma and spiritual experiences.

I was particularly taken by the talk of one Native American woman, Dr. Ruby Gibson. She used the body and Mother Earth as benevolent sources of biological, emotional and ancestral memory. She developed a somatic archeology and generational trauma recovery model. History was in the body. She field-tested and researched as part of her Doctoral work. This resonated with me as I used imagination in body movement and discovered past life ancestral trauma, the Roma holocaust.

The message was to slow down and go into our hearts where there is spirit and soul.

Gabor Mate noted that when the Native Americans were speaking, there was a different rhythm. I agreed. It had a calmness and sustained quality; one could access the feeling being spoken. In our culture, it is often the talking-head speaking. I heard another metaphor called "helicopter mind."

In their native Lakota language, there is no word for dominance. They emphasized rhythm as relationship: inclusion, community of the Earth. The symbol is the circle, the continuous beginning and end and the four directions.

Another presenter, Buffi Ste. Marie, talked about the disease of greed in society. That resilience and healing must touch the heart, be intuitive; go beyond the patriarchy. It is Quantum Physics, through connection and kindness and joy... away from dominance versus being dominated. Spend time not thinking. She said, *"Kindness, compassion, and strength versus smarter, better, richer."*

In summary: There needs to be a shift from the machine, a mechanized reality, a robotic rhythm, moving fast in time for dominance and control to being in the moment, a sustained rhythm, to be present, compassionate, able to empathize with the other, to become vibrant beings, dancing with life... from competition to collaboration. To not just think with our heads but feel from our hearts and have our feet on the ground. Feeling our vulnerability will give us the capacity to feel danger and to viscerally sense the need to save ourselves, others and the earth; to heal individually and collectively.

Repeating the quote by Thomas Moore from *The Care of the Soul* (1992), is relevant here:

When we relate to our bodies as having soul, we attend to their beauty, their poetry and their expressiveness. Our very habit of treating the body as a machine whose muscles are like pulleys and its organs engines, forces its poetry underground so we experience the body as an instrument and see its poetics only as illness. (p. 172)

Chapter 7

Mechanism in American Culture Rhythm of Illness: Masculine Mentality in Extreme

RHYTHM OF ILLNESS — Masculine Mentality in Extreme
    In the first book, I raised the question, could it be that the diseases of our time are symptomatic of our values for quantitative outcomes—-more is better, and the denial of vulnerability; the denial of human needs, limitations, feelings and death? The intent of this chapter is to explore the psychodynamics of our most prevalent diseases to show how they could express mechanism. Second, the intent is to show how the movements reveal a linear mentality through fast use of time, direct use of space, no intention toward weight, and the binding of the flow, strangling the life force.

Heart Disease: The Aggressive Lonely Heart

    Heart disease, viewed as a metaphor of mechanism. In my experience, patients with heart problems often guard their vulnerability with aggression. When asked about their feelings or needs they would skillfully touch your vulnerable spot. For instance, student nurses would introduce themselves to patients with heart disease. During the conversation the students would ask, "How are you feeling?" Because the patients felt vulnerable in responding to a question about their feelings, they would say something like, "You're new at this," pointing out the student's inadequacy. It's often called pushing someone's button. This is a protective mechanism and attempts to guard vulnerability.

Another way to avoid facing vulnerability of oneself is to handle many things continuously, to factor out subjectivity, to maintain an objective stance to move continuously like a machine. The end result of this style of thinking is that one does not have time to think about the quality of their life. It's as if the person lives up to the external values of society — but are they his values? Dossey (1982 ,1993), in his book *Space, Time Medicine*, made a similar analogy, and also referred to heart disease as hurry-up illness. He also defined illness as reflective of our mechanistic values. This mechanistic view, "sees the body as a clockwork mechanism in which illness is caused by a breakdown of parts." Our obsession with time and our belief that time flows may profoundly affect our health. He calls this "time sickness" — becoming an accepted medical concept, a possible cause of the greatest killer of heart disease. He recommends change, sense of time; people have been able to positively affect the course of disease. He says medicine needs to be updated. He asks the question, "What is the role of consciousness in health and illness?"

In a book called *Language of the Heart* (1985), Lynch described calling people out of the audience in a large auditorium filled with professionals who jogged and ate healthy. He would take their blood pressure sitting down and it would be normal. He would then ask them to talk about their family. They would talk about their family saying nothing was bothering them, but their blood pressure would increase to dangerous levels. This definitely exemplifies a split between body and mind. It also means that many of these clients were isolated from themselves.

In an article called, *Broken Heart Syndrome, Everything Explained,* the Japanese author Hashem Al *Ghaile (2020) said that excess response to stress effects the heart. He was the first to describe Broken Heart Syndrome.

In an article on Heart Syndrome from Preventdisease.com (October 25, 2015), students report:

In biology we described heart, and our teacher told us the heartstrings can sometimes break after a deep emotional trauma causing the heart to lose form, and as a result be unable to pump blood efficiently. You could literally die from a broken heart. The body is very literal, heart strings (tendons) inside the human heart can cause chronic pain after deep emotional trauma. Activated cells in the tendons are themselves responsible for producing biochemical substances that can cause pain and tendons even break due to surge of stress hormones. Thus, a broken heart can be very real due to emotional trauma.

Robotic Rhythm

Years ago in the '80s, aerobics was popular. I wrote that aerobics symbolized this hurry-up rhythm, a robotic rhythm. The impulse to move is external as the instructor tells you exactly how to move. Her commands are like a drill sergeant. One of my friends aptly called aerobics Nazi rock. The expression is taken out; one moves to the rhythm of an empty heartbeat. Could this be an expression of fear? The emphasis is on fast-paced movements, often moving ahead of the beat and out of synchrony with the music. This future orientation to time — meet that goal faster, harder; and don't have fun! When a person is moving fast in time and is out of rhythm, there is a greater chance of imbalance, and thus a greater chance of injury. Increased injuries have precipitated the development of non-impact aerobics. When the rhythm is too fast, the tendency is for people to be tense and bind the flow in their movements, making organic and emotional feeling during the dance impossible. The high in aerobics is the feeling afterwards. It is an expressionless dance, and it is not surprising that many aerobics instructors are bulimic, or anorexic.

Aerobics is symbolic of your mechanistic culture with the emphasis on being externally motivated, going fast in time, and being driven, binding the life force and human expression. It is push-button movement:

do-respond. We will become the machine computers, push-button war. This is robotic philosophy and expression of our present-day mechanism.

Lastly, the movement lacks intention. It is passive versus active in quality, thus, aerobics dance lacks a statement of purpose. It is motivated by the need to look good, rather than to feel good. The quantitative outcome of looking better, losing more weight, is more important than the activity itself. It is not surprising, that these dynamics are symptomatic of people with eating disorders. The issue here is emotional emptiness, and passive versus active intention.

Western dance celebrates the triangle in most of the forms: ballet, modern, and jazz. The triangle is a symbol of strength. Western dance is the adulation and triangulation of movement seen from every pose.

Running can be viewed as a mechanistic expression. This is particularly true if the intent in running is for speed and distance. This is a linear expression. A film that demonstrates this idea profoundly is the story of an American Indian who was a talented runner. When he was accepted on the running team at the University, the coach emphasized, winning in and the number of races he won the Indian boy lost his motivation to run because running lacked meaning. When he went home to his people, he realized he wanted to run for them. His running then was filled with intention and spirit.

In the first book I commented about break dancing being robotic and perhaps could express the alienation in the ghetto. It does have a robotic rhythm. However, in reading about it recently, it was a unifying force for those in these neighborhoods. It changed the street culture by putting their effort into an art form. Michael Jackson's Moon Walk became a cultural phenomenon.

There is concern about how the heart is functioning. Telemetry equipment invaded the health clubs. What are they trying to control? Our level of health, our heart? Our vitality is in question. Does the pulse rate give us answers to quality of life? Is quality of life doing things faster in time? Is more better?

When our heart is treated like a machine, we become the machine, and the prize is the mechanical heart.

Where is our heart? How is it that we do not define quality of life in terms of our ability to touch one another? How is it that quality of life is defined through speed and productivity?

When one talks about technology, it is talked about as if man responds to machines. The idea that one can make decisions about how we use technology is less common. Does this indicate that we feel controlled by machines, that structure is more important than purpose? This is truly dead philosophy. New life comes from the birth of a new machine. Have you visited the nursery of computers and witnessed their birth?

Eating Disorder: The Empty Heart

An anorexic patient jogs ten miles a day. She is bleeding internally from the continuous running. In therapy she describes the obsessive need to run. The therapist comments, *"Perhaps you are running from your life."* The patient says. *"Yes, I'm running away from my relationships, responsibilities, my job,"* and proceeds to name several other things she is running away from. It is clear that her repetition compulsion, running symbolized the unconscious conflict in her life and a way to escape her depression. After a few sessions, she began to get in touch with feelings of depression and connected this with her impulse to run.

The style of this anorexic patient was direct use of space, no intention toward weight, fast use of time, and her flow was bound. The bound flow of this patient connotes an inability to "let go" or have fun. By moving fast in time and using direct use of space characteristically, there is no time to smell the flowers along the way, nor a chance to even notice them. The lack of intention toward weight is related to the patient's feeling discounted. *"I feel like nothing."* It also symbolized a dissociation or split from the body.

Many women with anorexia may feel like ballerinas without grace and a sense of aesthetics; puppets on a string, skeletons in motion.

At the time this was written (2003), ballet often symbolized movement of anorexia. The emphasis in ballet was technique, and consequently lost much expression, leaving the ballerina beautiful, perfect but untouchable.

MECHANICAL BALLET DANCER
Illustration by Mathew Kimmoins

To touch the beautiful ballerina means death to her and she is carried off to heaven. This is the virginal myth and exemplifies the splitting of sexuality from normal relationships.

This is one dynamic of persons with eating disorders. At this time, some companies deleted stretching from their workouts, thus emphasizing strength but not flexibility. Consequently, movements are more bound, and lack freedom of expression. It takes away from the flow of life. Ballerinas often gain weight after they stop dancing. Could it be the dynamics of perfectionism that eats them up and leaves their heart empty? (See illustrations, p. 170)

In the movie *Run like a Girl, Identity and Adolescence*, teenage girls on a synchronized swim team would hold their breath till they thought they might die but felt they would prefer to die versus not be perfect. Their movements were perfect, robotic, and at one point, unintentionally included a Nazi salute. Many of the girls on the team suffered from bulimia, self-injury, suicide, broken homes, teen pregnancy and crime.

Cancer: The Protected Heart

This case study of the following patient was diagnosed as terminal when I interviewed her.

The patient said she was feeling very alone and started to cry. She stated that *"she always worries about something. If she didn't have something to worry about, she'd worry that she didn't have any worries."* She is presently worried about her daughter, who has been sick with back problems.

On the second visit, the patient said she could not talk to her husband about her feelings: she felt very alone and began to cry. When I asked the husband about his knowledge of nursing care, the patient angrily remarked, *"He would not even hear me hemorrhaging; we sleep in separate rooms."*

Her daughter wrote on the back of her questionnaire:

I broke my neck, back, and hip, and had six operations. Due to my extreme abilities and empathy, I was assigned to patients with terminal illnesses, mental disorders, and heart patients. I prepared my patients for death. I prepared myself for death; but I seem unable to prepare or break the bond with my mother. Yes, I know she's 72 years old. Yes, I have a husband and children, but I can't seem to find solace in that. I am a very emotional person. I find tears coming more frequently than I would like. I sought professional help, but I was told I was an unusually loving and emotional person — "Your normal crazy person." I feel I need to cry freely but find this outlet upsetting to my family. I hold it to the exploding point. You may not care in looking over what I wrote — it seems needless — but thank you for the opportunity for allowing me to release this small amount of feeling without obvious frowns.

This patient and family have difficulty with open expression of feelings. The mother could not share feelings of loneliness or fears with her husband, and the daughter had difficulty with sharing tears with her family.

In a second case, patient's cancer occurred just after her mother's death. She talked at length about their relationship. She said her mother was very controlling and condescending to her. To be accepted, the patient always tried to please her mother. She felt much underlying resentment and guilt about this. Her mother's demands were also related to financial contingencies. Relations were strained for a while when she told her mother she could just keep the money; she was going to live her own life. There was some resolution between them, however her mother became sick soon after. Her mother's death was difficult for her; she experienced tremendous guilt. She had asked the nurse to give her mother morphine to relieve her pain and her mother died a few hours later. She felt the morphine might have contributed to her mother's death.

Family members and patients with cancer had long-term patterns of coping with stress by being strong and independent, having a stoic front, and withholding feelings of vulnerability. Both patients and family members often could not be direct in asking for their needs or communicating they were in pain. The inability to express feelings or to be vulnerable was often projected onto the other person. "Don't tell him or her." This dynamic was true for both patient and family members and created a protective, tense atmosphere.

The underlying fear often was due to fear of loss. Patients and family members would withhold for fear that their loved ones would leave them. One woman withheld her anger with her husband for thirty years. She told me that when she was young, she lost her mother, and she would never lose anyone close to her again. This woman protected her heart.

The metaphor for the cancer patient is that of walking on eggs. This style binds the flow and strangles the life force.

In some of the most prevalent diseases of our time: heart disease, cancer, and addiction, there is an incapacity to express needs and feelings; one's vulnerability. The defense against this vulnerability is the stoic or strong front. In illness, this fear of vulnerability is expressed in bound tension in one's movement, which binds the body's ability for open expression and consequently binds the life force. This collective fear is often expressed by being achievement-oriented, and thus quality of life is not defined in terms of the quality of relationships but in being productive and strong. These values have been traditionally defined as masculine values. The feminine principle: values for relationship, caring, touch and open expression are often seen as weak and ineffective, particularly in patriarchal systems that are closed and unhealthy systems. It is the preference for hard versus soft values. The soft voice goes unheard.

These illnesses can thus be seen as symptomatic of problems in our culture that value production and perfection. It is as if the rhythm of our voices and movements imitates machines, thinking we are tough and strong and thus cannot be broken. To quote one of my patients: "Thought I was as strong as iron."

These values are reflected in the ideal masculine body: muscular, angular, reflection strength. However, this is not ideal for health, as there is no flexibility with a rigid body, making body expression very limited and crippling the person's ability to let go in tears, anger, or love. This exacerbates tension. These values also affected the ideal feminine image – Psyche — with soft and tender curves, have turned into flat and angular lines, turning softness into hardness. Women are now getting men's diseases.

Illness is rigidity reflected in rigid body structure. Choice of direction and emotional expression is thus limited. Relationship on a deep level is impossible. This is defense against vulnerability, the ultimate vulnerability being death. These are contemporary American rhythms.

At the same time my first book was written, Gabor Mate wrote a book titled, *When the Body Says No: Exploring the Stress Disease Connection,* 2003. He noted that repressed anger will lead to disordered immunity. Other criteria included the tendency to serve the needs of others first before even considering one's own needs, which he says is a common pattern with people with chronic illness. It is a type of enmeshment that prevents autonomy. There is an inability to process or communicate feelings effectively. The immune system is disabled by chronic emotional stress. (p. 175) He also notes that sympathetic nerves are activated in rage states; narrowing of blood vessels occurs with excessive sympathetic arousal, fight or flight activity, thus increasing blood pressure and decreasing oxygen supply to the heart, increasing lipid levels and increasing cholesterol, increasing clotting mechanisms further heightening the risk of blockages in the arteries. (p.270). *"If we cannot articulate our life experience, our bodies speak what our minds and mouths cannot."* (p. 273) So, this underlies the importance of understanding nonverbal expression and the importance of expressing ones feelings.

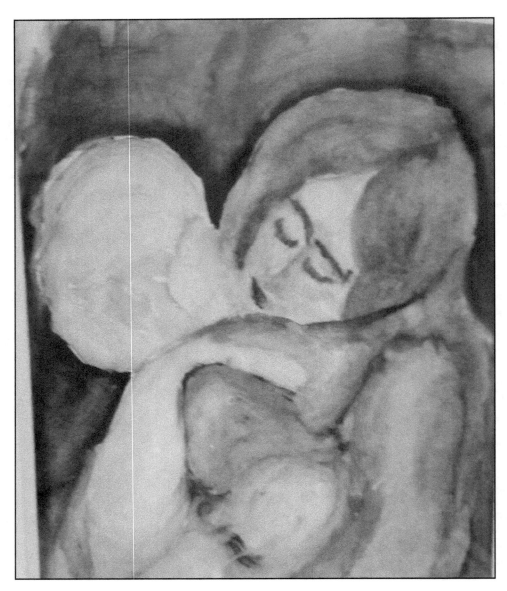

MOTHER AND CHILD
Watercolor Painting by Christina

Chapter 8

Child Development and Cultural Healing: Pregnancy and Early Infancy

I AM CONCERNED for pregnant mothers today who are fully employed. At most, there are just three months of leave time for a mother who has a newly born infant. Neuroscience tells us that babies need contact with the mother for normal brain development for a period of three years. They need the emotional resonance of their needs and feelings. They need contact with the mother's chest so they can normalize breathing and heart rhythm by hearing the mother's heart and feeling her breath. I can remember a colleague stating that there is "a rhythm that nurtures the brain." (Amini, 2000.) I recall a story told of a twin thought to be dead. The mother picked him up and put the baby on her chest and the baby revived. It was so profound. The dance therapists call this embodied parenting.

I worked with a mother who had postpartum depression. She felt inadequate when her baby was born prematurely. She felt she had done everything right during her pregnancy — nutrition and avoidance of bad substances. I did instruct her to put the baby on her chest as much as possible. The situation triggered a lack of nurturing from her own mother. This left a feeling of insecurity internally. We worked with this underlying self-esteem, "I'm not good enough." This helped her identify the origin of the insecurity and release the grief related to this.

She began to feel more confident with the care of her infant and both were now thriving. She more easily nurtures her baby through soothing, holding, placing baby on her chest, and breast feeding.

I can also recall a book titled, The General Theory of Love (2000), written by Fari Amini, MD, and two other MDs (Lewis, T. and Landon, R.) before he died. He was a psychiatrist, Medical Director, I worked with on the adolescent unit as s psychiatric nurse. He acknowledged that this synchrony of rhythm was important to the life of the child.

He theorized that crib death (SIDS) could be related to separation of mother and baby. The baby does not survive because the baby needs the contact of the mother to stimulate heart and breath rhythm. This is why holding the baby in a carrying halter needs to face the mother for chest-to-chest contact.

I also get concerned when I see baby carriages face outward versus toward the mother. My colleague, an ER doc, told me a story of a baby coming into the emergency room because she failed to see the baby stop breathing when the baby was in a carriage that faced the opposite way. The baby needed to see the mother's face to feel secure and the mother needed to see that the baby needs to reposition the child when the baby slumps into a position where it cannot breathe. Mom needs to attune to the baby's emotional and physical needs, attune to the baby's rhythm. Attuning to rhythm is related to survival.

This resonance starts in the womb as the baby moves to the rhythm of the mother's voice as I have described in a previous chapter. This is primal attachment. It is the first dance to mother's music; it is the origin of the Dance of Psyche. Psyche is dance, is music, is theatre.

Is society attuned to the baby's needs? I am concerned especially for single mothers. In one state, they are depriving single immigrant mothers of birth certificates for their children. (Hennis I. M., Oct 16, 2015) Planned Parenthood is constantly being threatened. Babies are often separated from their mothers when mothers have to work. Child-care is extremely expensive.

The emphasis on young children even in preschool is often on competition. In Norway children have no homework and are encouraged to play. The school day is short. They are in the world in terms of learning. Play is an important part of brain and social development. When I read this, the effect was that children's learning was enhanced. This was written in an article by Rune, S. and Sandseter, E.R.H. (2019) titled "Well Being and Involvement. How Children Play Indoors and Outdoors in Norwegian Early Childhood Education and Care Institutions."

Adolescents show up in psych emergency from being bullied at school. There is also pressure for performance without emotional support. There is a new program where I live where the emphasis was placed on emotional support and trust and the scores increased more naturally.

The implication is that the brain requires face-to-face interaction to be healthy. Emotional resonance is important to health and learning. The overuse of computers may contribute to depression or anxiety because of less personal contact and over-emphasis on competition.

This emotional resonance can be stimulated through art, music and dance, which in many schools have been cut from the curriculum. My cousin who was an art teacher had to buy her own supplies. This all indicates the need to provide more support and resources for our children.

Lastly, we are neglecting the next generation of children when we do not consider their injuries and deaths when bombing their countries. Restitution is needed.

In Stephen Levin's book *Waking the Tiger* (1997), he related to healing trauma. He quotes Dr. James Prescott (then with the National Institutes of Health). He presented important anthropological research on the effect of infant and child rearing practices on violent behavior in aboriginal societies. He reported that the societies that practiced close physical bonding and the use of stimulating rhythmical movement had a low incidence of violence. Societies with diminished or punitive physical contact with their children showed clear tendencies toward violence in the forms of rape, war, torture. This was reported in an article titled "Body, Pleasure and the Origins of

Violence" in *Atomic Scientist* in November of 1975. This helped engender trust by parents in themselves and each other, which then is emotionally transferred to their children to then feel safe in the world. Levine, S. (p. 228) described a group process in Norway was utilized to transform traumatic encounters opposing factions in the room, including religious, racial, and political issues. A mixed group of mothers and infants take turns teaching simple folk songs from their respective cultures. Holding their babies, the mothers rock and dance while they sing songs to their children. A facilitator uses simple instruments to enhance the songs. The movement, rhythm and singing strengthen the neurological patterns that produce peaceful alertness and receptivity. As a result, the hostility produced by generations of strife begins to soften.

Mirroring pleasure between mothers and infants generates feelings of security and pleasure. It is here that the cycle of traumatic damage begins to transform, babies are blissed out. (Levine, p. 229)

As I have said previously, the first song and dance starts in the mother's womb. The fetus moves in rhythm to the mother's voice, so this is primal attachment, and then it is understandable why holding, singing, dancing rhythmically is so powerful. Also recall the dance therapist Janet Adler's work with an autistic child, mirroring their unique gestures. You can then see the children skipping together. It was an effective way to bring these children out of their autism, their separation from others.

Daniel Seigel reports in his book, *The Developing Mind* (1997), how relationships and the brain interact to shape who we are. He notes that quality of mothering attentiveness and resonance for newborns in the first two years is related to secure attachment. It is the mother's ability to pick up on non-verbal cues the baby's need for comfort through holding and soothing, and physical needs for food, water, diaper changing. He emphasized emotional resonance... to feel what the other is feeling and to respond.

He notes, this also enables the child, and then can develop the left brain, the logic and language functions. This helps in formulating speech as right intuitive brain development is important for the left-brain development.

He Notes:

Primary emotional states are often directly expressed via nonverbal components of communication, including facial expressions and tones of voice. Primary emotional states are directly shaped by bodily response and directly influence bodily responses. These two basic somatic functions of primary emotions have been demonstrated to be mediated and perceived by the right hemisphere of the brain. (Seigel, p. 151)

So, to access emotions by the way the body moves is intuitive knowledge and gives credence to the use of authentic movement for insight into one's emotions. It also underlies the importance of the way the body moves for insight, attachment and healing. This enables mothers and primary care givers to pick up on non-verbal cues of the child's internal states. This is also important for frontline workers — Doctors, Nurses, Psychologists, Teachers and others in health care and education.

Non-verbal expressions, including those of the face, tone of voice, gestures, can transfer information about the internal states more fully to the outside world than words. (Siegel, p. 150)

Lastly, I would like to mention the concern of Dr. Bessel Vanderkolk (2014, p. 37).

He notes that half a million children take anti-psychotic meds. Low-income children are eight times more likely to be on psychotic meds through Medicaid. This includes a higher percentage of foster children as well. As a result, they have decreased motivation, play and curiosity. Drugs are so profitable, non-drug studies are not explored. They are marginalized as alternatives. Play and curiosity are important for normal development. Studies do not include natural methods. They are not funded; only drug studies are funded, he states.

In conclusion, there is a great need to give our children more care. Increase time for mothers to care for their children like other countries do. Attention to attachment of mother and child in the womb, at birth and during infancy, attention to picking up on cues for attention and physical needs. I am recalling a quote by Starr (1992, p. 105) that says it well:

The crooning, cooing, and rhythms which most mothers use when addressing babies are initially more significant in cementing relationships between them than words which accompany these vocalizations.

Khan (1961) further describes the power of rhythm to heal.

When a child's rhythm and tone are disordered, the healing that a mother can give often unconsciously, the physician cannot give in a hundred years. The songs she sings, however insignificant, come from the profound depths of her being and bring healing power. Infants respond to the pitch, intensity, and timbre of the mother's voice, all of which is part of music.

Chapter 9

Knowledge of Nature and the Divine

SIGNIFICANCE TO THE PARADIGM SHIFT. In the preceding chapters, the focus has been on "man as machine." Since the time of Decartes, the collective of man as machine has shaped all aspects of the way we live. This was described in previous chapters. It has affected science, technology and health, architecture, lifestyle, and the arts. The major assumptions of this paradigm are that mind, matter and spirit are split. Nature is understood by separation and classification and can be controlled. Predictions are made from static properties of things because nature is physical and essentially dead.

However, if an understanding of the new paradigm were acquired, the importance of rhythm would take a central place because rhythm is a vibration. The assumptions would shift — matter and energy are interchangeable — one is the other.

All life has vibration and energy, and nature is therefore alive. Nature would be understood by the connection between things. Rhythm is connection that organizes the universe. Mind, body and spirit are one. All life is connected through energy. Rhythm makes this possible. It is the way the mysteries are communicated to us. It is the language of the mystics. Dance is a way to embody nature and the divine.

Rhythm as Vibration. Gerber (1988) in his book *Vibrational Medicine,* states these assumptions quite beautifully.

Matter is composed of highly complex infinitely orchestrated energy fields (p. 59).

Human organisms are a series of interacting multidimensional energy files that interface with cellular systems. (p. 91)

Consciousness itself is a kind of energy that is integrally related to the cellular expression of the physical body. (p. 44)

He further describes that the etheric body acts as a hologram and poses the question, might not the entire universal energy interference pattern represent a vast cosmic hologram? Consequently, every piece contains the whole. The implication is that information is being stored in seemingly empty space and what happens in just a small fragment of holographic energy interference patterns affects the entire structure simultaneously. Thus, Gerber concludes that there is a tremendous connecting relationship between all parts of the holographic universe.

Through holographic interconnectivity of space, God could simultaneously get in touch with all creatures. (Gerber, pp. 60-61) He theorizes that we could tap into this information through meditation and that perhaps scientists could be trained in meditation techniques to access this knowledge.

My most recent experience in trance states is seeing portals of energy spinning in spiral movement that represent the universe communicating. I also had a vision of the planets in the Universe. On the History channel recently, they acknowledged attempts by other beings to contact us to help the planet survive. Many others have had these experiences. It is on the program, The Unexplained.

The implication is that meditation is a rhythm and a way to acquire knowledge in the universe, then music and dance, which is rhythmical can be a means to acquire cosmic knowledge. Also, the change in major assumptions is revolutionizing the way knowledge is acquired which includes an intuitive way of knowing.

Health and healing would be understood in terms of energy. According to Gerber, increased levels of organization in the body accompany increased energy. The implication here is that the body would be more rhythmical, as organization could be understood as a regular heartbeat, deep rhythmical breathing, rhythmical exchange of body fluids, etc. The body in this respect is a musical instrument. Rhythm heals and improves health.

Thomas Moore (1992) states:

Every disease is a musical problem. It's cure, a musical solution. The more rapid and complete the solution, the greater the musical talent of the doctor. They were concerned with the rhythm, tonalities, discords, and concords of the body and soul. The doctor must know the patient's music, the tempo of his disease. What is the nature of the dissonance that the patient feels as pain and discomfort? (p 170)

According to the Sufi author, Hazrat Inaryat Khan (1961):

Illness is an inharmony, either physical inharmony or mental inharmony; the one acts on the other. What causes inharmony? — The lack of tone and rhythm. Prana or life, or energy is the tone, circulation, regularity is the rhythm, regularity in the beating of the heart, of the pulse and the circulation of the blood through the veins. In physical terms, the lack of circulation means congestion and lack of Prana, or life, or energy means weakness. These two conditions attract illness and are the cause of illness. Rhythm is the action of the mind, whether the mind is active in harmonious thoughts or in inharmonious thoughts. (p. 15)

Thus, illness is lack of music which we call order. Does it not show that human being is music — that life is music — which we call order? In order to play our part best, the only thing we can do is to keep our tone and rhythm in proper condition.

Movement is life and stillness we see the sign of death. (p. 22)

Sourcing Ancient Healing Ritual
Connection to Nature and the Divine: the Light appears

Rhythm is a harmonious division of space and time that vibrates, sounds, organizes, communicates, and imparts knowledge. According to alternative theories and ancient mystics, there is a vibration or energy in space that holds knowledge of the universe. Human beings are also energy fields that are organized through rhythm. Rhythm keeps us alive — the beating of the heart and the movement of the air through the lungs. The stars and sun circle in a rhythmic pattern. It is as if the universe dances and we are part of this great mystical dance. According to recent science and ancient mystics, we can acquire this knowledge through the rhythm of the breath, sound and movement. One can make daily life a moving meditation, which is in concert with oneself, culture, nature and the divine. Knowledge can be acquired through the rhythm of the body, and to become conscious one becomes the dancer. (Campbell, C., 2003, p. 25)

I AM THE FLAME, the candle at sacred ceremony;
Sustained and quick,
The flicker of Lit,
Glowing in the dark,
Lit bright within,
Shaped with arms of ancient dance,
Accepting the light, from my Archangel Uriel and Ancestors and Kitties over the rainbow bridge.
Filling with light and love,
Beams of Light radiating from heart and hands....
The eye of Light within.
Filling with Kindness, Love and Laughter, with much to share today.
This flame shaped with arms of ancient dance.
I will become the ancestor in the sky and join Uriel, Boots, Cocoa and Cognac and Nona, shining bright with them.
They tell me, I am the Universe
Bright and free,
Through love and kindness
The flame in me
Shaping fire with arms of ancient dance.

The Dance of Wind and Fire

In order to create this choreography, I observed patterns of wind and fire. I watched the eagles ride the airfoils on the mountains at Tennessee Valley, I observed candles flicker, I used Persian dance to create the feeling of wind and fire (see photographs, p. 188-200).

The symbolism of this dance is to be in union with nature, the elements, and the divine. Fire symbolizes the divine and living life fully with passion. This dance is a prayer to the Goddess to keep us safe from destruction. Being in union with nature, there is respect for human need and an understanding of limitations and boundaries, thus being consumed and destroyed is less likely. The assumption here is that we are vulnerable to nature, and we must love and respect her, respect life. The dance also symbolizes the shift from moving to the rhythm of a machine to one that *"dances with life — from alienation to a state of being."* See photograph (p. 162-173, Dance of Wind and Fire). The Dance of Wind and Fire shows the life force dwelling beneath the surface.

THIS IS THE DANCE OF WIND AND FIRE

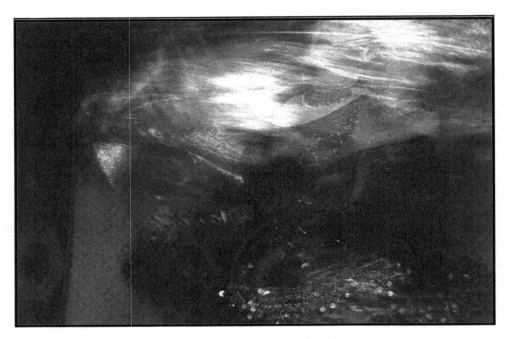

PHOTOGRAPHS SHOWING THE LIFE FORCE OF THE DANCE
By Christina, Dancer
Photography by Carl Johnson
Oakland, California

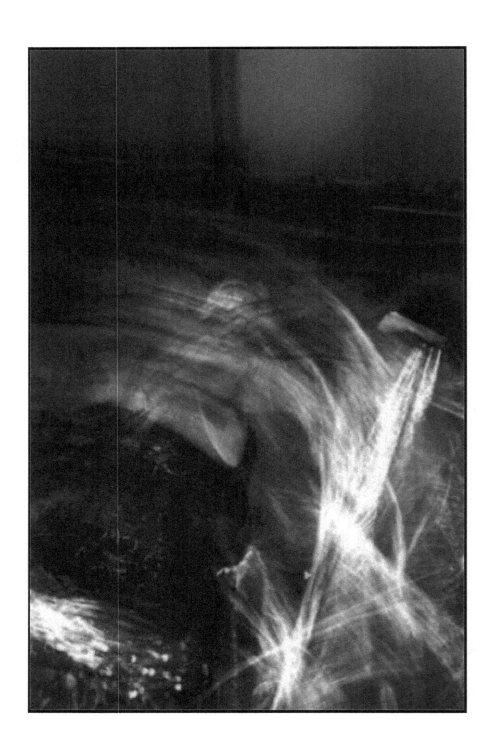

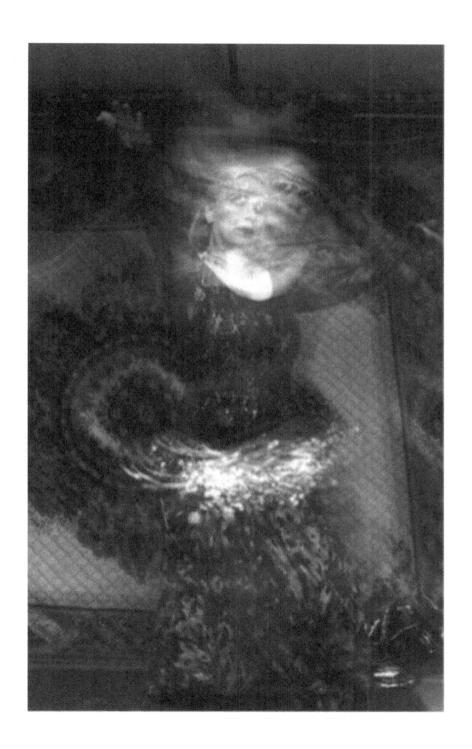

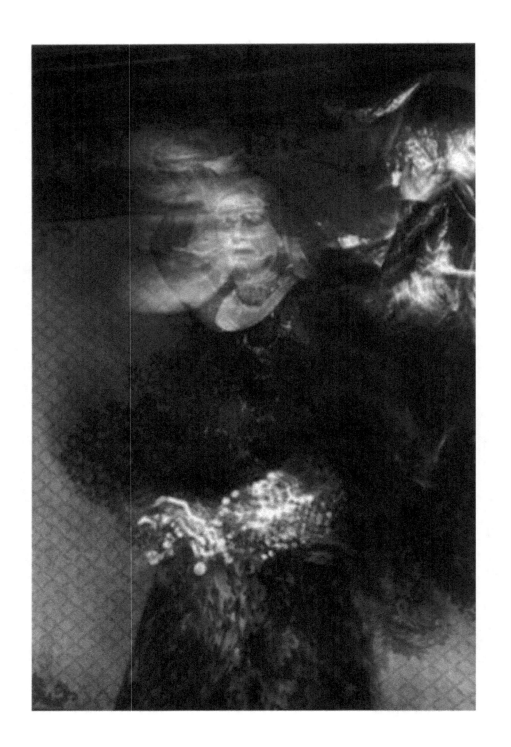

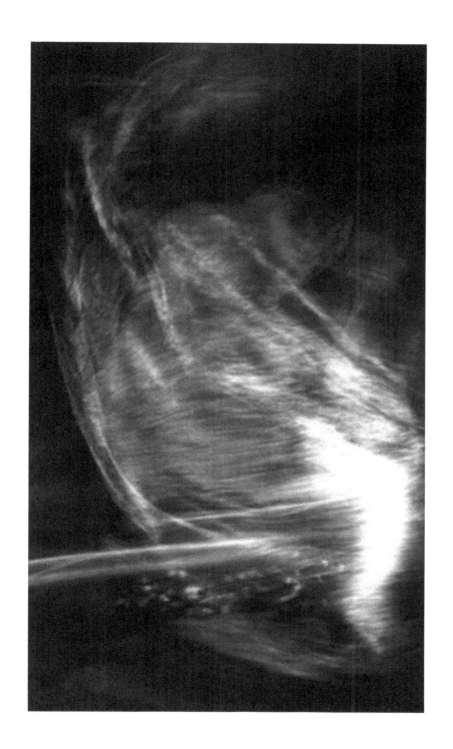

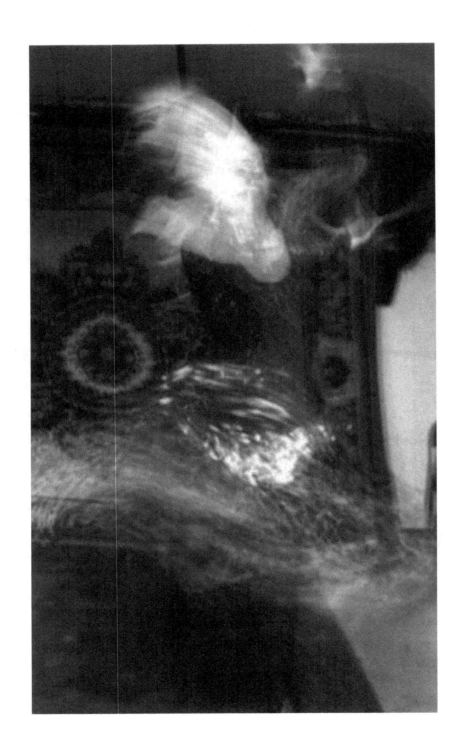

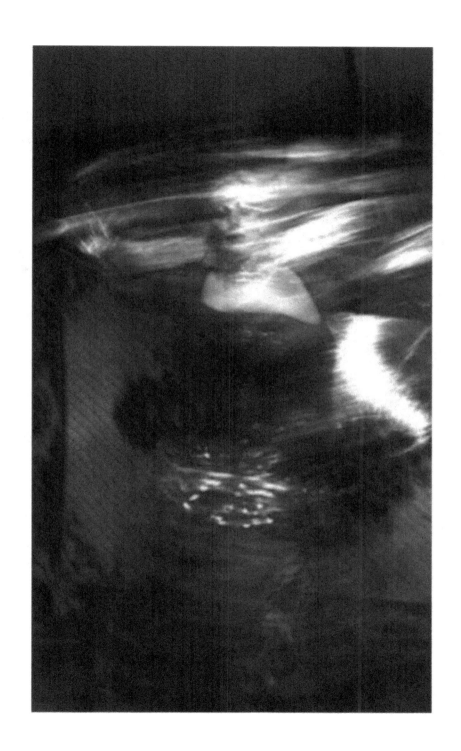

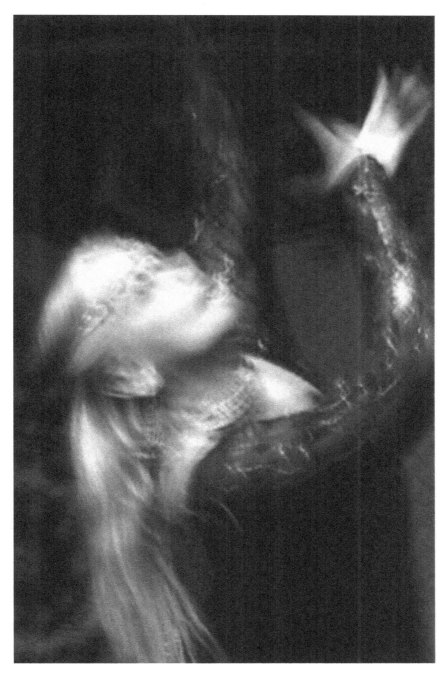

Choreography of *The Dances of Psyche* were developed from Persian, Middle Eastern, Flamenco dance.

FIRE DANCER
Watercolor Painting by my Aunt Nettie
Jeannette Fragasso Masi

Sharing Dance Performance Pictures: Persian, Tunisian, Middle Eastern

DANCERS:

Christina Campbell

Jasmyne Mabalatan

Noelle Duncan

Dannhae Habibi Maya

PERSIAN DANCE
Christina and Jasmyne performing at the Legion of Honor

TUNISIAN DANCE
Christina — Dancer
Felt Love at this Moment

PERSIAN DANCE
Christina — Dancer

PERSIAN DANCE
Noelle Duncan — Dancer

BEDOUIN DANCE
Christina — Dancer

BEDOUIN PAINTING
By Jeanette Fragasso Masi (my Aunt Nettie)

BEDOUIN DANCE
Jasmyn – Dancer

BEDOUIN DANCE
Noel Duncan

PERSIAN DANCE:
Noel and Christina — Dancers

Ready to Perform Russian Dance

Venus: Mystical Dance / Goddess of Love and Peace

I saw a beautiful cobalt blue costume; I was attracted to the music by Holtz, the planets, particularly Venus. The following mythology surfaced from moving to the music.

It's night and the stars have appeared in the sky and Venus becomes visible on the horizon. Venus is turning. The stars sparkle and the moonlight is shimmering in the mystical blue sky. She is the Goddess of Love and Peace. The stars are the jewels embedded in her gown.

She stepped out of the sky and stepped down to earth to heal those who wish love and peace. She crosses over the abyss of fear, and then uncovers her veil of heavenly grace to see the earthly burdens. She searches and pulls inward gathering sacred light.

She opens from the heart and opens to the heavens, holding the earth under her feet. She arches in prayer for love. She pulls her bow, sending it and piercing her own heart. Injured and in pain, she understands the suffering of the earth.

She turns inward, spiraling to the center, whirling in trance, transcending time and space. This is sacred prayer.

The stars open themselves and scatter shimmering light upon her dress. She realigns her chakras and creates healing light and energy.

Energy and light pour from her palms. She creates artistic gestures and hand movements as she plays with the light. Done with her journey, she turns to shed light upon the earth, so they may find love. This mythology symbolizes the reappearance of the sacred feminine, which is needed for spiritual growth. Stepping down to earth symbolizes the descent, to embody the feminine to cross over the abyss of fear and to ground through pain and suffering.

When the suffering is understood, compassion for others and love becomes a reality. When the darkness is understood, the light appears. When fear and pain are felt, the feelings are less likely to be split off into a dissociated self, the machine. (See also Schmookler, A.B., 1988, *Healing the Wounds that Bind Us to War*)

The dream that resembles the Dance of Venus was as follows: I was sitting underneath a waterfall, and I was feeling very serene and peaceful, happy. I was making a dance costume, and the skirt was cobalt blue and decorated with stars.

Stars symbolize the origins of life and the universe. They may also represent connection to nature, to the cosmos. Jungian psychologists have talked about the stars symbolizing individuation. There were two other dreams I had that were connected to the cosmos. In both dreams, I was feeling really free, flying around in space in a ship that was powered by vibration. I could go in any direction in the cosmos. The sky was lit up in beautiful geometric patterns. In another dream I was looking up at the sky and could see what others could not.

At this time, I would like to recall a quote about the dancing god, Shiva. Shiva was written in Capra's (1975) book, *The Tau of Physics*.

The metaphor of the cosmic dance has found its most profound and beautiful expression in Hinduism in the image of the dancing god Shiva. One of the most popular Indian gods appears as the King of dancers. According to Hindu belief, all life is part of a great rhythm process of creation and destruction, of death and rebirth, and Shiva's dance symbolizes this eternal-life-death rhythm which goes on in endless cycles. (p. 242)

Dancing God Shiva

VENUS DANCE: GODDESS OF LOVE AND PEACE
Christina — Dancer

VENUS DANCE: GODDESS OF LOVE AND PEACE
Dannhae and Christina — Dancers

Dannhae Habibi Maya — Dancer

Jasmyn Nabalacam — Dancer

In the book titled *The Revived Greek Dance*, Ginner (1944) describes the modern dancer.

Present day thought is prone to separate the physical from the spiritual and also, to one part of the body to the neglect of the other parts. Such separation breaks the rhythm of the whole and prevents perfect balance.

The ultimate aim of all dance must be to move the whole being together in harmony, Therefore, having made the body sensitive, let it be swept by rhythm the rhythm of music by moving to a good, singing simple tune, the rhythm of nature, by floating in the sea, and surrendering to the will of the waves, or by lying under the branches of a tree in the wind, to feel its effortless swaying. In this way the outer and inner being will be harmonized and learn that in nature there is no division — all parts move as one.

Afterwards, in imagination, the dancer can reconstruct these movements, the memory of the dance of nature will sweep the body as a wind, and all the being will move in perfect rhythm.

It will then it will not be difficult to express emotion and thought. The command of the mind will pass through every nerve like water through a tube and the instant response will produce the joy, or sorrow of the sensitive spirit.

The blending of mind, body and soul is both the result of and the only way to attain that poise of the human entity which brings it into true relationship with art and life. This is that divine unity which flows in the eternal rhythm of the universe. (p. 48)

For Christina:

A poem written by my dear friend Patti Szerlip who has been a witness across time.

In the middle of the floor is a dancer
who with her moves gives an answer
to the question of giving expression to life's hunger for the impression
of the link between beauty and light
when a lovely soul takes flight.

She begins to give meaning to grace,
her trance gives light to her face.
Her hands are the brushes that paint
the emotions that start as a feint
Glow, as a mist, as an amber
that grows into things we remember
from hundreds of years of emotions
shared by women across the oceans

She dances their sorrows and tears
She expresses their pain and fears
Her magical dance embraces them all
to honor their lives and the call
To lead them from darkness to light
and make valid her sister's long fight
For justice and power in the female heart.

Her dance of sorrow is a heavenly art
In the middle of the floor is a dancer
and with delicate grace, there is the answer.
She is every woman who longs to be free.
The light from her hands honors all who see!

Hands with Gold Light Dream

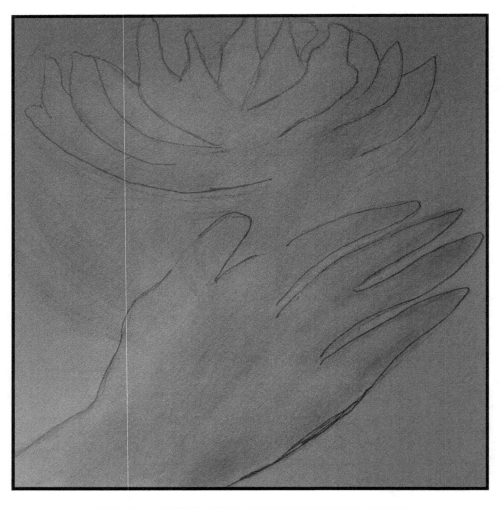

DREAM / LOTUS SPINNING WITH GOLD LIGHT
Water Color by Christina

Chapter 10
Miracles Appear in the Synchrony of Experience across Time Romani (Gypsy) and Tibetan Medicine Journey

THERE ARE TWO JOURNEYS, one from past life as Roma and a Tibetan Shaman journey in this life, maybe past life as well. Both validate my continuing journey as healer.

Romani Journey continues. My curiosity about the Roma (Gypsy) people peaked after my holocaust dreams. I was thinking I would like to meet the Romani people and hear about their experiences and their persecution/ holocaust. I decided on Sunday to go Greek dancing at Papa's Cafe in Petaluma. They had Greek music, dancing and were singing Greek songs which I loved. I went into the restaurant and sat down. There in front of me was the President of the Voice of Roma, an activist nonprofit organization dedicated to the Romani people. We had a wonderful dance together to Serta and with others in the restaurant. We became friends. He introduced me to the Romani culture. I was invited to Herdelezi festival which was in Spring celebrating when their wagons would begin to roll after the winter in the forest. He gave me articles about Romani Holocaust, called Parajmas.

I met his friend Julia, a Roma from Hungary; her husband was Zdaphco from Serbia. He took me to her restaurant called Bistro E. Europe with Gypsy flavor in San Francisco. There were fiery paintings of Flamenco dancers on the wall. We had many good times there celebrating holidays with many patrons from many countries. I heard many gypsy musicians there. Their music seemed like a blend of Middle Eastern, Balkan, Greek, Spanish rhythms, a fusion of many lands, like their travels. I met Dushan there who was Roma from Serbia. He played a beautiful violin. He was also an artist, graduated from college majoring in art. I started taking violin lessons from him. I started violin lessons when I was eight, and on and off throughout life. I always love Hungarian Gypsy violin since childhood. I can now play it on my violin myself. I am, I would say, at an intermediate beginner level. Once I heard a program on the radio about past life; that the love of music from past life can carry over into the next life... perhaps. This does seem likely for me about Romany (Gypsy) violin.

Synchronous Experience: Unexpected discovery of the Baro Than on my trip to India, the place of the Ancestors of the Romani people. I was going to a restaurant called Avatars in Sausalito where I live. The family was from Punjab, India. Avatar, the owner of the restaurant, had family there. He recommended I write to Saroj Ponti after I told him about my interest in writing about rhythm and healing. Saroj, his relative there, had done her dissertation on the dancing God Shiva in the caves of the Himalayas, a mountain range along the border between India and Tibet. She told me that Shiva is known as Gypsy as he is the King of Rhythm that connects with the Cosmos/Universe. This connection would come alive in my sacred dance across many years.

Her quote from one of her letters:

I did my research on the iconography of Lord Shiva, the god of destruction. I identified his various rupees with the help of ancient Indian texts. He incarnates in the ordinary form of men and women. Shiva as a family man, (wife Parvati, sons: Karltikeys and Garnish, Aanes) on one side, etc.) and Shiva as a Yogi on the other hand fascinate me.

She resonated with what I was writing about. Here is another quote from one of her letters:

Your writing was a great service to humanity. You realize that speed and mechanization is clinging to man and is killing consciousness. That human being can pave way toward the invisible world who realize the value of sentiments, feelings and emotions.

Art is the only means to get liberation, and it carries one's soul to be one with the self. So far as my field of research is concerned, it is very close to your subject. I am working on the folk art, myth and iconography of India. Women of the remote areas are the carriers of my field. They express their passions, desires and dreams through the folk media. They used to draw motifs and symbols on specific occasions and festivals. Interpretation of the symbols and motifs and the folk legends are of my special interest — Folk. Folk festivals, games, pharages, and dances, etc. weave symbols which are deeply related to the psyche of the ladies of the particular areas. I discovered some symbols which help us to explore the various dimensions of the specific culture.

Then she invited me to come to India to see the great Gods of the people of the Himalayas.

After writing to each other for several decades, I was invited to go to India. I was teaching and had private practice at the time but was able to carve out three weeks of time in December of 1999. I got on the plane, flew over the arctic to Germany, and then took another plane to New Delhi, India. A friend of Saroj, also named Saroj, met me at the airport. She greeted me with roses. They were very warm and loving and treated me like a very special divine guest. Their greeting, Namaste, means honoring the divine within. Their custom is to treat guests as divine. I stayed with them for a day or so. They took me to the train station in Delhi that went to Patiala, in the Punjab region.

The train ride was five hours long. I remember passing the beautiful fields of mustard greens and rice across the miles in India. My friend and colleague, Saroj Ponti, greeted me when I got off the train in Patiala. I was a guest in her home for three weeks, at Punjabi University where she worked. She would tell me once again that Shiva is known here as the King of the Gypsies because of Shiva's Rhythm and Dance.

She also told me that Punjab is where the Roma started their journey. It is known as the Baro-Than, meaning the place of the Ancestors of the Romani people. There was a conference there on the Roma to study their migration, origin, and patterns. The Romani language was found to have its origins in Punjabi language. There was a large number of Punjabi words that are still preserved in the Romani language. While I was there, I bought the book describing the conference in 1971 titled: ROMA by W.R. Richi, (1996). Richi noted that the Roma preserve the Hindu Religion; the Gods and Goddesses come alive in their dance. Shiva, the King of the Gypsies, God of the Rhythms of the Universe. Kali, the black goddess of time and death. She is considered the kindest and most loving of the Hindu goddesses as she is regarded by her devotees as the Mother of the Whole Universe. Because of her terrible form, she is also often seen as a great protector. Goddess of Creation, destruction and power, destroyer of evil forces. She is portrayed as dancing on her consort. (Wikepedia, Kali).

Kali is celebrated by the Roma all over Europe who come together at a Gypsy festival.

In my dreams an Indian man was taking me to meet Santa Sara/Kali. She comes alive in my dance as protector of evil and rage against these negative energies. This was the dance of Guernica: the Nazi and the Roma. In my fire dance, I relate to fire as protection and destruction. The fire also surrounds Shiva in a circular form. It is the fire from passionate rhythms in dancing. I also see this as protection and regeneration connecting with the rhythm of nature, creation and destruction, and the cosmos.

I met with her students who showed me their art, oil paintings. One assignment the art students had was to go into the jungle and draw nature as communicating. The women were painting their images of what liberation meant to them. The significance of the paintings was to maintain their cultural identity and its roots in the process of modernization. I enjoyed meeting and talking to these students. Saroj arranged trips for me with students as guides.

Students taking me to visit a Rajas Castle. There were many rooms in this castle. One room was designated for meeting his many wives. I remember going to many museums. I was introduced to a Romani scholar who took me on tour to meet Romani (gypsy Tribes) of India. I met the cobra tribe. They were dressed in pink cotton garb with pink cotton turbans on their heads. They had their cobras there for tourists to see and would make some money from tourist contributions. I evidently gave them a bit too much over the recommended amount and they followed us; Romani Scholar, student and myself went to the car. Two of the Romani men and cobra followed us and came to the window. We both leaned to the right, away from the window to protect us from the cobra as the professor drove off. Later I was to find out that the fangs of the cobras are removed.

We drove to another Romani tribe, and I was introduced to them. They had their wagons still drawn by bison. I knew only a few words in Indian but was making an effort to express in their language and to include facial expressions of acceptance and excitement about meeting them; it went a long way. *Namaste, aap kaise hain.* Hello, how are you? The other word that was powerful was Sunder (beautiful!) as they showed me their clothing that they made... Sunder!! They invited me to sit on their wagon. I expressed delight as I climbed up and sat there. They showed me their dance which was derived from the movements of planting in the fields. It was slow in contrast to the exuberant stereotype of Gypsy dance. I felt honored. I performed my Fire Dance for them. I spoke to the Tribe leader who told me that they may have to stop their traveling. The metal they used and sold did not have a competitive price.

Dance of Psyche: Presentation to Students. Saroj asked me to present my ideas to her art and mythology students at Punjabi University. I was writing the first book at the time. I did present many of the ideas in the first book to them which are reviewed here. I performed my dances for them. I was surrounded by their beautiful artwork. See dance pictures.

I also went to their Indian Kathak dance classes where there was a live drummer and sitar player. I was to learn that the root of the Flamenco was

the Kathak dance. Flamenco is definitely part of Gypsy culture now.

I am very thankful to Saroj for being her honored guest in India. I was treated like a Goddess... Namaste, greeting the Goddess within.

Remembering her quotes from her letters, the synchrony of events with the Romani culture as it may have been related to past life is experienced as awe and as a miracle. I was honored. It is definitely part of healing to see and feel the synchrony and miracle in your life.

The Journey of Tibetan Medicine:
Journey Toward the Light as healer, Cleansing past life holocaust and the trauma of being a Nurse in the Medical System.

My Tibetan Medicine Journey started with my mother who had a guru in California. We lived in Florida, and I was a teenager at the time. She was a member of the Meta-physics Group called Joshua Tree which was based in Tibetan Medicine. She would receive educational material from them and be in touch with her teacher.

She would say to me, *"What keeps you alive?"* I was perplexed. She would say, *"Your breath."* She taught me meditation then and she would say, *"Make your breath like a wheel."* She would meditate every day. She would pray for family members and be very intuitive about their fate. One example was my Aunt Lina, her sister, was sick and she said, "It's not her time now," meaning it was not her time to die now, and it was not.

Years ago, after my father's death, she had a mental health breakdown and became very delusional and paranoid. She was placed in a psychiatric hospital against her will by her sisters. She lived in fear that this would happen again as I have said previously. She would go in a rage, sometimes for hours, days, at the time. I could not challenge her feelings about my aunties. If I did, it would set off the rage and I would be rejected.

So, getting involved in Buddhist meditation quelled this fear and she became very functional. She started working in the garment industry using her fine art, draping, and design skills. She graduated from fine art and dress

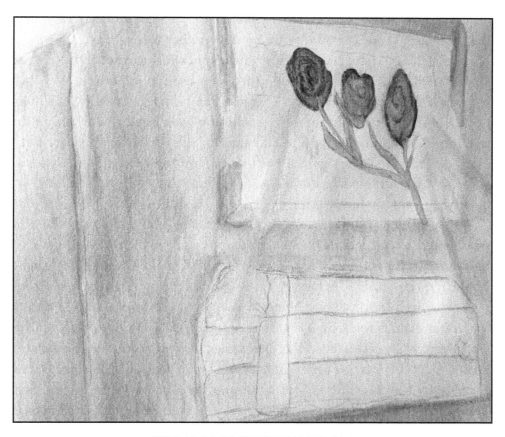

**DREAM OF MOTHER'S ROOM
WITH GOLD LIGHT POURING THROUGH**
A Spiritual Light Becoming More Vibrant

design school when she was young. Later, she had a close friend who had an exclusive shop on Miami Beach. She used her design and draping skills as well there. She sent me beautiful dresses and outfits during this time. I remember her sense of humor when she talked about her experiences with the customers there. It was very funny. My mother was very witty

So, I learned that meditation and connection to the divine source empowered intuitive and healing powers for herself and others — myself included. Her mother, Angelina Fragasso, my Nona (Grandmother), mentioned in the preface of the book, was also a healer. As I have said in the initiating ideas, families used to take their babies/children to her for healing. The story goes, she would hold them, and their fever would drop. I was to learn later that she studied with other advanced healers in Italy... so healing runs in my family.

My brother also continues the family tradition in healing and Tibetan medicine. He received his Masters in acupuncture in the 90s as he finished his career in the airlines. He retired and started his Doctorate in Chinese Medicine when he was in his 60s. He commuted by plane (as retired airline person) from Florida to my home in Sausalito, California, once a month attending classes for four days, across three years. He then received his Doctorate in Chinese Medicine. Interesting... he did his dissertation on the health effects of flying at high altitudes across the years of airline personnel.

He had a close friend and colleague, Dr. Daniel Wong, at the Five Branches Institute of Chinese Medicine. He studied with the Monks in Tibet. His teacher was the teacher for the Dalai Lama. I thought it would be great to have him compliment my trauma psychology practice. He treated the patients in my practice with acupuncture and herbs and taught Tai Chi and Qigong meditation once a week on Fridays. Of course, I would do the trauma work.

I also received acupuncture with him and took his Tai Chi and Qigong classes. Before the acupuncture treatment, he would suggest an issue and I would dream about it. As I mentioned in the section on healing trauma, the pendulum swings from dark to light, from dark traumatic dreams to dreams of a new reality, more in the tradition of the Shaman according to Daniel. The dreams represented the shedding of trauma of my experience in the medical model and shifting to another reality related to spirituality.

The Romani (Gypsy) journey continued as well in the cleansing holocaust dreams to dreams of vibration, light, and sacred dance ritual across the world and dreams of nature; this was empowering.

There were cleansing water dreams: The pendulum swinging from dark water to clean sparkling water, Nazi dreams of fear and danger shifting to being safe; travel dreams representing the launch of a spiritual journey; several dreams of diving off high places, losing my purse and then recovering it. Many dreams of resilience and dreams of light and sacred dance across the world. There were snake dreams representing the Tao which was also a symbol of the Shaman. Then gold light appeared in my dreams which is considered a symbol of transformation. In the Jungian tradition, your lead, your wound, symbolically speaking, transforms into gold. It is an alchemical process.

Daniel (Dr. Wong) gave me the monk's pills. These were the pills the Tibetan monks chanted and prayed over, the Monks of the Dalai Lama, the holiest of the Tibetan monks. Some residue from the Monks funeral pyre was also included. I was already seeing auras around my patients and students in Psychiatric Nursing clinical; taking the Monks pills amplified the aura's light. I saw pink auras around students when presenting my writings; pink light signifies love; gold auras around Psychiatric Nursing students in conference; gold signifying the divine. I also noticed the auras coming out brighter when using a combination of EMDR (eye movement rhythm) and authentic movement in psychotherapy with patients. I let patients know if it seemed appropriate for that person's belief system. Mostly I kept it to myself. The ceiling and room in my home light up with a beautiful green gold light, pink, or more recently blue light when trancing in sacred dance or belly breathing. Much later on, I saw violet and aqua colored light also when trancing. Now, years later, I see spirals of energy, portals representing the Universe and I have had a vision of the planets in the Universe.

Healing Journey through Tibetan Medicine: Dreams from Trauma to Vibrance, from Dark to Light. I will highlight some of the more significant dreams here. As I mentioned previously...after acupuncture Daniel (Dr. Daniel Wong, Dr. of Chinese Medicine) would suggest an issue, and I would dream about it. As I reflect back, often the medical model dreams represented the trauma of working in the hospital, the dark side, and then it would swing into more hopeful dreams. In Shamanic tradition, the process may represent the bridge between mainstream medicine, and a new world that is being co- created (Hines, R. (2022). Sacred Science.com)

In my first meeting with him, he said I looked burdened. I said, "Yes, I work in nursing. I was teaching Psychiatric Nursing at the university at the time. Students were in Psych Emergency, a locked psychiatric unit, and at a hotel for the mentally ill in the community. I was also in private practice specializing in trauma as a psychologist.

I had the following dream: I was in a Pediatric floor and feeling overwhelmed, not knowing whether I had a patient assignment and possibly not taking care of my patient. The dream changed. I was observing nurses in white uniforms taking care of medial patients with lots of tubes and I was feeling relieved of not making the decision to be a Medical Nurse, not wanting to deal with the tubes. As a Medical Nurse, there was more emphasis on tasks; I was more inclined to work with the patient's trauma of medical procedures and surgery. I was interested in healing relationships.

The dream continued. I walked back to Pediatrics and looked into a child's crib which was in the croup tent. I pulled the tent aside, and the child had no arms and legs.

I felt grateful that I was born whole in this lifetime... had a strong feeling of gratitude. However, I have some survivor guilt about being whole as I remember veterans with arms and legs missing as a Navy Nurse working on the amputee ward. This was motivation to write about healing violence and war in society.

At the end of the dream, I was feeling overwhelmed about what to do. My resolution was to help other nurses. This calmed me down.

The dream represented my nursing experience as traumatic, seeing so much suffering, trying to keep up with overwhelming patient assignments. No matter how much energy put out, it never seemed enough. The underlying feeling of this was "I'm not good enough." Daniel said, "One could see this as a cleansing dream."

On the second meeting with Daniel, he said I would acquire knowledge of the Universe. I had the following dream.

I was back at a housing project where I lived with my mother and brother; I was in my early teens. I was looking up at the sky and could see what others could not. The pendulum swings to the dark. I was in a beautiful home by the ocean, a one-family unit with Spanish tiles. There was a Latino man there who said he loved me. A Latino woman was there too, and I loved her too. Then I felt so much fear in my body. We went outside, and we were in the car in back of the home. A tidal wave came, and it was a dark wave about 50-60 feet high, perhaps 3-4 stories high. I was observing that one wave brought the house into the back of this cave with several people in it. I was looking on. The waves were large, but I was safe. On reflection of the dream, a cave is a place where healing rituals would take place in ancient times.

The significance of the dream was that I had fear attached to love and cosmic knowledge, but I was able to handle this terrifying fear and heal it. I was thinking about the paradox of water that flows and fear that binds... the pendulum swinging from dark to light. The message was "if you move through the enormous dark wave of fear and grief, you will get through it and survive."

The other paradox of opposites that the dream shows is dark and light, bound and free, earth and sky, life and death, fear and love, vulnerable and strong. stillness and movement... fear and grief towards love.

In the next dream, the pendulum swings to vitality from fear. I was hanging off a ledge at my Aunt Nettie's house, and it was a little scary. Aunt Nettie's house was a place of warmth and love, many get-togethers with aunties, uncles, and cousins. Aunt Nettie was my mother's close sister.

In the next scene I was watering the lawn with the hose; the water had a strong feeling. The water was going into the earth and the lawn was getting very green. Water represents depth of feeling and cleansing of fear... and life, and the green color represents vitality. Lessening fear increases vitality.

The pendulum swings again. I had a dream of a creek that was beautiful, clear, green-blue, and then there was one that had man-made rocks and was dirty. This may represent the collective psyche as well. Man has dirtied the waters through pollution and chemicals from oil refineries and other corporations. It represents my personal psyche, cleansing the darkness.

In the next dream I was in a house with a funeral going on. A friend was there in the room, but she was unavailable. The meaning of the dream was that I had loss and grief, but the feeling was I was dealing with this on my own.

Cleansing dream related to the Medical Model. I was a supervisor at a psychiatric unit; I was exhausted. I arrived there and the place was toxic. There were no walls around the bathroom. In my discomfort I urinated on the floor contributing to the toxic environment.

As a supervisor of students in the psychiatric unit, there were staff that were defended and unavailable and I was on guard. I felt I would be exposed for not being good enough.

The initial bullying experience as Navy Nurse contributed to this feeling of not being good enough, being defective. This feeling stayed with me throughout my career; I was on guard. I feared being a target again. The fear of being exposed as defective was part of the toxicity.

After a day at the hospital orienting students to the Psychiatric unit and some of the Nurses were a bit cold, I had the following dream.

2022. This dream went back to an experience on a psychiatric unit years ago. My colleague and friend, Mary Ann, asked me to work at this new psych unit that was opening in Santa Rosa. I was in another toxic situation where I was scapegoated. Controlled medications went missing from the locked medicine cabinet. However, I was cleared, found clean as they found the nurse who was taking the meds. It did reenact the early trauma from my

Navy Nurse experience. I was considered part of the team after that. The head nurse who took over wrote a letter of recommendation for me, and I was hired on an Adolescent Psych unit at UCSF. This helped me heal my sense of competence as a nurse. However, the wound was still there.

In the dream, Mary Ann and I were up high in the mountainous area, and I was swimming in black industrial water. She encouraged me to climb up this steep mountain/cliff. Looking down at the water, it looked dangerously high. I wanted to get down. Mary Ann jumped. Then, I jumped what seemed like 1000 feet and made it safely. I was swimming in the black water where the dream ended. This was metaphor of what it was like working in toxic environments. The energy field was emotionally toxic; and going through the feelings of fear to heal was like jumping from a 1000-foot cliff. I made it safely.

Significance of the dream to the collective psyche. The black water reflects the water poisoned by oil. To confront this as an activist is dangerous, like jumping 1000 ft. This is what is being done by the gathering tribes of the Dakota Axis pipeline. They are fighting for clean water and put themselves in danger by fighting the oil industry. Their fight is our fight for health and safety. They are very brave, and I appreciate them.

A dream that is related to indigenous activism. I was in the jungle surrounded by trees. I was standing in front of a stream with beautiful clear water with a huge black snake. I found out that there was an indigenous tribe in the Amazon that had a black snake as their symbol. They were fighting to get the oil and gas industry from ruining the Amazon. The black snake represented toxic oil ruining clear water and the forests. (See p. 236)

Cleansing Nazi dreams. I was in a fascist camp and in danger. I had this Nazi woman guard by the feet, and I was banging her head against the wall and stairs killing her. I put her dead body on the chair with other dolls and no one noticed the dead body at this restaurant. I had a family, husband and a daughter. They were loading our furniture into a truck without incident.

This was a healing dream representing power over the Nazi experience, the holocaust. This dream and several other dreams were about

BLACK SNAKE IN CLEAR WATER IN JUNGLE DREAM
Symbolic of toxic water from oil pollution
Watercolor by Christina

cleansing lower chakras related to survival. Dreams about shame, fear, and rage, and the shame and fear of being exposed before others... the underlying feeling of being defective.

More Roma dreams. I was on a Gypsy wagon on top of a diving board. As a Roma person you were at risk of being a target. So many Roma experiences were fearful experiences like being on a high diving board. For me as a young person I was diving off high boards challenging my fears: 1- to 3-meter boards and 5-, 7-, and 10-meter towers. So, perhaps it showed up to represent challenging the fear of being a possible target as a Roma being found. Many years later, I found out that my Russian Romani grandfather on my father's side left Russia/Lithuania to escape persecution. This is the root of my ancestral inheritance, trauma, fear of persecution. Many bullying experiences throughout my career, the most painful occurring as a Navy nurse was my trauma reenactment. Afterwards, I lived in fear of being persecuted again. This showed up in my dreams of Holocaust. In the next dream I was lying in bed next to a Roma man who was ill. When he got up, he was able to walk. This might have been a message that I may have the ability to heal; heal Romani holocaust, experience from past life.

In the next Romani dream, I may have been in a Gypsy camp. There was chaos and I was running from the Nazis. I ran into a hole in the ground, a latrine. There was soap on the top and the smell was OK. I felt I would be safe.

Romani dreams continue. I was sitting in someone's living room and there was a couple who had a son. They said their son died in a concentration camp. I went outside to the pool, and the water was deep and dark. This was a dark water cleansing dream. Dark water signifies deep moods of grief related to holocaust.

A Roma grave. I dreamed of a Roma grave. It was fresh dirt just recently dug-up and the dirt was loose. There was a figure of a tall 40-ish man, Roma, slim, black shirt, hat and pants. Then there was blood dripping on the ground. In the dream, the feeling that it was a Roma grave was very strong. There was also a feeling of recognition and validation as a Roma that I was feeling looking at the grave.

In the next dream my mother and her friend opened a hotel. There was a wall there by the bay. It had had Nazi numbers there (perhaps the numbers tattooed on people's arm). It was a Holocaust memorial for those who were killed.

Another repetitive dream was of having to pack because the fascists were coming.

I feel these dreams were cleansing the horror, fear and grief of Holocaust experience.

The collective significance: This persecution is still going on in Europe now. Roma children continue to be separated from their families; Roma still are subjected to discrimination and unlawful arrests and harassment.

This is also relevant in the United States as I have described in previous chapters; the rise of Nazi groups, White Nationalists. It is a warning of the suffering that can occur from authoritarian leadership stoking hatred, division including Racism, Classism, Misogyny.

These last four years were a wake-up call on how fragile democracy can be.

Chapter 11

Dreams of Vibrance and Sacred Dance of the Silk Road: Pendulum Swings to the Light

*D*REAM OF VIBRANT FLOWERS. I was in L.A. at a huge building. I looked out the window and there were beautiful flowers there... colorful pansies, very vibrant. There were huge fields of these vibrant, colorful flowers. The dream signifies to me vibrance, greater life force, and the flowers signify creativity.

Dance Levitation dreams. In the next scene, I was practicing my dances in a large room. I was then levitating, going up to the ceiling, flying and coming down. Initially, the movement was simple, but then I was in the air and then back down on the ground.

Daniel's interpretation was that they are similar to other dance dreams that represent the silk road. He sent a link of the paintings in Dun Huang Caves in the Himalayas where the dancers levitate to the ceiling. They are called the Sky Dancers and represent wisdom.

A few days later I had the following dream: I was in Persia studying the ancient spiritual ritual. I had a veil and a long dress on. I was being evaluated to see if I remembered the steps of the ritual. I was unsure, but able to pick up cues from the other dancers in the ritual as to what came next. Mirroring movement of others is an intuitive way of knowing, and also represents connection to others and ancient Persian culture.

Then, I was in a spa dressing room, getting ready to dance, learning the sequence of an Asian ritual. My dance teacher, Lorna Zilba was there. We were getting dressed. The experience was finding a place to get ready.

Indian Dance Dream. I was working on Indian choreography. Another dancer suggested two quick turns to the left, and I suggested three or four turns to the right. When I think of left, I think of linear movement. When I think of right, I think of intuitive movement. I have always been an intuitive dancer, moving from impulse, feeling, versus remembering sequence of movement from someone else's choreography.

The next scene of the dream was making a costume out of palms. The significance of the costume out of palms means the dances are sourced from nature. Hawaiian dance is a good example of this. Their movements represent the waves of the sea and make tribute to earth and sky. Their attire is grass skirts.

I had a dream that there was this full stretch of material in front of me and it was full of a powerful force. I could see the material move from this powerful force. I put the material around me, and the material shaped itself into gaucho pants. There was a small black snake that got caught and was near my inner left thigh. I felt that the snake would bite me, but the dream ended abruptly.

The significance of these dreams represented to me that my future lies in understanding the ancient dance ritual for healing. From the dances I have learned across the years, and from around the world: Greek, Persian, Egyptian, Tunisian, Indian, Flamenco, the movement of these dances was used as vocabulary to create through spontaneous movement dances that showed the way through trauma into the light, Dance Mythos, a story about healing

Submarine into ancient Greece dream. I walked into this submarine ready to go into the ocean. I noticed there was an ancient Greek statue peeking out from the top of the submarine, half hidden. I went inside; the crew and the captain were there — some gathering for my lecture. Then suddenly this woman burst forth saying she had a vision about an ancient Greek statue of a woman Goddess being on the ship. She ran toward the left side of the ship. There it was right there. I was starting my lecture, and it was about something mundane, perhaps the medical model. I thought to myself, *"no, it's about this ancient knowledge; this is what I need to be talking about."*

The next scene in the dream: I was with Alexandra and the Captain of the ship talking about the Greek artifacts on the ship.

Daniel told me to pay attention to and connect with artifacts, pottery and stone sculptures. I experience so much depth in Greek dance... so much joy and the depth of sorrow. My Dance of Gentle Sorrow was done to very soulful Greek music. The ocean represents the depth of feeling. The submarine represents the ability to dive deep into the depths of feelings and the unconscious through Greek music and dance in representing feminine intuition and the ancient Greek Goddess. Coincidently, my friends started calling me Christina Athena.

Cosmos dream. I was on a ship last night in outer space. The feeling was it was a very large spaceship. I was talking to the other crew members. We landed the ship on earth. In sacred dance one honors sky and earth, earth and sky. One looks up to the heavens and the Universe but has reality with feet firmly planted on the ground, landing on earth. According to Mendel, author of *Dream Body* (1982, p. 33-35), *the Universe was considered the Body of God.*

Shaman Dream. I was in the mountains in a secluded cabin there. I was looking out the window and could see the animals. There was a herd of caribou. They appeared mystical in how they seemed coalesced, bonded together with an energy wave above their heads. An eagle came to the hut. It was wounded, but it was coming to me for healing, familiar with me and the cabin. There was an overriding feeling of being a Shaman. There was then a party, and someone there called me a Shaman. It was an overriding sensation; that the connection to these animals in the mountains had to do with Shamanism/healing.

THE EAGLE COMES TO ME FOR HEALING DREAM,
CARABOU LOOKING ON
Watercolor by Christina

In reading these dreams to Daniel (Dr. Daniel Wong), he said that I am continuing to develop as a Shaman. It was not until years later that this prediction of developing as a Shaman seemed more real as I reviewed the snake dreams going back to the 1980s.

Snake Dreams related to Shamanic Tradition.

The very first experience was actually a daytime dream/image. I was running in a field and stepping on branches that turned into serpents. At that time, I was to find out that Snakes represent energy channels. So, in this way the medical image of Aesculapius, the two snakes winding up a shaft and then facing each other may represent channels of energy. The significance to the medical profession, however, is a symbol of renewal. The snake's ability to shed old skin and renew with new skin. The perfect metaphor for healing...as we shed the toxic old trauma's and renew our sense of self, with new identity and new energy and vibrance:

Joseph Campbell describes this well:

The serpent is universally symbolic of consciousness bound to the field of terrestrial life. Serpent shed its skin to be born again, as death/life themes throws off death to be renewed as the moon sheds its shadow to be reborn.

I continued seeing sticks on the ground as serpents. It occurs with great frequency, and I have been thinking about the symbolic nature of the serpent. In meditation, I felt an image of a cobra coming up inside of me and its hood hovering above my head. I could sense its dreamlike outline within and above me. I also felt a rattle in the first chakra. The sense I had was one of power and the feeling I could defend myself. The threat of snake venom, the ability to strike when threatened. I was miffed by the meaning of the rattle but later found out that the rattle is used by a Native American tribe for trance states. Later images/dreams were both cobras and rattlesnakes. The meaning of the serpent is also instinctive knowledge. The strike would be knowledge.

At the end of 1999, September 25th, I had the following dream: There was a group of women who pointed their fingers where the book of knowledge was. I walked there somehow being aware that when I put my hand in the book, there were asps, snakes there and they bit me on the forefinger. I felt it. It hurt physically. It felt real, that it was happening. The snakes crawled away and lost their energy. I survived. The dream ended. The significance for me at the time was that my vitality was strong as I survived the snake bite. According to Shamanism, initiation as a healer is being bitten by a poisonous snake and surviving.

Stephen D. Farmer, PhD (1999) wrote an article: *The Artist and the Snake.* He said the snake is deeply embedded in our consciousness, a powerful symbol of major transformation. In some traditions, if you are bitten by a highly poisonous snake and survive, you're considered to be a powerful healer. He also cited the AMA caduceus carried a snake as symbol. Kundalini yoga works with energies of the spine that can be likened to a serpent. He quoted Jeremy Neely in one of his favorite books, The Cosmic Serpent.

He proposed that DNA is often represented in indigenous traditions and art as intertwined serpents. There is richness to the physical and the spiritual stories with snake, snake energy and snake medicine.

He noted Paul Hiressinstamin's spiritual art (mandala art.com). He was inspired by Spirit/God source; a whole range of images from mandalas to deities from various religious and devotional practices helping others into inspirational source for their creations. He said:

In a room with Cobras all around me like Raiders of the Lost Ark ... I fell onto my belly and a Cobra bit him on the foot but did not kill him." I felt the poison go in me and felt I was going to die; instead, I felt elated, felt ecstatic, full of life initially The snake represented transformation."

Snake Dreams working with Daniel. When I was working with Daniel, (Dr. Daniel Wong) who studied with the Monks in Tibet, I had the following dream: I was walking through this room and there were very long thin snakes in the room, one white, one grey. They were both following me as I walked past them. I was a little frightened, but I walked quickly through the door safely. Daniel said it was an entrance into the spiritual door (November 5, 2010).

June 17th, 2011, I had the following dream: I was walking with my Roma friend Julia and another woman with golden blonde hair; she was youthful, perhaps 40ish. Someone came rushing in with a cobra as medicine. There was anti-venom serum that the women took. The snake came with the serum contained in a clear, perhaps plastic, container. It got loose and split into two parts. The snake was large, black and white, but looked grey against the black skin scales. It was about to eat the smaller snake. The large snake then curled up in a box resting. There was some unease about where it might be. I was in the dream and very much a participant.

Daniel said this was medicine for self-healing. It is an ancient snake that split, the one curled up in a box was an energy channel, and the small snake was qi, energy channel opening up. Qi, pronounced chee, is the life force that flows through nature.

I told the dream to my Indian friends at Avatar's restaurant, Karla and Ashook. They said the dream represented Shiva, the King of dancers, and the woman represented Shakti, his wife. Shiva has a Cobra next to him. He is playful with the Cobra, which is a defiance of death, and also compassion to all, including animals.

I would like to recall for a second time the black snake in the forest dream (see p. 236). A dream that is related to indigenous activism was: I was in the jungle surrounded by trees. I was standing in front of a stream with beautiful clear water with a huge black snake. I found out that there was an indigenous tribe in the Amazon that had a black snake as their symbol. They were fighting to get the oil and gas industry from ruining the Amazon.

I was talking to dance therapists in my dream about active imagination in movement. I articulated something about the patriarchy and women as complicitors. There was much agreement about this. It felt good to have a voice about it. Then I had an image of a beautiful rose-colored snake. Rose color meaning love, the snake, a nonlinear way of knowing. The significance of this was a symbol of feminine knowledge, also a symbol of the Goddess. Now, in this time, coming of age for the new world, challenging patriarchy.

A few days later I had a dream of a rattlesnake. It was large and its scales well defined and clearly seen. Walking around I did not know where it was. Then it was in a basket curled up. It was very large and beautifully defined. Could this mean that my energy inside was becoming larger and my identity as energy healer was more clearly defined, myself more clearly defined? It had an indigenous feel to it, particularly thinking about the basket.

Gold Light Dreams

According to Jung, Gold is a symbol of transformation, a metaphor for spiritual enlightenment. In these dreams I interpret it as on the path to enlightenment.

The first dream was in 2001. I had a dream that my kitty Coco gave birth to a golden kitty. I loved Coco so much. For me my love for her was a spiritual experience. At the end of her life, she seized, and I stayed with her and was with her when she died. She was surrounded with green and red light during this time. I had this dream shortly after her death. She was in a cabinet above my bed and jumped out and landed on my chest. I felt her land there, a body-felt experience in the dream. She was telling me she was with me in spirit. I experience enormous grief when my kitties die. I reached out to an animal communicator/telepath, and this began my journey in communicating with her and my other kitties and met my ancestors on the other side through this telepath, a birth of a unique experience. This included my Nona, my Italian grandmother, who was a healer in Italy. She guided me toward the light; how to expand my energy field.

Later, her brother, Cognac, went missing; I was heartbroken. I was walking with my feral, Boots, in the same place in our courtyard where Coco and Cognac would walk with me. All of a sudden, a puff of light came out of Boots. I sat down at nearby steps and felt the presence of Cognac. I felt him on my lap and I was surrounded with red and green light. I felt so much love. It was his goodbye to me, a beautiful experience. However, his spirit would stay with me too and I would stay in touch through the telepath. I would also see them in visions in my third eye.

Golden Coin Dreams. I had a dream where two coins — one in the shape of a sphere and the other in the shape resembling a heart — were emanating gold light. I interpret the sphere as a mandala of wholeness and symbolizing connection to all things. The heart emanating gold light was a symbol of spirituality. They were connected to each other by two small rings. (See image p. 252) When we are whole, connected to all things and the universe, we are perhaps on the road to enlightenment and love.

A dream that followed was one about my brother setting up a telescope, and I could see what others could not. I thought this signified connection to all things and to the universe,

Gold Light in Hands Dream. I had a dream that I was reaching out to Julia, my Romani friend, and there was a gold light around our hands. I was kneeling down and reaching out to her. This signified to me that there was love for my friend who was Roma and love for Romani culture.

Cousins in Gold Light. A few years later, I had a dream of my cousins visualizing me and seeing them with gold light between us. One cousin appeared with gold light then another with gold light, and another perhaps five or six cousins. Then at the end of the dream, there was a gold coin.

Wheel in Gold Light. I had a dream of a wheel in gold light. It could have been a Tibetan wheel or a Romani wheel. I think it could represent both, especially since my journey is a Romani journey and a Tibetan Medicine Journey. (See p. 251)

Lotus spinning in Gold Light Dream. Lastly, I had a dream of a lotus in my hand, and it was spinning from the gold light, energy, in my hand. I would like to say that gold light represents connection to the divine. It represented an energetic flower dance. (See p. 249).

Energetic flower dance. I was inside a gym. The man I was with was on an exercycle. He was trying to impress me with his strength. I, on the other hand, was mesmerized; I was playing with a soft paper flower that was a lotus, one in the left hand and one in the right. The one in the left hand took off as I was supporting it; it appeared to vibrate and twirled in this beautiful vibrant dance. It was powered by the energy in my hand. I was mesmerized by it. There was the paradox of physical exercise and energetic movement. Energetic movement became the obvious choice for me. I was then teaching a dance class. Later in the dream, I said, *"It's hard to just focus on physical exercise,"* then said *Quan Yin's name.*

The lotus is a symbol of transformation. The lotus grows in muddy water but blossoms into a beautiful flower ... so metaphorically speaking from trauma to beautiful being, darkness into light. When one faces the darkness, pain of trauma, compassion becomes stronger. Quan Yin is the Goddess of Compassion.

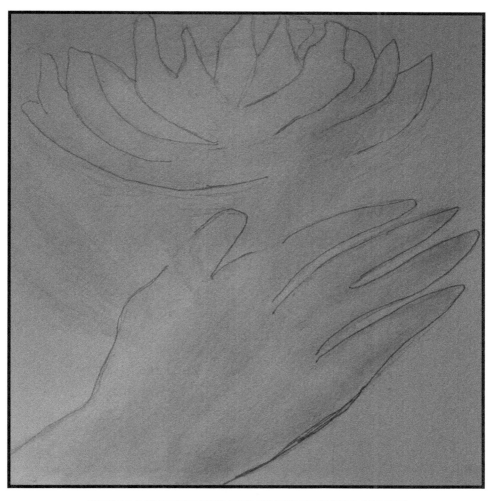

DREAM / LOTUS SPINNING WITH GOLD LIGHT
Water Color by Christina

DREAM OF MOTHER'S ROOM
WITH GOLD LIGHT POURING THROUGH
A Spiritual Light Becoming More Vibrant

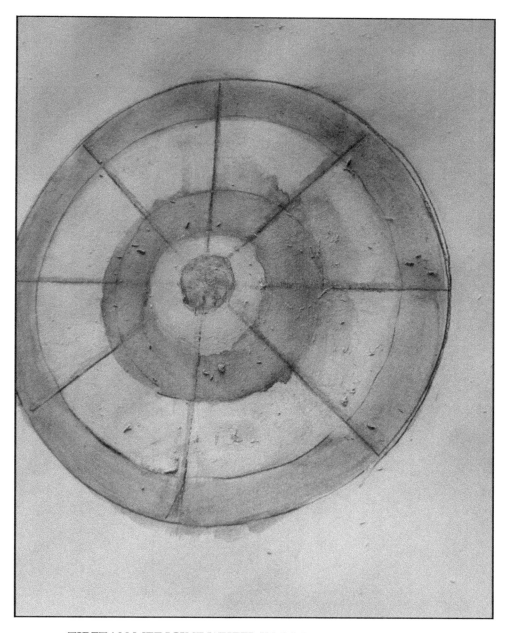

TIBETAN MEDICINE WHEEL IN DREAM IN GOLD LIGHT
Portal to the Other Side
Shows as ancient symbol

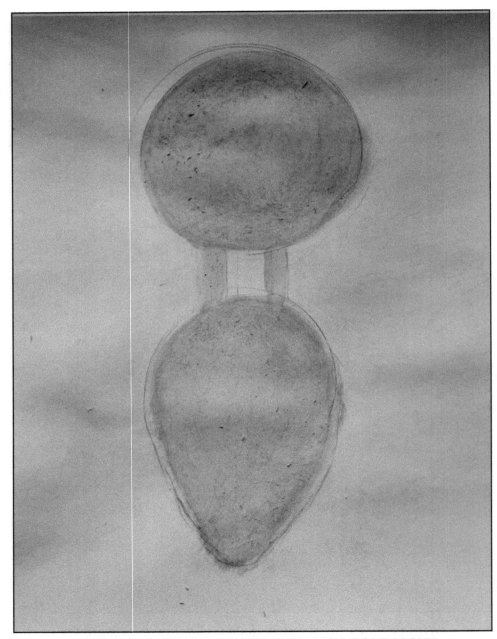

SPHERE AND HEART SHAPED DREAM IN GOLD LIGHT
Masculine and Feminine Connected
Watercolor by Christina

Chapter 12
Spiritual Healing:
Lessons in the Story of Jesus as a Target of Bullying

I WAS SEVEN YEARS OLD when I was asked to be in a Catholic procession with other children. We followed the priest who was carrying the host ceremoniously. It was to commemorate Jesus. I remember feeling so much love for him which is still there today. I carried flowers in a basket, kissed the flower in the name of Jesus and threw the flower where the priest walked with the host representing Jesus. The love is from Jesus as healer. There is some evidence that he studied in India and gained healing powers there.

There is powerful meaning in his story: his persecution, death, and resurrection that is relevant today. Firstly, his anger at the status quo, using the temple for money. In today's language for profit. The image of him turning over the table in anger is vivid in my mind. Secondly, he was a target of a mob led by Pontius Pilate and a crowd that ranted to persecute him. I think about all the whistle-blowers and peaceful protesters who are arrested for speaking out and wanting more human values.

Jesus represented a new philosophy of love and compassion that threatened the powers that be. In today's language, he was targeted for his new way of being that threatened the status quo. Even before he was born, he posed a threat. Harold had all the boy infants killed to eliminate this threat.

This is true today as artists, healers or those speaking out against the status quo are targeted and have been throughout history. Healers were burned at the stake during the Salem witch-hunts, and during the inquisition, to name just a few.

Jesus suffered against this brutality. He forgave them for they "do not know what they do." I find myself saying this many times in this life. I identify with the persecution of the healer, a sensitive spirit bringing in a reality of love and healing in a brutal environment. It is a combination of sensitivity, conscientiousness, creativity that makes you a target of the bully; and coming out with the truth or coming out with a new way of seeing or being.

Sensitive spirit affected more by the meanness and cruelty in society. Those who can shape a new reality from this sensitivity are often targets of the bully. Healers have been tortured, burned at the stake for this throughout the centuries. This is the story of Christ, shaping a new reality through love and kindness and is beaten and tortured but is resilient and rises to the light in the resurrection.

These are metaphors relevant for healing today. We experience the pain of not being loved, or through the brutality of others. Embracing the pain, letting it pass through us, we come to a new light; it is the type of death and resurrection, and like Jesus we let go of the resentment and anger. However, it is important to feel the fear, the anger, to experience it first and then it is easier to let it go.

The story of Jesus is an ancient story of healing from toxic environments and tyrants. It is relevant today. It is a story from darkness into the light, a powerful healing journey, Mythos, sustained across time.

Jesus Story: Tibetan Medicine

Jesus as Healer. I ran across an article titled, *"There is proof Jesus came to India, made a deep study of Hinduism, and taught when he returned to Jerusalem."* (J. Oakes, 2013).

He noted that the story is Mythological like Indian Mythology. There was a revision of Christ's story that the missing years of Christ from age 9-33 was spent in India as a Buddhist Monk, that his healing powers were acquired there. He returned to the Middle East to speak and there he was arrested and then crucified. However, according to this article, it was not clear that he died. Some accounts said he returned to India; his name was Issa. He was buried there and there is a tomb in his name, Issa. Speculation was that it was similar to near death experience. His healing powers may have been related to Buddhist meditation enhancing power, such as casting out the devil, healing the sick, may have come from this ancient knowledge. In working with Dr. Daniel Wong, Physician of Chinese Medicine, who studied with the Monks in Tibet, he described advanced powers of Tibetan Monks to cast out demons and heal the sick. Further, in our discussion about psychosis, he talked about advanced Buddhist Monk healers' power to exercise demons from psychotic people. So that I do understand the possibility of Buddhist healing very possibly could be related to Jesus's healing powers.

There is also powerful meaning in the story of his persecution, death, and resurrection that is relevant today. Firstly, his anger at the status quo, using the temple for money or in today's language for profit. Secondly, he was a target by a mob led by Julius Cesar who ranted to persecute him. He was taken from his prayer by soldiers arresting him.

I think about all the whistle-blowers and powerful protestors arrested for speaking out and wanting more human values, values for equality for Black lives, for women, for LBGTQ, for the poor, the sick, and homeless. Jesus represented a new philosophy of love and compassion that threatened the powers that be. In today's language, he was targeted for his new way of being and persecuted. This is true today for artists, healers, activists. They are targeted and have been throughout history. Healers were burned at the stake during the Salem Witch trials and during the Inquisition. Jesus suffered against this brutality. The story goes that he forgave them, for they do not know what they do. It has been my experience that being kind, sensitive, bringing a healing philosophy of love and healing makes you a target in a brutal emotional climate. This includes conscientiousness, and creativity.

These are metaphors relevant for healing today. We experience the pain of not being loved or the brutality of others. Embracing the pain, experiencing the hurt, resentment and anger and letting it pass through us, letting it go, we come to a new light; it is a type of death and resurrection. The story of Jesus is relevant today as an example of healing from toxic environments and tyrants… a powerful healing journey from darkness as passage to the light.

This is the story of Jesus being constantly reenacted:

A quote that is relevant to today's world quoted from the Christian Monitor, 2002:

Jesus made it clear to his followers that to follow him was to take the path that leads to persecution and hardship, going against the crowd and having the world hate you, because you represent the "light" that Jesus is in the world, which in turn exposes the evil of the world system ruled by Satan, the father of lies.

Jesus makes it very clear that the path he was walking down, being hated by the world because he exposed its evil deeds, was a path that led to his physical death/persecution via execution but resulted in eternal life in God's kingdom.

A sensitive spirit is affected more by the meanness and cruelty in Society. Those who can shape a new reality from this sensitivity are often targets of the bully. This is the story of Christ, shaping a new reality through love, compassion, and kindness… is beaten and tortured but is resilient, rises to light in the story of the resurrection. It is a powerful story, resonates across time — Mythos.

Resistance to Creativity and Changes. So, why is change and creativity so difficult? Years ago, I read *The Courage to Create* (1977) by Rollo May whose writing is relevant here and inspiration to be the change needed. He says, *"We are living in a time when one age is dying, and a new age is not yet born."* I would say we are giving birth to a new age, and we are having severe labor pains. Creativity is moving forward in spite of despair. *Art is revealing the emotional and spiritual conditions of human beings in that period of time.* (May, 1973, p.3, p.53)

In emotional change, moving forward also triggers pain as we let go of the past, so grieving is part of progress. We are shedding old skin and growing new skin. Moving through may also trigger old traumas and stir-up whether I am worthy of creative treasures. Many find this difficult because they are afraid of feeling the pain underneath; often, they say I might not survive if I go there. So, support and trust were important for them to experience the pain and grief... and for some to titrate it across time.

So, how is this relevant today? Could it be that we are in the process of shedding the need to have power and control over others? Are we about to then rid ourselves of classism, racism, sexism, corporatism and militarism? Is the violence today fear of survival, if we don't maintain the powers that be, including white supremacy? For those who are participating in the insurrection, this may be the case. So hopefully we make the shift, shift to honoring the values and needs of human beings through equality and diversity in creating a new world. Making the shift through accountability for violence but also getting underneath the violence and the addiction to the inner struggle, dealing with the fear and anger that people are struggling with. Creating a new identity that is based on inner strength, not power and control through force and violence.

Another quote by Rollo May (1977, p. 63) is relevant here:

Whenever there is a breakthrough of a significant idea in science or a significant new form in art, the new idea will destroy what a lot of people believe is essential to the survival of their intellectual and spiritual world. This is the source of guilt in genuine creative work. He quotes Picasso: "Every act of creation is first of all an act of destruction."

NEW GREEN LEAVES
An image of new growth that I had in sacred dance.

Chapter 13

Summary:
Reflections, Significance

THIS WAS A HEALING STORY for myself and my culture and my ancestors. I felt worried in the late 70s that a profit over people, over the needs and values of people, would get us in trouble. I described the traumatic effects of this profit motive on many institutions: banks, foreign policy, health, pharmaceutical companies, economic policy etc., to hopefully amplify the toxic effects of this policy. I used the arts, dance, watercolor of dreams to reach the collective unconscious of our times. I gave warning in the first book about the machine, efficiency and productivity that may lead to a numbing through robotic rhythm splitting us apart. The elite monopolizing most of the economic benefits, leading to classicism, racism, sexism. The society exploding in protest with George Floyd's murder reflecting the enormous racism in the society. The women also marching in the street in protest for women's rights. This is now amplified with the abortion rights issue being overturned.

The answer to the collective trauma was an internal journey.

Enter into my internal journey through dreams of holocaust, imagery of the Nazi, a premonition of the white supremacy to come, Charlottesville, the insurrection. In healing self, there was a mirror into the collective culture, the wounds of the American society and our need to heal. The message is that it is healing self that makes possible healing society.

The Dance of Psyche is to see the world through rhythm. The way people move in time and space. In this latest era before the pandemic, it was to move fast in time, a hurry-up rhythm, which can be numbing to the nervous system and shuts us down.

In experiencing this it brought up feelings and images that reflect the personal and collective psyche which was put in art, paintings, and dance theatre.

Thus, it was looking at trauma through the body and body movement, the visceral sensations through posture, rhythm images and dreams. This helped in understanding healing attachment trauma, health and illness.

Society was then in lockdown which had people confront their internal feelings. Many could not handle the underlying pain: addiction, depression, anxiety, suicides, shootings increased. It brought to the surface the enormous need for mental health services. I would say that isolation is the underlying reason. I would say that problems with Mental Health are perceived as weaknesses compared to physical issues such as injury from accidents, a broken arm or leg. Seeing mental illness as related to trauma may help diminish the stigma.

The purpose of my book was to trauma inform through both science and art.

Dance/Rhythm was symbol of the psyche in attachment, trauma, health and illness; a journey from trauma to the light of being through posture, rhythm, images and dreams that represent personal, collective and ancestral trauma. A story/Myth to heal: a journey that started in 1982 through to today… from the trauma of the emotional/spiritual conditions of our time. Dance was used as symbol of the psyche as the ultimate intention is to become a vibrant being. Going from production and efficiency, fast in time, for profit to one that is sustained in time and flows. Thus, enabling one to be in their body, to feel, to become a compassionate human being. So, healing trauma is important for paradigm shift: from the machine, a materialistic reality with an emphasis on separation and classification, splitting, to one of vibrance, energy that unites. Thus, it is rhythm, music and dance that is the unifying force; unites self, culture, nature and the divine.

I shared my experience as nurse, then trauma psychologist across 50 years. My intention is to pass down my knowledge/wisdom across these many years which is now part of the collective. I shared my personal trauma which was a window into the collective. I shared my experience of Father's illness and death as a young child and Mother's depression across a lifetime. My bully boss experiences as a young nurse with sexual harassment and then throughout my career, not limited to what happened but the experience of it. Had the insight that the bully was gatekeeper of the profit motive. I attempted to speak out the truth of it but was targeted. Many patients came into my practice with bully boss experiences as well. I would say, many became depressed and suicidal. So bullying is very toxic to the self. They would speak out, tell the truth and then be targeted too.

I would reach the creative unconscious through imagination in movement tapping postures, rhythms and dreams which were a portal to the collective, moving images that represented consciousness, the emotional spiritual conditions of our times. The dance was portal to the dream which cleared present and past trauma across time. Dance was the symbol of the psyche, movement in time and space, ancient ritual and present-day healing through rhythm, a force that unites self, culture, nature and the divine. Rhythm as symbolic of relationship between fetus and mother — the first song and dance, the fetus moves to the rhythm of the mother's voice. This is primal relationship. It is no wonder that dancing to music goes back to ancient ritual. Shamans sing songs to those who need healing. Present day times uses EMDR (eye movement rhythm) to help heal trauma. The dance therapist uses authentic movement, a healing process that uses spontaneous movement to access underlying feelings and memories from the body. Present day trauma work now recognizes the body as important for healing versus just analysis of it, more oriented toward the emotions through the body. What was profound was that ancestral history was in the body. This is an acknowledgment by Native American tribes. It tapped dreams of holocaust for me. It wasn't until years later that I learned my grandfather was a Roma from Eastern Europe who trained Polish Arabian horses for the Aristocracy in Russia. Left Russia to escape persecution there and came to the United States. He changed his name to Campbell when he came here. There are several Russian, some Greek, sounding names that were found: Kolosky, Kolocauskus ,Novich, to name a few. DNA testing also revealed Ashkenazi Jewish four to seven generations ago. I also considered the Holocaust dreams from past life.

In healing, the pendulum swings from the darkness of trauma, back and forth across years and perhaps a lifetime, and then the light appeared. This is the rhythm in healing the darkness.

It is my hope and purpose in writing this story that it helps us heal, personally and collectively. May others source their collective and ancestral trauma so we lessen the incidence of violence and war. That we heal the split between those who have and those who don't, thus heal classicism. We support those who are different: different cultures. Communicate that Black Lives Matter. That we acknowledge the trauma of their slavery, the unjust lynchings and killings, the injustice across several centuries. We acknowledge the Native American, the indigenous tribes, their injustice, their discrimination, the many breeches in our treaties with them in their right to their Native land. I think of Hawaiian indigenous tribes and think about present-day attack of Asian Americans on the streets. The Roma are still being persecuted in Europe and Russia. More recently, the Haitians are being demeaned/ I know there are others as well. We acknowledge all of our illegal wars and violence against those who have resources: thinking of: Viet Nam, Cambodia, Laos, Iraqi, Afghanistan, Chile, Venezuela, Libya, Syria and Yemen and also the sale of weapons for war, now in Ukraine, but also sale during WWII. We are now selling bombs to Israel contributing to the death of the Palestinians. It is now considered genocide by the International community. I feel for the victims of the nuclear bombing of

Hiroshima. Not surprising that the image of Guernica came up as well which evokes the suffering of the innocent lives that were bombed and destroyed. I would say our need for dominance and control fuels these collective traumas. Profit is a way to dominate. I question the profit motive made from the weapons of war. The need for strength comes from our weakness, the need to prove strength. The value for the strong man.

Acknowledging the suffering to release past traumas, have present impact, and have justice for future hopes. A powerful healing force is to be a witness of the other… to say I see you, hear you, feel your presence across time. The most critical theory to health is relationship through presence, a friend, a lover, a colleague who can see who we are and be a witness over time. Helping, remembering events of the past that shaped our lives, understanding the significance in the present and giving us hope for the future, someone is there for us… presence, being able to feel, resonant with the emotions that lie underneath, understand the suffering, offer emotional support. We need each other.

The dreams that gave enormous insight about collective trauma were the holocaust dream and the separation of children from their families. These dreams were reflected in the dance of Guernica, the Nazi and the Roma which gave insight into the dangers of production and efficiency over human values. The SS were ordered to get so many people into the gas chamber every ten minutes. They were oblivious to the horror taking place. Does moving fast in time shut down the nervous system, make people numb to others suffering? Does profit, winning at all costs, numb the psyche? The most recent example is Putin's aggression. He did not care about the suffering he caused.

So, Putin said the Ukrainians did not have a right to exist. Treating them as not being seen, heard, or felt. Numb to their suffering. Numbing caused by addiction to greed and power. Trauma reenactment for the Ukrainians to be killed, violated because they do not matter… to be used for the narcissist needs for him to be great at all costs. Profit over the needs of people, not in touch with their suffering.

"Suffering from one's own trauma enables one to feel the suffering of another." When one is numb, trauma is reenacted over and over — in this case through war.

Dictators see poverty as a weakness and an invitation to dominate and control. Fracturing the population, so they start fighting with each other; another tactic to dominate and control. The population is split through the gaslighting of information; it is done like a repetitive drum beat. People fall into a robotic trance and lose their grip on reality. They fight with those who have a different reality, the culture fractured.

This was true with the Covid epidemic. The split was between the vaccinated and the unvaccinated. The unvaccinated being scapegoated. Pharmaceuticals exploding with profit. The truth about effectiveness not fully disclosed.

How do you break the denial of people in lockstep delusion? In order to avoid war; it's diplomacy versus violence. If I have learned from working with delusional patients, no matter how delusional, it is helpful to form a trusting relationship, to be present, to communicate that they are worth spending time with, play a game with without confronting initially. Then, with trust and safety, clarifying reality may have a chance to get through. The trick is to know when they are ready — trust and safety first. Those who do not have serious delusion may be capable of connecting it with the original trauma. A skilled therapist is important here. In order to avoid war, it's diplomacy versus violence. Even in the throes of war... diplomacy. However, I would also say lack of accountability also fuels tyrannical actions.

The question is: What is the meaning underneath what they are saying?" I remember a schizophrenic saying he has snakes in his stomach. This may mean there could be physical problems there, or it may have emotional significance from his past experience.

So, the significance is to heal self in order to see clearly. Often, when injured by trauma, the underlying powerlessness is projected onto the other. Violence is about destroying the defective part of ourselves to come out victorious, to feel powerful through destruction. When one heals, we are more capable of seeing the other more clearly, both good and the bad. Less likely to project the bad onto the other and destroy.

Hitler was ashamed of having Jewish ancestors a few generations back. He projected this shame onto the Jews and destroyed them as if to destroy that defective part of himself. Putin invaded Ukraine because of the Nazis he said. He was the one acting like a Nazi.

The path to healing was an internal journey. Internal images, feelings, dreams were a portal to the collective trauma.

After cleansing the trauma, the Light appeared. The Tibetan medicine journey through dreams cleansed the trauma from the medical system and the holocaust. Then there were dreams of connection to nature, and then dreams of gold light appeared. I was able to see auras around my patients; in trance states the room filled up with green light from heart chakra, yellow light representing Archangel Uriel, pink light representing love, blue light truth and ancestors on the other side, and gold light representing the divine, a spiritual reality.

So, healing trauma is what is necessary for paradigm shift, to shift from a Materialistic reality, the machine, which separates to one that is energy and light/love… that which unites us with all living things. This is a way of knowing through intuition versus just linear, objective knowledge, and includes both art and science. This is done through movement from the visceral sensation in the body. The body is where human history resides. This is a way to acknowledge the feminine, spiritual reality. We are more than matter — we are energy/vibration that unites us with the cosmos and the earth, to all things. Nature is alive. We are human. We are vulnerable. We are capable of honoring others suffering versus domination and control. We are capable of compassion, expressing beauty, being warriors of the soul, through art, music and dance. Body rhythm unites us with self, culture, nature and the divine. Embracing vulnerability gives us the capacity to feel that the earth is in danger and thus save her… to be entranced by her beauty, to be in awe of life and its complexity. Through imagination in rhythm, one is drawn to this truth and beauty, one becomes a being of light and love.

Healing Collective Trauma

The need to heal a collective trauma is now coming out in the trauma psychology field. Many conferences through live zoom conferences, Native Americans talking about their persecutions and loss; African Americans also talking about their killings by police. Many practices heal the fear, terror, the fight-or-flight nervous system and restore, shifting to normal functioning of the parasympathetic nervous system.

For me, I wanted to give an example of a healing journey through my dreams and dances that represent a shift from trauma to vibrant being. It was a shamanic journey; the initiation dream and Tibetan Medicine dreams told me I was here as healer, to understand myself as a being of light and to experience that all things are energy, light and love.

The journey is consistent with Jung's Mythos, a journey of darkness into the light, metaphorically speaking from lead to gold. The process of healing is also consistent with the Tao in Chinese medicine also a journey of darkness into light. Both healing practices include the experience of opposites: dark and light, sadness and joy, chaos/clarity, fractured/whole, conflict/peace. This was the swing of the pendulum in healing… to eventually see the light, to experience the dreams of gold light.

POETIC REFLECTIONS ON THE DANCE OF PSYCHE: RHYTHM OF CONSCIOUSNESS

In this healing journey: rhythm, poetry, music and dance were the mirrors into the soul.

Rhythm as unifying life force/vibration, the music and dance within the soul comes forth.

We are music, the Dance of the Psyche
Unifying Self, Culture, Nature and the Divine.

Light and Dark united.

This is the Tao, darkness to light
The Jungian principle, lead to gold

The Mandala, as symbol of Unification:
The sphere, Unity
Spiritual reality, the Heart
The doorway to dreams, the spiral

The architecture of movement in space and time,
The geometry of the Universe
The spirals/ portals of energy, connecting to the cosmos.
Vision of the Planets experiencing
The universe as God

Opening to the divine through the dance as dream,
to the posture as gateway to the past,
amplifying present pain, the darkness,
feeling the depth of the wound,

releasing to the light.
The image, the gateway to depth of feeling,
messaging the memory, shedding light for the future.
Unifying past, present, and future.

The Eagle flies, seeing all fragments of the self unite.

Moving through past, forward to present,
sourcing meaning, existential purpose is met.

In the search, the gold is found, uniting with the other, and
        the collective culture
Uniting with the beauty of Nature and Truth
Brings Light

The Divine light appears, sourcing from the heart.
Able to feel it.

The Sun arises from the night and gives new life and light.

I am a being of light, reflecting, connecting through Rhythm, Vibration.
I am energy, a unifying force in Self, Culture, Nature and the Divine.

The Psyche, an inner experience. The images, gestures, postures and
        dreams take you on a healing journey.

Rhythm, poetry, music and dance were the portal to the dream,
        the inner story,
a unifying force with self, culture, nature and the divine.
Portal to the collective unconscious.
Helpful in connecting the dots across time and lifetimes
Capable of sourcing collective and ancestral trauma.

Takes you from dark into light, from trauma to vibrant being.
Capable of healing self, helping the other to heal.
Knowledge that I am a being of light,
A Vibrant Being
Communion through empathy
Understanding suffering
Emanating light and love through truth and beauty and Compassion

the Dance of Psyche: Rhythm of Consciousness

Dance is a reflection of the Psyche
Through rhythm, the soul is remembered.
Time suspends itself reaching infinity.
The present moment is past and future at once.

Temporal space becomes infinite shaping itself to endless cycles of
death and rebirth.

Here is a flow of life – surrendering.
We are the wind, fire, water, and earth.
Love, sorrow, anguish and joy.

The body relaxes, becomes softer.
Capable of experiencing life and vitality of
becoming vibrant human beings.

Because we are the life force that is the cosmos-capable of
experiencing ourselves, expressing the story of our culture,
being as one with nature and the divine.

This is the Dance of Psyche:
Rhythm of Consciousness.

— C. Campbell, 2002

ARCHANGEL URIEL TAKING ME TO THE LIGHT
Painting by Patti Szerlip

BIBLIOGRAPHY

Adams, K.A. (2019). *Trump and the Social Trance.* Journal of Psychohistory 17 (3), p. 252, p. 238. 252.

Adler, J. Quote, *American Dance Therapy website.* 1st Book Bib.

Aginse France Press (May 6, 2016). *Vandals Surrounded Nazi Swachikas and words, "Gas Them" in Germany's Memorial to the Half Million Runa and Sinti Murdered by the Nazi's.* By WWE Newsmaker, Head of the Roma Foundation. "An Aggressive Anti-Roma Act.

Amnesty International (July 18, 2017). *The Most Precise Bombing Job to Avoid Caribbean Casualties, False Narrative.*

Amini, F. (2001). *The General Theory of Love.* Random House, NY.

Associated Press (December 10, 2016). *Documents Shed Light on Sandy Hook Shooter, Adam Lanza's Tortured Mind.* CBS News.

Bartenioff, I. (1980). *Body Movement: Coping with the Environment.* New York: Science Publishers.

Birdwhisle, R. L.(1970). *Kinesics and Context.* Philadelphia: University of Pennsylvania Press.

Brady, Jack. *War Crimes – Representative. To Catch a Dictator. Special Tribunal about Aggression – ICC – DemocracyNow.com.*

BusinessInsider.com (July 9, 2015). *Employees Reveal 22 Awful Things about Working at Facebook.*

Business Insider (January 28, 2015). *Facebook Employees Reveal 22 Awful Things about Working at Facebook.* By Caroline Moss and Maya Kosoff.

Campbell, C. (1977). *Perception of Stress by Staff Members in an Adolescent Milieu.* Unpublished Master's Thesis, Jose State University.

Campbell, C. (1984). *Hospice Evaluation.* Unpublished doctoral dissertation, University of San Francisco 1984.

Campbell, C. (2003). *Dance of Psyche: Rhythm of Consciousness.* Sausalito, California. Campabella Healing Arts Press.

Campbell, D. (1998). *The Riddle of the Mozart Effect.* (Music therapy for illness care and prevention) *Natural Health* 27(6).

Campbell, J. (April 27, 2013). *The Power of Myth.* Interviewed by Bill Moyers. Joseph Campbell Foundation, https://jcf.org7Myth.Blasts.

Capra, F. (2010). *The Tao of Physics.* Boulder, Colorado: Shambala Publications Inc.

Chardorow, J. (1991). *Dance Therapy and Depth Psychology.* New York: Routledge, Chapman and Hall Inc.

CBS News. (December 10, 2018.) *Documents Shed Light on Sandy Hook Shooter.* By Adam Lanza

Chomsky, N. (2003). *Hegemony or Survival: America's Quest for Global Dominance.* New York, New York: Henry Holt and Company, LLC.

Chomsky, N. (2016). *Truth Emerges Tweets:* (April 3, 2016 @ 3:40 a.m.) Quote by Chomsky, Norm. "As Long as the General Population, etc."

Chomsky, N. (1999). *The New Military Humanism: Lessons from Kosovo.* Monroe, ME: Common Courage Press.

Chomsky, N. (1999). *Profit Over People. New York: Seven Stories Press.*

Chomsky, N. (2017). *Requiem for the American Dream. The 10 Principles of Concentration of Wealth & Power.* New York: Seven Stories Press. Classism, Corporate Greed.

Condon, W. and Sander, L. *(1974, January) Neonate Movement is Synchronized with Adult speech.* International participation and Language Acquisition. Science (p. 92-101).

CNN (2016/06/12). Orlando Shooting, 49 Killed. Shooter Pledged Allegiance to Isis.

CNN (Dec. 3, 2015). *You have to take out terrorists' families.* By Tom LaDiansi.

Cohen, D. (2003). *What's Behind the UN Cover Up of Picasso's Guernica?* artcritical.com.

Cruz, S. (2018). *Parkland Shooting Suspect. A Story of Red Flags Ignored.* (March 1, 2018). NPR.ORG.

Dell, C., Crow, A., & Bartelett, I. (1977). *Space Harmony.* New York: Dance Notation Bureau Press.

deMause, L. (1997). *The Psychogenic Theory of History.* The Journal of Psychohistory, 25(3), 128-129.

deMause, L. (1995). *The Personality of the Fetus.* (Winnicott, D. Eds.) Kahr B., & Varma, V.P. *A Memorial Volume for Mental Health Professionals.* London: Karnac Books, (PP 1-17).

Democracy Now (Nov. 29, 2015 @ 9 p.m.). *Quotes by Amy Goodman on the Bombing of Innocent People, the Resultant Carnage*

DemocracyNow.org (2017). Quote by Carl Schmitt, a philosopher (1930s). *Nazi Era Philosopher Wrote Blueprint for the likes of Donald Trump and Vladimir Putin: Mystical Connection between Leader and the Masses. The Leader Articulates the Internal Emotions of the Crowd, by Masha Grissen.* (March 10, 2017)

Democracy Now (Feb. 16, 2023). *Turkish/Syrian Earthquake.* HISYAR OZSOY. Government did not prepare. Corruption – Allowed construction – Cut corners – Were not Member of Turkish Parliament. Lebanese – Not Taking Care of People. Iraq and Egypt reduced economic nature. Pakistan – World Economic Crisis.

Diabetes Forecast (1999) *Artful Anesthetics* 52(8) p.46.

Dossey, L. (1982). *Space Time, &Medicine.* Boulder, CO: Shambala Press.

Editorial Board (Sept. 21, 2016). *The Epi Pen Outrage Continues.* New York Times.

England, P. (2015). *Ireland's Pots & Pans Revolution: Lessons from a Nation that People Power Helped to Emerge from its 2008 Crisis All Stronger.*

Evans, S., *Personal Communication. February,1999.*

Everytown Research Policy (2013 to 2023). *How Gun Safety and Prevention Measures are Researched. Violence in America, the health of it and its impact on Survivors..*

Facebook Post (November 12, 2017). *Wake-up, We Will Be Persecuted Worse than the Jews: Evoked by 60,000 for Right March in Poland Calling for "White Europe" by Gypsy Travelers & Muslims.*

Farmer, S.D. (2023). *The Artist and the Snake.* Drstevenfarmer.com (1999). www.earthmagic.net.

firstfinecalifornia.com *Education on Toxic Stress for Kids.*

Friedlander, I. (1975). *The Whirling Dervishes.* New York: Macmillan Publishing Co.

Gallia, K. (1999). *Beethoven's Babies Bill. Natural Health,* 29(1), 24.

Gerber, R. (1988). *Vibrational Medicine.* Sante Fe, NM: Bear and Company.

Gerber, S. (1998). *The Sound of Healing. Every Culture in the World also Used Sound and Music to Heal. Vegetarian Times,* 247(6), p. 68.

Ginner, R. (1944). *The Revived Greek Dance. It's Art and Technique.* London: Methuen & Co.

Gonzalez, E. (2018). *Parkland Students' Incredible Response to Enormous Tragedy.* March for Our Lives, Feb. 17. Anniversary of Columbine, Apr. 20.

Gonzalez, E. (2018). *March for Our Lives.* March in Washington, D.C. Anniversary of Columbine Speech. April 20. Guardian News.

Goodman, A. (November 29, 2015 at 9:00 p.m.). Quote re Bombing of Civilians. Guernica.

Goodreads.com. Neoliberal Democracy quote by Noam Chomsky.

TheGuardian.com (Jan. 24, 2023). *Tragedy Upon Tragedy. Why 39 US Mass Shootings this year?*

Gypsy/Roma Travelers (2017). Quote in Facebook, *Persecution worse than the Jews.*

Hale. S.E. (1990) *Sitting on Memory s Lap. The Arts in Psychotherapy.* 17(3), p. 269-274.

Hamel, P.M. (1976). *ThroughMusictotheSelf.* BoulderColorado:Shambala.

Hayward, J. (June 26, 2009). *The March on the Hudson – The Full Story.* Simple Flying Newsletter. The March on the Hudson Movie (Released September 2, 2016). Director, Clint Eastwood. Distributed by Warner Bros. Pictures.

Henderson, G. W. (1999). *Sit back, Relax, and Enjoy the Music.* In *World Disease Weekly Plus,* July 12, 1999.

Heisenbergen, C.V. (2004). *Guernica, The Biography of a Twentieth Century Icon.* Bloomsbury, USA.

Hines, R. (2022). www.sacredscience.com. *Inner Alchemy Program.* Principle/quote by Pollize, R.

Hitressinstamin, P. Spiritual Art (mandala art. Com)

Hoffman, J. (1997). *Tuning into the Power of Music.* (Use of music in medical care) R.N. 60^{N6}(3), p. 52.

Independent News. (Monday, 29 June 2015).

Independent Television Service, Corporation for Public Broadcasting. *Run Like a Girl, Smile Pretty Program Series, Identity and Adolescence.*

Judge, H.: *Texas Garden Birth Certificates for US-Born Children of Some Immigrants.* (By Molly Heddessy-Fiske. (October 16, 2015). Difficulty in access to basic services and full rights as citizens. National News 9, mollyh8. Los Angeles Times.

Jung, C. (1964). *Man and His Symbols.* New York: Doubleday Inc..

Keller, F. E. (1984). *A Feeling for the Organism: The Life and Work of Barbara McClintock,* New York: W.H. Freeman.

Khan Y. K. (1961) *The Sufi Message of Hazrat Inayat Khan: Mental Health Purification, The Mind World.* London: Barrie and Rockcliff.

Kharitidi, O. (2001). *Entering the Circle: The Secrets of Ancient Siberian Wisdom.* Charlottsville, VA: Hampton Roads Publishing Company, Inc.

Kharitidi, O. (2001). *Master of Lucid Dreams: In the Heart of Asia. A Russian Psychiatrist Learns How to Heal the Spirits of Trauma.* Charlottsville, PA: Hampton Roads Publishing Co., Inc.

Killing of Innocent Children in School Shooting. April 20, 1999 (en.m.wekipedia.org) *Sandy Hook Elementary Shooting.* December 14, 2012 (wekipedia.org.)

King, M.R. (2018). Quote by Martin Luther King, Jr.

Kline, N. (2007). *The Shock Doctrine: The Rise of Disaster Capitalism.* New York, Metropolitan Books. Henry Holt and Company, LLC.

KRCB (2015) *Bombing of Cambodia Anniversary Report.* KRGB.org. (Aug. 23). Newsweek.com-delivere

Independent News. (Monday, 29 June, 2015)

Ireland's Pots and Pans Revolution: *Lessons from a Nation that People Power Helped to Emerge from the 2008 Crisis all Stronger* by Phillip England.

Lanza, A. (2012, Dec. 14). *Sandy Hook Elementary School Shooting.* A l s o called Newton Shooting, CT. Wikipedia.

LA Times (May 27, 2017). *White Supremacy Assisted in Fatal Shooting, Stabbing of Two Men. Anti Muslim Ranking in Portland* by Thatcher Schorid. May 22, 2017.

Levine, P.A. (1997). *Waking the Tiger Healing Trauma.* Berkeley, California: North Atlantic Books.

Levine, P.A. (2010). *In an Unspoken Voice: How the Body Releases Trauma and Restores Goodness.* Berkeley: North Atlantic Books.

Long, C. (1996). *Doctors Find Music Works Well with Sedatives and Anesthetics.* Insight on the News. 12(1) p. 41.

Lynch, J. J. (1985). *The Language of the Heart.* New York: Basic Books.

Martin, R. (2003). *Picasso's War: The Destruction of Guernica and the Masterpiece that Changed the World.* Plume Books publisher. Dutton Imprint. New York City.

Mate, Gabor. (2022) *The Myth of Normal, Trauma, Illness & Healing in a Toxic Culture. Avery,* Penguine-Random House.

Mate, Gabor (Sept. 30, 2003). *When the Body Says No: Exploring the Stress-Disease Connection.* Hoboken, New Jersey: John Wiley and Sons.

Mate, Gabor. (Oct. 10, 2021). *The Wisdom of Trauma Summit* (conference). Trauma Research. Current Clinical Practice.

Matien, Keller Omar (NY Times 6/17/2016) *The Orlando Massacre Turned Sanctuary of Fantasy, and Europe into a Sobering Scene. All too Familiar in America.*

May, R. (1969). *Love and Will.* New York, W.W. Norton & Company.

Meyers, J. (2016). *Dark Money,* New York. Doubleday Press.

Meyers J. (2017). *Dark Money. The Hidden History of the Billionaires Behind the Rise of the Radical Light.* NY City. Double Day Publishing. Corporate Greed.

Mendelson, R.S. (1979). *Confessions of a Medical Heretic.* McGraw Hill Company.

Moore, T. (1992). *Care of the Soul.* New York: Harper Perennial.

Moyers, B. (2013). *Interview of Mark Liebough, Author of This Town,* Penguin Audio.

Moyers, B. (2017). *Interview of Mark Leibough, Author of This Town, A Town Where Money Rules.* Producer, Gina Kim, Editor. Corporate Greed.

Narby, J. (2021). *The Cosmic Serpent.* Audio Book. https://www. audiobookstore.com.

Nazaryan. (2017). *Timothy McVeigh, Extremist New Hero.* Southern Poverty Report. The New Extremist.

Nelson, D. & Weatlers, R. (1998). *Music and Healing in Psychotherapy.* In *Journal of Humanistic Psychology.* 38(8), 101.

NPR (April 24, 2017). *The Warfare May Be Remote, But the Trauma is There.* By Sarah McCammon.

NPR.org (March 1, 2018). *Parkland Shooting Suspect: A Story of Red Flags Ignored Cruz Shooter.*

NY Times (2016) *Avoidance of Clues Related to Intent to Commit Terrorism by Relatives and Family.*

NY Times (June 18, 2016) *Oakland Nightclub Shooting.*

NY Times (June 20, 2016). *Gunman Calls to Police to be Partially Released.*, p. 8, by Loretta Lynch.

NY Times (2020). *Daniel Prude Police Shooting. What We Know about Daniel Prude's Case and Death.* By Michael Gold and Troy Glossom. (April 16, 2021)

Oats, J. (March 25, 2013). This is proof Jesus came to India, made a deep study of Hinduism and taught it when he returned to Jerusalem. (Christianity.org)

PBS (2016). *Amazon Empire: The Rise and Fall of Jeff Bayoff* by James Jacobe.

Pearce, C. J. *(1980). Magical Child. New York: Bantam Books*

Pouliot *(1998). The Power of Music. In World and I, 13(5) p. 146(8)*

Perkins, J. (2004). *Confessions of an Economic Hit Man.* San Francisco, Oakland, California. Bennett Koeler Publishers. Corporate Greed.

Picasso, Guerenica's History. http://www.tamw.edu/moc/picasso/ study/ history.html. *Gypsies & the Holocaust.* http//www.remember. org/witness/wit.vic.gyp.htm. *Sinti and Roma: Victims of the Nazi Era.* http//www.holocaust.trc.org/sinti.htm.

POC (Physicians Organizing Committee), San Francisco, California.

Pope Francis Quote, (1988),

Pots & Pans Revolution (2012). https//m.youtube.com. *Uptraded by Magical Marques*

Dr. Eric Punhart. *Medical Anthropologists.* Physician Northwestern University. Medical System Corruption. U.S. Mortality Rate. Patients deprived of care due to not being able to pay. 30 million, 5 cure. Insurance, Pharmacy.

Rage Against the War Machine Rally Held in Washington. (Feb. 19, 2023)

Redens, S. (1978) *Eustathios Stratis Pontus: an Ethnographic Sketch,* unpublished paper.

Righi, W.R. (1996). *Coma: The Panjabi Emigrants in Europe, Central and Middle Asia, the USSR and the Americas.* Publication Bureau, Punjabi University, Patiala.

Rosan, D., M.D. (1996). *The Tao of Jung: The Way of Integrity.* New York, Penguin Books.

Rust, F. (1969). *Dance in Society.* London: Routledge & Kegan, Paul.

Sagan, Carl https:www.space.com.15994-Ca.

Savastio, R. (2013). *Icelanders Overthrow Government and Rewrite Constitution after Banking Fraud.* Scotland: … Corporate Greed. Guardian.com.

Schmid, T. (2017). *White Supremist Arrested in Fatal Stubbing of Two Men after Antiracist Rant in Portland.* **(May 22, 2017).** *www.latimes.com* Thacher Schmid.

Science and Health (2017). *Dehumanization allows Us to Dismiss Peoples Feelings and Experience.* Commentary on Eric Trump Comments, "Not Even People": https://www.rox.com / Science and Health. 6/7.15755852.

Schmookler, A. B. (1988). *Out of Weakness, Healing the Wounds that Bind us to War.* Toronto: Bantam Books.

Shapiro, F. (1989). *Efficacy of the Eye Movement Desensitization Procedure in the Treatment of Traumatic Stress. Journal of Traumatic Stress* 2, 199-223.

Siegel, D. (1999). *The Developing Mind: How Relationships and the Brain Interact to Shape Who We Are.* New York, London. The Guilford Press.

60 Minutes (11/27/2011). *Constructive industry Recession (2007 1 in 4 in poverty.)*

Stanton, C. (1983). *Origins of Attachment, Culture, and Cue-Sensitivity.* Presentation given to Stanford Medical Center Nursing Research Staff.

Starr, A. (1992). *Music and the Mind.* New York: The Free Press, A division of Macmillan, Inc.

Susan J. (11 August, 2022). *Birth Registration of White Supremacy.* Cambridge Core University Press. Part of History. Southern states used Birth Registration to fix racial identity in order to determine access to school, moving and other benefits. Identity important to land titles… Important to the allotment of land to the indigenous tribes.

Stewart, Jan (2017). *The Price of Inequality.*

Stiglitz, J. (2012). *The Price of Inequality.* Audio Book. Falcon Press. Narrated by Connor Goff. Quotes: *How Today is Divided Society Endangers Our Future.*

Stiglitz, J. (2012). *Inspiring Quotes by Joseph Stiglitz, Nobel Laureate in Economics… (10/11/22)* www.goodreads.com Author – *The Price of Inequality. How Today's Divided Society Endangers Our Future.* Publisher – Tantor Media, Old Saybrook, Connecticut.

Sullenberger, C. (2009). *The Hudson River Landing, Flight 1549, U.S. Airways, January 15, 2009:* Sullenberger landed in the Hudson River. The movie *"Murder on the Hudson"* - https://liberty / 35P9R27.

USA Today (2015). *Pope Francis quote about Greed for Money,* Sept. 25, 2015.

Vanderkolk, B. (2015). *The Body Keeps the Score: Brain, Mind, and Body in the Healing of Trauma.* New York, New York: Penguin Books.

Vanderkolk, B. (2021). *The Body Keeps the Score.* Trauma Healing, 2-day workshop. May 6 & 7.

Washington Post (Feb. 23, 2018). *Democracy Dies in Darkness.* Gov. Matt Beurn statement – by Scherer.

Wallace, H.A. (1944). *Harry A. Wallace Quotes.* New York Times. W. Norton & Company. Midtown, Manhattan, NY, New York

The Guardian.com (2013). *Icelanders Overthrow the Government and Rewrite the Constitution after Banking Fraud.* By Sauastio, R.

The United Ukrainian Ballet. Gisell – Ballet Director. Dance their feelings. Ballet gives line life purpose. Keep Ukraine in Mind.

USA Today (2015). *Pope Francis quote about Greed for Money*, Sept. 25, 2015.

Washington Post (Feb. 23, 2018). *Democracy Dies in Darkness.* Gov. Matt Beurn statement – by Scherer.

Wallace, H.A. (1944). *Harry A. Wallace Quotes.* New York Times, April 9. 1944.

Wertenbaker, L. (1967). *The World of Picasso.* New York: Time-Life books.

Westley, M. Gedeonse, T. *Music is Good Medicine. Newsweek* **132(1), 103. Whitmore,B.** (1997). *Musical Birth: Sound Strategies for Relaxation.* In Mothering, 84(4), p. 56.

Wikipedia (April 20, 1999). *Shooting, Columbine High School.*

Wikipedia (December 14, 2012). *Sandy Hook Elementary School Shooting, Also Called Newton's Shooting* by Adam Lanza, the Shooter.

Wikipedia (Feb. 14, 2018). *The Parkland Students. Stoneman Douglas High School Shooting.*

www.TruthDay.com (2017). *Ear & ground / item / and book. What Austerity Does to a Child's Brain* by Alexander Read Kelley. June 14, 2017. Journal Ac to Pediatrics.

Zenko, M. (2015). *Report: Council on Foreign Relations in 6 countries.* Jan. 7.

INTERNET

Gypsies and the Holocaust.wit.uig.gyp.htm.

Gypsies and the Holocaust. https/wit.vic,gyp.htm

 Sinti and Roma. *Victims of the Nazi Era.http//www,holocaust.trc.org/ sinti.htm.*

Al Jazeer. *Black People Killed by Police in the U.S.* By Alison Chughtail. 2014-2022.

Southern Poverty Law Center Report. (April 21, 1995). The New Extremist.

FILMS

Patch Adams (1998) Robin Williams plays Patch Adams. He was admitted to a Mental Hospital with depression. He enjoyed talking to fellow patients. He found the Medical Profession separate and cold and does not address their emotional needs. He strove to be a Doctor and opened his own Medical clinic.

Adler, J. (Author and Narrator) (1970) Looking for Me(film) Available from Mental Health Materials Center, New York.

The Doctor (1991) William Hurt plays a self-centered Doctor that undergoes transformation in his views about life, illness and human relationships when experiencing being a patient in a hospital. It is based on the book, "A Taste of Your Own Medicine."

Million Dollar Baby (2004) Frankie Dunn (Clint Eastwood) is a veteran boxing trainer. Maggie Fitzgerald (Hilary Swank), a working-class worker arrives at his Gym to seek his training. He reluctantly accepts her. They develop a bond that changes them bot. Maggie breaks her neck leaving her on a ventilator dependent, She is quadriplegic. She requests Frankie to euthanize her.

Dr. Zhivago (1965) Starring Omar Sharif as Dr. Zhivago and Jul ie Christi as Lara. It was an historical story during the Russian Revolution. Significant was the Dr. Zhivago dealt with the tragedy all around him by writing poetry and tuned into the beauty of nature.

www.ingramcontent.com/pod-product-compliance
Lightning Source LLC
LaVergne TN
LVHW081446080825
817983LV00001B/5